BORDERS   18.71
LA GRANGE   1.45
            20.16
JANUARY 12, 2006

Divine Madness

Jeffrey A. Kottler

Divine Madness

Ten Stories of Creative Struggle

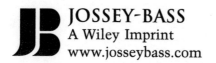

JOSSEY-BASS
A Wiley Imprint
www.josseybass.com

Published by Jossey-Bass
A Wiley Imprint
989 Market Street, San Francisco, CA 94103–1741   www.josseybass.com

Jossey-Bass books and products are available through most bookstores. To contact Jossey-Bass
directly call our Customer Care Department within the U.S. at 800-956-7739, outside the U.S.
at 317-572-3986, or fax 317-572-4002.

Jossey-Bass also publishes its books in a variety of electronic formats. Some content that
appears in print may not be available in electronic books.

Permission credit lines on page 312.

Library of Congress Cataloging-in-Publication Data

Kottler, Jeffrey A.
  Divine madness : ten stories of creative struggle / Jeffrey A. Kottler.
    p. cm.
  Includes bibliographical references.
  ISBN-13: 978-0-7879-8149-5 (alk. paper)
  ISBN-10: 0-7879-8149-4 (alk. paper)
  1. Mental illness—Case studies. 2. Mental illness—Anecdotes.
  3. Genius and mental illness—Anecdotes. 4. Art and mental illness
  —Anecdotes. 5. Insanity—Anecdotes. I. Title.
  RC465.K68 2005
  616.89'09—dc22   2005021193

Printed in the United States of America
FIRST EDITION
HB Printing   10 9 8 7 6 5 4 3 2 1

Contents

⎯∿⎯ Preface

My most closely guarded secret is that I'm crazy.

As long as I can remember, I feared that one day I would just flip out, lose control, and never return from never-never land, or wherever people go when they're gripped by insanity. Growing up in a home with an alcoholic, depressed, and sometimes suicidal mother, I felt as if I didn't have the choice of indulging my own madness, because I was too busy trying to keep her from hurting herself or one of my brothers.

This was a delusion in itself, as I later learned in therapy: I wasn't nearly as powerful as I thought I was. This made me feel even more depressed.

During my years in college, I could barely keep things together, especially after the breakup of a relationship, which devastated me. I either had a psychotic break for a few days or maybe the flu; even today I am not sure which had hold of me. But that experience of not being able to tell what was real—and what was my fantasy—was so terrifying that I knew I finally had to get my act together. It was writing that ultimately saved me.

During these college years, I studied creative, crazy people with a desperate vengeance. I became fascinated with deviance, not the kind that leads people to commit antisocial acts, but rather the sort that produces revolutionary advances in some domain. My heroes were all wounded, imperfect, flawed, but brilliant, innovators. I thought that van Gogh's being driven to carve off his own ear as a statement of unrequited love was incredibly romantic. When Marilyn Monroe killed herself by swallowing a bottle of sleeping pills, I secretly harbored admiration for her courage; for some time I had thought seriously about doing myself in but just couldn't muster the energy or the commitment—or whatever it takes to go that far.

I was writing by then, every day, putting all my restless, frustrated energy into creative self-expression. I devoured biographies of other writers who I imagined shared my vulnerabilities. I poured out my heart, trying to make sense of all the crazy thoughts, secret fantasies, and overwhelming feelings that swirled around in my head. Sure, I still thought I was crazy—but by that time, I felt that that was all right for a writer; for some of the things I'd been reading, it might even work to my advantage.

I began studying psychology in the first place less to help others than to try and save myself. I was too embarrassed at this point to disclose to friends how fragile I felt. I could never confess my fears to my parents, who had their own troubles, and already looked at me as if I were an alien. And the thought never occurred to me that there were professionals who might be of assistance. The only solution seemed to be that I would have to try and save myself, through my work, but also through the study of others who had struggled with similar terrors and insecurities.

——w——

It turned out that this was not such a bad plan. It wasn't until I became a psychologist and started listening to everyone else's troubles that I learned I wasn't nearly as weird as I had ever imagined. I realized how perfectly normal it is to fear going crazy. From working with a number of writers, artists, and musicians, I also heard again and again the belief that a certain amount of deviance is not only tolerated among creative people but is actually expected. It even has a special name: *eccentricity.*

The people whose stories are told in this book are far more than eccentric. They were by almost anyone's definition mentally impaired to the point that they were dysfunctional a good portion of the time. They were so depressed that there were times they could barely get out of bed. Their intimate relationships were seriously compromised. They resorted to using drugs or alcohol and other self-destructive behaviors to soothe themselves. In more than half the cases, they eventually surrendered to their madness and took their own lives. We can romanticize their pain and anguish all we want, but these individuals paid such a dear price for their exquisite sensitivity that in most cases it literally killed them.

Most of us have an unbounded fascination with eccentric geniuses. The success of books and movies about the likes of Jackson Pollock, John Nash, Virginia Woolf, Howard Hughes, and Vincent van Gogh testify to the public demand for interesting stories about creative individuals who struggled with demons and yet still managed to remain so productive. Such narratives offer hope to the rest of us, reminding us that we too can overcome adversity and self-limitations in order to accomplish something important.

It is perhaps one of the most intriguing paradoxes that great creative achievements can occur within the disordered, tortured minds of the mentally afflicted. In many cases, it is precisely the gifted person's pain, not to mention a rather unusual view of the world, that leads to innovation, whether in the fields of art, music, drama, film, or literature.

———

How is it that some extraordinary individuals manage to overcome disabilities to find brilliant creative expression that is sometimes even enhanced by their madness? This book examines the age-old relationship between creativity—what Plato called *divine madness*—and various forms of mental illness.

Marcel Proust, a French writer of the early twentieth century, who was perhaps justifying his own emotional turmoil, once said that "everything great in the world is created by neurotics." Although that is certainly not always the case, there are indeed a number of prominent examples of individuals who suffered severe forms of mental illness—depression, bipolar disorder, anxiety, phobias, obsessive-compulsive disorders, even schizophrenia—and yet still managed to make major contributions to the world.

The particular individuals selected for this book were chosen based on the diversity of their artistic expression, personalities, and backgrounds. There are writers (Virginia Woolf, Ernest Hemingway, Sylvia Plath); artists (Mark Rothko); musicians (Charles Mingus, Brian Wilson); and performers (Vaslav Nijinsky, Marilyn Monroe, Lenny Bruce, Judy Garland). They represent an assortment of psychological maladies, including mood disorders, schizophrenia, bipolar disorder, eating disorders, and personality disorders. Their lives and their artistic contributions span most of the twentieth century. And they operated in quite different cultural and artistic contexts. (See the following chart.) Yet what they all had in common, regardless of their afflictions, is that they managed to harness their disabilities in such a way that they seemed to power their creative energy. It is highly likely that without their particular maladies, they never would have accomplished what they did.

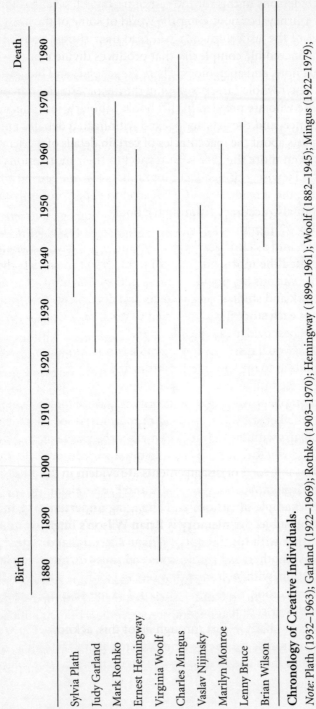

Chronology of Creative Individuals.

Note: Plath (1932–1963); Garland (1922–1969); Rothko (1903–1970); Hemingway (1899–1961); Woolf (1882–1945); Mingus (1922–1979); Nijinsky (1890–1950); Monroe (1926–1962); Bruce (1925–1966); Wilson (1942–).

There are lessons in this for the rest of us, but I'll save that for the end of the journey. For now, enter the world of some of the most creative minds of the last century. As you read their stories, you can appreciate the incredible complexity that produces divine madness.

One final note, and an apology. There are scholars and biographers who spend their whole careers studying the life of a single individual, such as those who are profiled in this book. Scholarly journals in literature, science, and the arts are packed with heated debates among various experts about the inaccuracies of certain details of a celebrity's life; this is even more the case with respect to their motivations and intentions. Likewise, critics assail biographers for not getting all the details right, and a reader has every reason to expect not only thoroughness but also accuracy from such a book.

In this book, therefore, I have taken great pains to be both factually accurate, and as clear as possible, about how I have understood and interpreted the motivations and intentions of the artists themselves. As the various notes and citations in the book testify, I've done my homework and studied various texts and documents that provide most sides of each story. Then I've tried to reach my own conclusions based on the best evidence available.

There is, as you'll discover, considerable controversy among scholars and experts as to the best interpretation and most realistic portrayal of some of these individuals. Marilyn Monroe, for instance, has hundreds of biographers, who come down on one side of the debate or the other as to whether she was really mad or misunderstood, whether she really had affairs with the Kennedys, whether she was sexually abused as a child, and whether she died as a result of suicide, or accident, or murder. The same sorts of disagreements are evident in the analysis of the lives of Virginia Woolf, Sylvia Plath, and Ernest Hemingway.

Another example of various and changing understanding that is based only on subjective memory is Brian Wilson's interpretation of his relationship with his therapist. Wilson's feelings and statements about this psychotherapist changed several times during the span of their association, with Wilson at first seeing Landy as a demon, then a savior, then a crook, then again as a kind of messiah, and more recently as both self-serving *and* helpful.

So my job has been to sort through all of this, acknowledge where there have been disagreements and differences in facts and interpretations, and then reach my own subjective but (I hope) balanced conclusions.

⎯⎯

The major task has been to explore the connections between creativity and so-called madness in ten notable individuals by examining available texts about their lives. As in all such studies, I have brought with me my own experiences and knowledge base, as well as a particular lens that is very different from that of a biographer or even a psychohistorian.

I am a psychologist but also a writer, who seeks to explore the ways that personal experiences are informed by professional involvements and likewise by the ways that our professional behaviors are influenced by what we encounter in our daily lives. I have spent particular time examining this phenomenon within the field of practicing therapists.

Psychobiographies, like those contained in this book, can be conceptualized along a continuum from those that attempt a search for "truth," or some illusion of objective reality of what "really" happened, to those that are evocative accounts that seek instead to describe events with no apology for subjectivity. I have tried to seek a balance between both extremes, sorting out controversies and discrepant reports as much as possible (such as what really happened during the last hours before Marilyn Monroe's death or to what extent sexual abuse really occurred in Virginia Woolf's childhood home) but also interpreting the available data from my own viewpoint. The overriding goal is to understand the links between creativity and madness (which I am already assuming are present) through the lives of ten individuals from different artistic professions and eras within the twentieth century.

Even if you disagree with my particular interpretation of any single event, keep in mind that I am a psychologist who is primarily interested in the connections between art and madness. I'm interested in not only finding greater meaning in these incredible lives but also helping others with inspiration to rise above their disabilities and limitations and express themselves more productively. I ask the reader's forgiveness for any and all errors that I have made in telling these stories. Whereas I have made every effort to get as many of the facts and details as right as I can, my own limitations have likely resulted in only a few (I hope) inconsequential errors and omissions. I am optimistic that such mistakes will compromise neither the essence of the stories nor the overall ideas that are presented in that context.

Acknowledgments

After having done more than a half dozen books together, I am grateful beyond words for the wise counsel of my editor, Alan Rinzler, who first came up with the idea for this book and then guided it, lovingly, through every step of the journey. This has truly been a partnership, more than any author could hope for.

I would like to thank Mary Read, David Shepard, and Brad Keeney, three colleagues of mine, for their thoughts about the clinical implications of the narratives in this book. I am also indebted to Mary Halunka for her assistance as a research assistant, as well as for her contributions in developing the *genograms* (graphical devices that plot multigenerational patterns in families) for Virginia Woolf and Ernest Hemingway.

I am most grateful for the expertise and guidance of the Jossey-Bass/Wiley staff: Catherine Craddock, Helene Godin, Seth Schwartz, Carol Hartland, Jennifer Wenzel, and Marcy Marsh, as well as my permissions editor, Sheri Gilbert.

Huntington Beach, California   JEFFREY A. KOTTLER

Divine Madness

CHAPTER ONE

The Nature of Madness and Creativity

Myths and Realities

What is the fascination we have for disturbed geniuses? Even decades after their death, there are more biographies written (and read) about the likes of Marilyn Monroe and Judy Garland than anyone else, including political figures. We seem utterly spellbound by the stories of people who, against improbable odds and unimaginable challenges, manage not only to survive but to thrive. Unfortunately, this success may be severely limited to only one narrow area of career productivity.

What Is the Connection Between Madness and Creativity?

In examining the correlation between the artistic temperament and manic-depressive illness (as an example), one finds that there is a virtual catalogue of prominent artists and writers who suffered debilitating, suicidal depression or bipolar disorder. Going back into history, the list is a "who's who" of celebrity poets (William Blake, Robert Burns, Samuel Taylor Coleridge, Hart Crane, Emily Dickinson, T. S. Eliot, John Keats, Walt Whitman, Dylan Thomas, Anne Sexton); writers (Victor Hugo, Edgar Allan Poe, Ernest Hemingway, Ezra Pound,

Charles Dickens, Mark Twain, Virginia Woolf, William Faulkner, F. Scott Fitzgerald, Henry James, Leo Tolstoy, Tennessee Williams, William Styron, Hunter Thompson); composers (Tchaikovsky, Schumann, Rachmaninoff, Mahler); musicians (Charlie Parker, Charles Mingus, Irving Berlin); artists (Michelangelo, van Gogh, Gauguin, Gorky, Rothko, Pollock, Munch, O'Keefe). Look further at the number of actors (Marilyn Monroe, Judy Garland, Rod Steiger, Patty Duke) and contemporary musicians (Michael Jackson, Brian Wilson, Kurt Cobain), who all suffered (or still suffer) forms of emotional disturbance, and the link between artistic temperament and madness seems quite obvious. When you see the complete list, you might very well get the impression that mental illness is a *requirement* for creative success.

In fact, the relationship between creativity and madness is often exaggerated. There are many more well-adjusted, emotionally healthy, high-functioning creative artists than there are those who end up in mental hospitals. As you can imagine, it is hard to get a lot of work done when you are so depressed that you can hardly crawl out of bed, much less find creative inspiration.

Nevertheless there is a basis for the association we make between creative personalities and a certain eccentricity, if not burgeoning insanity. Among the general public, only about 1 percent of the population is diagnosed with manic-depressive illness, whereas that percentage can be as high as 38 percent among artists and writers.

In another extensive survey of creative individuals, the lives of over a thousand prominent contributors in the arts and letters were studied, as well as those in business, politics, and sports, as a basis for comparison. Sure enough, it was found that only about 5 percent of the politicians, scientists, athletes, and corporate moguls suffered the onset of mental illness during their childhood or adolescence, yet the percentage skyrocketed to over 30 percent among the creative artists and musicians. Once they entered adulthood, the differences were even more profound: well over 60 percent of the creative geniuses experienced full-fledged mental illnesses, most often in the form of mood disorders.

The various disorders common to creative individuals all involve tremendous suffering. Such individuals learn not only to tolerate pain but to live with it in such a way that they can continue to be fruitful. In many cases, what gives their life its greatest meaning is converting their anguish into useful contributions. This is what existential psychiatrist Victor Frankl observed when he tried to sort out why some of his brethren died at Auschwitz, the Nazi death camp, while others survived. It wasn't just that people were randomly murdered, but Frankl also noted that some of the inmates just gave up and died of despair. They seemed to be unable to find any meaning to their suffering.

> *We who lived in concentration camps can remember the men who walked through the huts comforting others, giving away their last piece of bread. They may have been few in number, but they offer sufficient proof that everything can be taken from a man but one thing: the last of the human freedoms—to choose one's attitude in any given set of circumstances, to choose one's own way.*

This same attitude is what distinguishes those who somehow manage to overcome their emotional disabilities in order to devote their lives to creative efforts: they find some meaning in their pain. Among the subjects of this book, you will immediately notice the difference between those who surrendered to their illnesses, taking their own lives, and those who managed to endure. Compare, for instance, the difference between rock icon Jim Morrison of The Doors, who slipped into a melancholic stupor supported by drugs, and Brian Wilson of the Beach Boys, who eventually rediscovered his creative energy after decades of depressive darkness. As you will see, Wilson was able to negotiate some peace, largely as a result of not only creating music but also finding personal meaning in his pain.

What Privileges Are Afforded the Creatively Mad?

Keep in mind that many creative innovations and new discoveries appear downright crazy at the time. Many scientists, artists, and writers have been branded as heretics. Galileo, Copernicus, Columbus, Freud, Darwin, Picasso, and Einstein did not exactly enjoy a receptive audience to their radical ideas. It takes a certain amount of single-minded devotion (read compulsivity) and thick skin (immune to others' disapproval) to overturn the status quo.

It can be seen from these examples that madness can afford the individual certain resources and abilities that are not available to others. The fantasy life, free flight of ideas, distortions of reality, and heightened senses that are associated with mood disorders offer a unique perspective on the world. If we rename the mania that accompanies bipolar disorder as a kind of *intense creative experience*, then we have a description of a state that does indeed lend itself to inspiration and productivity.

In interviews with prominent artists and writers, it was found that almost all of them reported periods of intense productive output in which they could go without sleep and work almost to the point of exhaustion. Rather than calling them manic states, they described them in terms of creative ecstasy, characterized by euphoria, enthusiasm, boundless self-confidence, fluency and speed of ideas, physical and emotional sensitivity, and emotional intensity. Sounds pretty good if you want to get a lot of work done, doesn't it? And haven't many of us experienced this kind of productive experience at some time in our lives?

When questioned further, however, these creative artists also mentioned some rather annoying symptoms as well, including fear and anxiety, suspiciousness, excessive drug and alcohol use, impulsivity, uncontrolled sexuality, restlessness, irritability, grandiose ideas, argumentativeness, reckless spending of money, and breakneck speech. What now emerges is not just a picture of artistic license but something approaching a more psychotic mania.

As described earlier, that may very well be one reason why people with this capacity gravitate toward artistic professions, not only among the eminent but also in those industries such as advertising, entertainment, and journalism that permit flexibility in work styles and tolerate eccentricities.

Is Madness Truly Divine?

The evidence may be compelling regarding the link between creativity and madness, but there are also critics who question this and believe that it is essentially a myth. The question we should be asking is not whether creative individuals are helped by their mental illness but whether some people can be so resilient that they manage to accomplish remarkable things in spite of their handicaps.

The National Alliance for the Mentally Ill, an organization particularly concerned with the ways that these awful diseases were being portrayed as helpful in some ways, conducted their own study in which they asked twenty-four artists what happened to their output once their symptoms were brought under control by Lithium. One-quarter said there was no change in the quality or quantity of their work, and one-half reported that their creative efforts actually improved. Other studies have supported this result, suggesting that only about one-quarter of those who begin treatment notice a drop in their creative productivity.

Ancient Greek philosophers such as Plato, Socrates, and Aristotle lauded the benefits of *divine madness,* which they believed was literally a gift from the gods, the source of creative inspiration. But the condition is not nearly as much fun or as entertaining as it is cracked up to be. There is no way to romanticize or gloss over the debilitating severity of symptoms nor the depth of despair that is prevalent among those with serious mental illness—no matter how productive they may have been in one domain.

As you will see in the stories contained in this book, emotional disorders are best described as a living hell, an existence of daily life so excruciatingly painful, so devoid of hope, that death is often seen as the only way out. And the chances of those with mental illness killing themselves are about twenty times greater than the general population.

Contemporary novelist William Styron writes about his own struggles with lifelong depression, which became so merciless that killing himself seemed the best and only solution:

> The pain is unrelenting, and what makes the condition intolerable is the foreknowledge that no remedy will come—not in a day, an hour, a month, or a minute. If there is mild relief, one knows that it is only temporary, more pain will follow. It is hopelessness even more than pain that crushes the soul.

Just imagine what it must be like to be so desperate, so *accepting* that your plight in life will never change. All you can do to give yourself even a few hours of satisfaction (but never peace) is to give vent to your creative expression.

In What Ways Are Creativity and Mental Illness Related?

There are many different kinds of mental illness common to the creative professions, each with its own unique set of tortures. Perhaps most prevalent of all among artists and writers is *manic depression* or *bipolar disorder,* a biologically based cycling of moods that takes someone from a state of crippling depression to euphoric agitation. Next most common would be *major depression,* the diagnostic name given to those who experience terrible and lengthy periods of melancholic misery that appear without any precipitating event. Both of these conditions are often not only biologically based but also passed on from one generation to the next. Someone like Ernest Hemingway, who suffered suicidal depression, had two other siblings who killed themselves, not to mention a father and a son with the same condition. Philosopher William James and his writer brother, Henry James, were both afflicted with major depression, as were their father and two other of their siblings. Vincent van Gogh had three other siblings with psychotic or mood disorders that led to suicide or insane asylums.

Less severe but still incapacitating conditions that are common to the creative include *dysthymia,* a milder but still chronic form of low-grade depression, *schizophrenia* (most famous examples are the Nobel Prize–winning mathematician John Nash and English poet Richard Dodd), *obsessive-compulsive disorders* (think Howard Hughes), *anxiety disorders* (John Steinbeck, Charles Darwin, Barbra Streisand, Woody Allen), *drug or alcohol addictions* (Jackson Pollock, Sigmund Freud, Thomas Edison, Edgar Allan Poe). The latter often begins as a form of self-medication for distressing symptoms and then becomes a hard-to-break habit that becomes a problem in itself.

Although these mental illnesses manifest themselves in unusual, different, and confounding ways, there are several common symptoms:

- Impaired or dysfunctional relationships with family and friends. Not only is the creative person distressed, but likely so are the people around him or her who have to deal with the erratic behavior.

- Apathy and diminished pleasure in most activities. Mental illness is a grim business. It is a major chore just to get through the day, much less to derive any satisfaction from the experience.

- Significant changes in appetite and eating patterns. People often lose or gain weight, further compromising their health and well-being.

- Disrupted sleep in the form of either chronic insomnia or constant waking. It is difficult to concentrate and remain focused, much less feel very good if you can't get enough sleep to function well.

- Chronic fatigue and lack of energy (except during mania). Not only does the sleep disruption take its toll, but even for those who sleep constantly, it is still hard to find the energy to crawl out of bed.

- Feeling totally worthless inside, no matter how much you accomplish or how much recognition you have. Self-esteem and confidence take a huge hit when you realize you are noticeably different (and a burden) than everyone else around you.

- Presence of auditory or visual hallucinations that destroy your ability to experience the world the way that others do or to see what others describe as "reality." If you can't trust that what you are seeing and hearing is real, it takes a tremendous effort to negotiate daily activities without getting yourself in big trouble.

- Self-defeating behavior in the form of acting out or self-medicating. When you have little to lose anyway, when you have problems with impulse control, when you believe yourself to be special, it is predictable that you might do some things that are hurtful to yourself or others. Especially common are attempts at self-medication through addictions and eating disorders.

- A sense of abject hopelessness and despair such that the future seems like a prison sentence that must be endured—until you have the courage to end it once and for all.

A picture now begins to emerge, not of someone who is "gifted" but rather is afflicted with a chronic disease. Writing in a letter about his episodes of insanity, Edgar Allan Poe talked about his attempts to medicate himself with alcohol, to the point that he was regularly seen about town as a drunk: "During these fits of absolute unconsciousness I drank, God knows how much or how long. As a matter of course, my enemies referred the insanity to the drink rather than the drink to the insanity."

As you will find in the stories that follow, it is challenging to sort out the cause-effect relationships between madness and creativity. Do some forms of psychopathology help promote greater creativity? Or is it the other way around: Does deep creative work lead to madness?

Regardless of which way the process flows, you will find within the biographical narratives some fascinating themes that will generate as many questions as answers. You may also find some interesting parallels to your own life, perhaps not to the extremes that are represented in these particular individuals, who are chosen for their uniqueness, but nevertheless inspiring in that they remind you what can be accomplished under the most challenging circumstances.

CHAPTER TWO

Sylvia Plath

Perfected in Death

At age thirty, at the very height of her creative powers, and just beginning to earn international attention, Sylvia Plath took her own life, in what was to become not only a final act of madness but also the seminal event that finally brought her the recognition she so desperately sought.

To fully appreciate the magnitude of Sylvia Plath's desperation, one must remember that she was at the time the mother of two young children, Nicholas and Frieda, both still in diapers. Picture their mother calmly putting them to bed, reading them stories, and tucking them in. She sits in a chair in their room, watching them sleep, tears falling down her cheeks, but still with sufficient control to avoid any sobs that might disturb them. After some minutes, or maybe hours—she has completely lost track of time—she stands unsteadily on her feet and kisses each child on the forehead. She feels so exhausted, so utterly spent and depleted, that she can barely find the energy to move. The chair beckons her to sit again, but there is much to do as the night slips away.

It was the winter of 1963, and Plath had been living with her husband, Ted Hughes, in Devon, several hours outside London in the English countryside. Hughes had insisted that they move there so he could have his solitude. She had just published her autobiographical novel, *The Bell Jar*, under a pseudonym.

The previous months, Plath had been progressively deteriorating in her mental state, and her marriage was ruined beyond repair. Yet in spite of this pressure, she continued to forge on in her creative work, producing some of her best poems. Plath had been prolific since her first writing binge at age ten, but nothing like the kind of work she had been turning out these last weeks, when the world seemed to close in on her, and she could no longer think clearly about anything else except putting words to page.

Her behavior had become increasingly alarming; she was described as "raving" or "psychotic" by Jillian Becker, a neighbor, and even her husband, Ted Hughes, who had left her several months earlier to live with his girlfriend. During the days, she might be lucid and clear-headed, but as darkness fell, she would become disoriented, confused, and erratic, problems that were partially related to chronic insomnia. There was genuine concern about her ability to care for herself, much less her children.

Plath took tranquilizers and sleeping pills to help ease her anxiety; they did seem to numb her, but not nearly enough. She still felt resolved to follow through on the plan to end her life that she had been considering since she was a teenager. For quite some time, she had thought about sleeping pills as the best option, but that had already failed her once as a college student. Hanging had been considered and rejected. For a period, she thought about following the lead of her role model, Virginia Woolf, by drowning—she even tried that once but couldn't quite complete the job. Guns and razor blades were far too messy. But now she had finally settled on a plan that gave her some relief—finally, there would be some end to the torture she endured. She was supposed to have died ten years earlier during her first serious suicide attempt, so she considered that everything that had happened since then was an unexpected bonus. Now, not her poetry, not even her young children, seemed enough to keep her going any longer.

Plath opened a window in the children's room, even though there was a chill in the winter night. She took one last look at her little boy and girl, backing out of the room and closing the door carefully. She tested the handle one more time to make sure it was closed securely; then she studied the crack at the bottom and the seams along the side.

Returning with supplies, she stuffed a towel under the door and taped the edges all the way around, working carefully and methodically. Once satisfied with the result, she shuffled toward the kitchen, where she took a seat to gather her strength.

It was now the time of the night—or early morning—when she usually did her best work. As she was always plagued by insomnia, it was not uncommon for her to be up at this time, writing line after line of verse. It was for that reason that her landlord, Trevor Thomas, who lived in the flat downstairs, thought little of the relentless pacing he could hear through the floorboards. Sometimes it would go on all through the night.

Just a few nights earlier, Plath had completed her last poem, "Edge," at the same table where she now contemplated an act of destruction rather than creation. Like so much of her writing, the poem was painfully and brutally descriptive of her current emotional state. She now lived without hope. Her marriage had just ended through one last act of betrayal—her husband going off to live with his girlfriend. Plath felt totally worthless as a mother, believing her children would be better off without her. There is even evidence in that last poem that she considered taking her children with her on this journey of total self-destruction, writing about dead children coiled at her empty breasts. It would seem that she decided on a reprieve, at least for the little ones.

"The woman is perfected," Plath wrote in the opening line to her last poem. "Her dead body wears the smile of accomplishment." Then two stanzas follow, "Feet seem to be saying: We have come so far, it is over."

It was not just her feet that had surrendered but her whole being. Plath rose from her chair and shut the door to the kitchen with deliberate intention. She placed another rolled towel at the space at the bottom and then repeated the process of taping the door's edges. She studied the result carefully until she was satisfied. She seemed to find some small satisfaction in doing this final job as perfectly as possible. She might be a failure as a wife, a mother, and a poet, but in this, her final act, she would get it right. Plath returned to her chair to rest from the exertions and gather one final surge of strength and resolve. She stood up, walked slowly over to the oven, and turned the knobs all the way to their highest settings, without lighting the burner.

Getting down on her knees, Sylvia Plath, one of the most innovative and ultimately most venerated poets of the last century (even though at this point she still lived in relative obscurity), gave in to her madness. The creative work was no longer enough to sustain her. The pain was just too much—she could not endure another day, not even another hour. Plath took the very last towel and placed it on the oven door where she rested her cheek, taking deep breaths until unconsciousness claimed her.

The pain had finally ended.

Early Beginnings

Much of what we know about Sylvia Plath comes not only from interviews from friends and relatives who are still living but also from her own voice and writing. Plath was an inveterate letter writer. She produced thousands upon thousands of letters, sent to her friends, lovers, pen pals, and relatives over the years. Several thousand such letters were sent to her mother alone during the years she spent away at college and living abroad.

Plath was not only an accomplished and highly disciplined poet by the time she was eight years old, publishing for the first time in the *Boston Herald,* but she was also committed to keeping a journal since childhood. By the time she was twelve, Plath was writing entries almost daily, including everything from the poems she had completed and the projects she was working on to the most detailed descriptions of her clothes, teachers, friends, fantasies, sexual impulses, and innermost thoughts. By the time she died, there were something like twenty-five separate manuscripts containing her journals, all but the ones that were kept the last two years of her life, which were destroyed by Ted Hughes to protect their children (and most likely himself).

When you consider that so much of her writing was in fact autobiographical, we can add these artistic works to the stacks of material written in her own voice. The result is that there are few artists about whom we know so much about what she thought and felt, not only about her creativity but also about the despair that drove so much of her artistic work.

Plath's earliest memories were of a happy childhood with plenty of time spent reading and enjoying the beach near where she lived along the coast of Massachusetts. She was born in Boston in 1932, where her father, Otto, was a distinguished professor of German and biology at Boston University. Her mother, Aurelia, was an English teacher, who also became a professor of literature. The family settled in a small town north of the city, with easy access to the beach.

In spite of the way that Sylvia Plath attempted to romanticize her early life and gloss over the hardships, there is little doubt that her father was one very strange guy. He ran the household with both German efficiency and autocratic control, isolating his wife and the children from others. He was a selfish and self-centered man who was described as stubborn, controlling, opinionated, and antisocial. He required complete obedience from his wife, and his children.

Sylvia's mother, Aurelia, had dreams of being a writer and novelist but was not permitted to do so because she was obliged to take care of Sylvia; her younger son, Warren; her irascible husband; plus her work responsibilities. Otto ran a tight ship, and no such extravagances as discretionary writing were to be permitted unless it somehow contributed to his needs. When Sylvia was born, Aurelia, the frustrated writer and English teacher, tried to live her unfulfilled desires through her daughter. By the time Sylvia was five, she had already written her first poem, and by eight, she was producing rhymes and couplets at a regular rate. These efforts were kept secret from the controlling Otto, who would not have approved.

When Otto became ill during this time, he was so stubborn—as well as depressed and self-destructive—that he refused to consult with medical authorities. He was convinced he was dying of cancer, and so there was no sense in seeking any treatment. By the time he realized that he had diabetes, which could have been treated, the disease was far too advanced. He died when Sylvia was nine, and it was from this time onward that it felt like her childhood ended.

Although Otto's death certainly had a huge emotional impact on the family, Aurelia and the children must have also felt some relief from finally being out from underneath his complete dominance. One devastating consequence, however, was the poverty they faced, as Otto had refused to make any long-term financial provisions for his family. This worry about money, and concerns about where and how they would live, would follow Sylvia Plath for the rest of her life.

The family was forced to relocate to the town of Wellesley after Otto's death so that Aurelia could find suitable work. None of these dramatic changes in residence, financial status, or her father's death had an appreciable impact on Sylvia's school performance. Throughout her life, from the earliest years all the way through graduate school, she continued to excel academically at the highest level. She demonstrated a degree of intellectual precociousness that was off the scale, a potential that was also realized in straight A's throughout her school years.

While in high school, Sylvia Plath's creative gifts were already emerging. She began publishing her poems and essays not only in school newspapers but also in mainstream print publications, like the *Christian Science Monitor* and *Seventeen.* Most young poets would be thrilled for such an exposure at such an early age. But following a pattern that would occur throughout her life, no matter how much success she enjoyed, it was never enough. For every publication acceptance she received, there were twenty or fifty times as many rejections—normal for any working poet—but with the young Sylvia Plath, each rejection was a personal blow to her psyche. Her moods were volatile and unpredictable, sometimes the result of disappointments, and other times the beginning of what would soon develop as major depression.

Notoriety

Based on her superior academic record, Plath earned a full scholarship to Smith College, entering in the fall of 1950. Smith was one of the best private institutions in North America, one of the famous "Seven Sisters" colleges (at a time when the Ivy League did not allow women students) and a breeding ground for the brightest, most privileged women in the country. Interestingly, she chose to move away from home—and her mother—even though she lived within walking distance of another esteemed institution: Wellesley College. Sylvia wanted to have greater independence and to get away from her mother's stifling influence.

To say that Plath distinguished herself at Smith would be a gross understatement. Even among the most talented women in the country, she stood out as extraordinarily gifted as a thinker and a writer. She continued to write poems at a blistering pace, discovering how this creative expression helped her cope with depressions that were becoming both more frequent and more intense. Her primary mentor and scholarship sponsor, Olive Higgins Prouty, even suggested that Plath concentrate on writing about her own experiences as much as possible. This became the signature theme of her writing career.

By perusing her journals during this time, it can be seen that she was in many aspects a pretty normal college student. She ruminated a lot about men, sex, love, friends, her ambitions and dreams. She also started documenting her emotional states. In one entry, she even made a connection between the frequent physical illnesses that would plague her throughout life and the depression she felt.

For the first time, during her sophomore year, the depression became so severe that she could no longer write. And this sent her spiraling into even deeper despair. Her journal entries are replete with brutally self-critical statements, calling herself "pitifully stupid" and "inadequate." She also began writing about an increasingly paralyzing sense of helplessness, as if she were drowning. In one entry, dated November 3, 1952, she writes:

I am afraid. I am not solid, but hollow. I feel behind my eyes a numb, paralyzed cavern, a pit of hell, a mimicking nothingness. I never thought, I never wrote, I never suffered. I want to kill myself, to escape from responsibility, to crawl back abjectly into the womb. I do not know who I am, where I am going—and I am the one who has to decide the answers to these hideous questions.

As if she didn't already have enough to deal with, sleeplessness was the next symptom to take hold, a condition that would persist throughout her life. It is challenging enough for anyone to deal with the problems of daily living, especially when under considerable pressure and suffering from a mental condition, but having in addition a chronic lack of sleep makes it almost impossible to think clearly, make sound decisions, and cope effectively.

Plath sought psychiatric care for the first time after a suicide attempt, with limited results. Like most such organically based depressions, the episodes would appear and disappear of their own accord, often without any precipitating event. Because this was a time before effective antidepressant medications, there was little to do but wait for the mood disorder to run its course and hope that talking helped (which it usually did not). It certainly didn't help matters that Plath was often perceived by peers, and her few friends, as arrogant, aggressive, demanding, volatile, and difficult to get along with. This only contributed to her sense of isolation.

Plath continued to excel in her studies throughout the next few years, all the while managing to produce an astonishing body of work for someone so young. Many of her poems continued to appear in major magazines. She earned honors and prizes, one after the other, culminating in the 1953 invitation to serve as guest editor of a special issue of *Mademoiselle.* Even though this was certainly the high point of her brief career up to that time, the experience was ultimately disappointing, if not completely disillusioning. She was introduced to the commercial aspects of the magazine publishing business, which appeared to compromise the integrity of the work selected and produced. In *The Bell Jar,* a thinly disguised version of her experiences in novel form, Plath described how she began to obsess about various ways to end her life during this period. As she was already in New York, the land of skyscrapers, jumping off a building seemed like a good option, but she figured that it would need to be at least seven stories to be safe. Too messy and undignified she considered, especially for a Smith girl.

The next best option was to follow the lead of the ancient Roman philosophers, who used to open their veins in a warm bath. "But when it came right down to it," Plath wrote, "the skin of my wrist looked so white and defenseless that I couldn't do it. It was as if what I wanted to kill wasn't in that skin or the thin blue pulse that jumped under my thumb, but somewhere else, deeper, more secret, a whole lot harder to get at."

She finally settled on pills, and lots of them. But she had to wait for the right time and place.

Once back at home with her mother, Plath realized her depression seemed intractable. Even worse than the pain was the realization that she was so sick she lost the ability to write. Because this was the only reason she had for staying alive, there seemed to be no sense in continuing. She wanted to die. Very badly. And now was the time.

Sylvia Plath wrote a note to her mother, saying that she went for a walk. She went down into the cellar, where she had discovered a small cranny she could crawl into; her body would remain undiscovered for some time. Then she swallowed close to fifty sleeping pills before she passed out.

When her mother came home to find the note, she waited several hours, then several more hours, before eventually calling the police. Sylvia Plath was missing, disappeared, couldn't be found. During the next few days, headlines were all over the newspapers and media, speculating on what had happened to the coed who had vanished in thin air. Police, and even the Boy Scouts, launched searches in the vicinity, but without success.

It wasn't until Aurelia noticed that the sleeping pills were missing that she began to suspect that Sylvia was somewhere around the house. They began a more thorough search that soon uncovered the hiding place where Plath's body lay hidden. By the time they found her, she was barely alive, a mass of bruises, filth, scrapes, and sores. Although only barely conscious, she had entered a state of catatonia.

Sylvia Plath was now famous on campus, and throughout the region, not only for being a talented poet but also for being mentally unstable, a mad woman.

Treatments

By this time, Olive Prouty was gravely concerned about her protégé and so agreed to foot the bill for the best mental health treatment that could be found. Sylvia's depressive condition was so grave that the doctors decided to use electroconvulsive shock treatment (ECT). At that time, this was a terribly primitive procedure that resembled a medieval form of torture. There were no restraints or tranquilizers employed. There wasn't even a doctor present. Just a piece of wood between the teeth so that the patient didn't bite her tongue off during induced convulsions.

It was an utterly terrifying experience that left Sylvia literally speechless. One of the greatest poets of her generation was subjected to repeated shocks to her system to the point where she completely lost touch with words. For a month afterward, she could neither speak nor seem to recognize words spoken to her. Even worse, the shock treatment not only didn't cure the depression, but her personality seemed to fall apart. She began showing the most florid signs of full-fledged mania. A few years later, she would describe her life as being run "magically by two electric currents—joyous positive and despairing negative." During these manic spells, she would become agitated, her mind racing with ideas she couldn't begin to form into words. She was not yet able to channel this energy for creative purposes; a few years later, she would stay up into the wee hours of the morning, pacing up and down, writing poems with a fury. But at that time, confined to a hospital, she seemed at times as if she would explode. She seemed far worse than she had been before the suicide attempt.

Plath's recovery was slow and very gradual. She seemed to improve more because the illness ran its course than because of any particular treatment the doctors attempted. Psychotherapy with a female psychiatrist, Ruth Barnhouse, did prove useful to her in some ways, mostly because the doctor gave her explicit permission to begin talking about her feelings openly, as well as exploring her repressed sexuality toward men. This had been a situation over which she had been feeling considerable guilt.

Now that Plath had a benevolent sponsor, she was afforded the opportunity to enter the famed McLean Psychiatric Hospital, described as the "Mad Poet's Society" because it had housed some of the greatest living poets, like Robert Lowell, during their mental breakdowns. One writer observed that for several of the hospitalized poets "sojourns at McLean provided not only needed respites but also creative material. Madness came out of the closet in their writings, and even acquired a certain cachet."

A second round of abbreviated shock treatments proved more helpful. For reasons that nobody could explain (the workings of ECT still remain a mystery), she made a complete reversal, regaining both her composure and her spark. In spite of her recovery, however, Plath remained painfully insecure. She could never seem to get past the idea that in this land of "blue bloods" and privileged women attending Smith, she would always be a "scholarship girl," who was never good enough and never deserving. No matter how hard she worked, how perfect her grades, or how many poems she published, it was never enough to make her feel anything more than barely adequate. She believed it was only a man who could complete her and make her whole.

England

Upon graduation from college in 1955, one year late because of her hospitalizations, Plath was further distinguished by winning a prestigious Fulbright scholarship to study at Cambridge University in England the following fall semester. This was also a time when she continued to explore her sexuality. Unfortunately, because of her unusually low self-esteem, fragility, and self-destructive tendencies, she made some spectacularly poor decisions about choosing her lovers.

Plath's first sexual experience, a few weeks before leaving for England, was with a man who ended up raping and abusing her physically. She actually spent the evening after the experience in the hospital, after which she continued dating the man! She blamed herself for the episode. Maybe she had done something to deserve it, or she had led him on, or she had misunderstood his intentions? In any case, the bottom line is that she ended up seeing this man who had treated her so abysmally.

Professionally, Plath's career received a large boost as she made preparations for her new life in Cambridge, England. She had poems accepted in the *Atlantic Monthly,* the *Nation, Harper's,* and *Mademoiselle,* among others. She was only twenty-two years old and had already written hundreds of poems, dozens of short stories, magazine articles, and published essays. She had been awarded a most prestigious scholarship and was graduating from one of the most elite universities summa cum laude.

Once settled at Cambridge, Plath devoted herself to her studies and writing with total devotion. More than anything the doctors had tried—shock treatment, medications, psychotherapy, bed rest—it was writing poetry that seemed to calm and stabilize her the most. It was the only reason she could find to keep living. Without that, there was nothing else to live for.

But Sylvia Plath was a complicated person, living during a transitional time for women. As much as she wanted a career, she also wanted to find love with the right man. She had been told all her life that it was OK to have poetry as a hobby, but her real purpose was to settle down, raise a family, and make a good home for her husband.

The weather in England was predictably miserable—cold, dark, and wet—which didn't seem to help matters any. Plath again felt herself slipping backward into depression, as if this illness had a life of its own (which in a sense, it did). She began to exhibit delusional and paranoid thinking, believing at one point that children assaulted her with snowballs because they could sense she was rotten to the core. She found it difficult to make eye contact with anyone for fear they could see inside her. If the poetry was not enough to save her, she reasoned, then perhaps a man might do the trick. She was ready to meet someone.

She was first attracted to Ted Hughes because of the violence in his poetry. Writing in her journal about his poem "I Did It," she said, "Such violence, and I can see how women lied down for artists. The one man in the room who was as big as poems, huge, with hulk and dynamic chunks of words; his poems are strong and blasting like a high wind in steel girders."

If her first lover raped and abused her, then perhaps it is not surprising that she picked a future husband who, although a brilliant poet on the verge of recognition, was also a noted philanderer. Hughes was tall, dark, handsome, and charismatic. He also seemed to exude a kind of dangerous violence and unpredictability that Plath found both alluring and a little frightening. It was an inauspicious start to their relationship that Hughes roughed up Plath during their first lovemaking, leaving her bruised and battered as she later described in her journal. To add further humiliation, he mistakenly called her by another woman's name. Sylvia was appalled by the way he treated her, but like many wounded, insecure women, she went back for more.

Once their relationship solidified, they both agreed that Ted's career was far more promising than her own, so she took on the responsibility for being his literary agent, as well as his typist. That this would compromise her own creative output seemed to be worth the price: finally, she wouldn't be alone any longer.

There has been so much written about the Plath-Hughes marriage, most of it scathingly derogatory. Sylvia Plath is portrayed as a helpless victim and Ted Hughes as a beast who took advantage of her. But as in so many relationships, conflicts are almost always an interactive effect: Sylvia Plath played some role in the destructive relationship and shaped Ted Hughes, just as he did with her.

Certainly, there were some aspects of their relationship that were highly dysfunctional—for both of them. Hughes was an abusive fellow, given to fits of rage and violence. He also held some very weird ideas about the occult. He experimented with hypnosis as a form of mind control, and his wife was his most frequent subject. The two of them frequently consulted crystal balls and tarot cards before making important decisions. They believed that they were in contact with the spirit world and even had names for the favorite spirits that guided them.

Yet with all the weird goings-on, Plath felt the healing power of love as an anecdote for her despair. She believed in her heart that Hughes could save her. He believed it, too.

Domestic Life

Plath and Hughes began their life together, marrying in the summer of 1956, just three and a half months after they met. Despite their agreement that his work was most important, both intended to pursue their parallel careers, working to support each other. It is obvious that they both had tremendous affection and respect for each other, especially for each other's writing. Throughout their life together, they always resided in cramped quarters, working practically on top of each other. Their emotional life was rich, their sexual life satisfying, and for at least six years that they lived first in England and then briefly back in the states, they enjoyed a relatively stable, happy marriage.

Some critics and biographers have reviled Hughes as the villain in their marriage, but in many ways he was an excellent and patient companion for his wife, who, in her own ways, was not exactly easy to be around. Sylvia Plath's dependence on Ted Hughes was sometimes so smothering that by his own count, she interrupted him 104 times in a single afternoon!

During the years they were married and living together, Hughes's career as a poet eclipsed that of his wife. His first book of collected poems, *The Hawk and the Rain,* was published in 1957, championed by no less than T. S. Eliot, who represented the publisher. This brought Hughes a lot of international attention. Meanwhile Plath stopped writing altogether, trying hard to support them both with odd jobs, because being a poet never paid much—then or now. It was not just the responsibilities that crushed her creative urges but domestic life as a whole. She felt as if she were dying "in the world of pies and shin beef." She felt stuck, stymied, admitting, ". . . my whole being has grown and interwound so completely with Ted's that if anything were to happen to him, I don't know how I could live. I would either go mad, or kill myself."

Because Plath's husband was another poet, who did not hold regular employment, responsibility fell on her to earn the stable family income. Soon after they were married, the next year, in 1957, she was offered the dream job—to teach English at her alma mater. Hughes agreed that the change of scenery might do them some good. For the first time in her life, she had a stable source of income, as well as the kind of respectability for which she so long yearned. She also followed in the footsteps of her mother, who was a professor at Boston University at the time.

Yet while teaching her classes and keeping up with all the grading, Plath could feel her creative energy being drained away. During the period when they first boarded the ship for America, she could feel the urge to write returning again, but the feeling did not last. At the time, she not only had little time to write but had even less inclination. She might have enjoyed some degree of financial and emotional stability, but it came with the cost of losing her creative voice. Her mother was proud. Her husband was grateful for her financial support. Her colleagues and students were impressed. But inside, Plath felt she was dying.

Like so many creative geniuses who attain exalted status, Sylvia Plath cut loose from the moorings that grounded her life. She risked everything, certainly the idea of a stable home, and—even more dangerous—her sanity, in order to pursue her art. She quit the teaching post at Smith after one year and took a job as a secretary at McLean, in the same hospital where she was once a psychiatric patient.

Needing to remain intellectually stimulated during this stifling domestic life, Plath attended a seminar at Boston University by famed
poet Robert Lowell. Lowell talked not only about his art but also about
his struggles to deal with his own severe depressions. It was there that
Plath befriended another up-and-coming (and depressed) writer,
Anne Sexton, who was to become her confidante as well as competitor. They compared notes about the best way to commit suicide and
swapped stories about their previous attempts. Sexton and Plath
closely followed each other's careers with an equal measure of admiration and envy. They also shared a dark secret in their mutually dis-
abling depressive episodes. It is more than a little eerie that at various
times in their lives they both ended up at McLean Psychiatric Hospital for treatment, along with their former teacher, Lowell.

After Plath became pregnant with their first child in 1959, Plath
and Hughes decided to return to England so that both of them could
continue to write. Plath wanted to keep her husband away from the
Smith coeds with whom he was often seen flirting, and Hughes
wanted to flee to the countryside, where he could escape the distrac-
tions of bourgeois life in America. For Hughes, this would mean almost complete freedom to spend all of his time doing whatever he
liked (some of which had more to do with an extracurricular love life
than in writing poetry). In contrast, Plath had to work various menial
jobs in order to support the family, writing mostly in the wee hours
of the morning when she could not sleep.

In spite of her efforts to maintain her own separate identity and
writing career, over time Plath grew more and more dependent on her
husband. She began crying frequently, with little or no provocation.
There were more ominous signs as well—all the warnings she had
heard about Ted's seductive proclivities seemed to be played out in
sightings with other attractive women. He denied any involvement,
but Plath became convinced that he was having affairs. Her already
erratic behavior became more pronounced. At one point, she became
so desperate to make sense of what was going on that she ripped up
several of her husband's manuscripts, mixed them up with a few of
his fingernail shavings and dandruff from his desk, and burned them
together in a cauldron while uttering witch's incantations. When the
fire died down, there was one particular scorched piece of paper that
caught her attention. She reached down to retrieve the paper among
the ashes, noticing to her horror that there was a single legible word—

Assia—which she recognized as the name of a woman that she suspected of being her husband's new lover.

The relationship between Plath and Hughes began to deteriorate, even as their first child, Frieda, was born in April 1960. Plath wrote a few months earlier, "Dangerous to be so close to Ted day in and day out. I have no life separate from his, am likely to become a mere accessory." Once their daughter was born, Plath's already fragile emotional state was exacerbated by postpartum depression.

Hughes had by this time resorted to his previous behavior, again earning his reputation as a womanizer, having juggled a number of affairs about which Plath was dimly aware but chose to ignore as much as possible. Plath realized that she was being lied to, and she stopped being able to trust her husband. She became more angry and resentful in direct ways, and all the while she entered her darkest and deepest depression yet.

In spite of the tensions and conflicts between them, the love-hate in their relationship, they produced a second child, Nicholas, who was born in January 1962. Sylvia could sense that she was losing her husband, her lifeline, and this may have been a last attempt to keep him around. Unfortunately, the presence of another crying baby only magnified the claustrophobia she felt, as a captive within their little cottage. She tried to take on the responsibility of motherhood, maintain their family home, earn sufficient income to support them, and yet still find time for her own writing. Even under the most ideal circumstances, Plath had a difficult time with stress. In these circumstances, she was in way over her head.

Whereas previously her depression would take its toll on her creative capacity, this time she had crossed some sort of line where her artistic output became not diminished but enhanced. She was somehow able to write her heart out throughout all the sleepless nights and early mornings, preoccupied with dark thoughts. But this time, the emotional "self-repair" that is possible through creative expression was suspended when she delved too deeply into what psychoanalysts might call *narcissistic regression*. This means that she lost touch with reality and lost control of the usual ways that she had structured her world. In simple terms, she began to unravel.

A few years earlier, Plath had written in her journal about the power she wielded in her creative writing, and the accompanying fear: "I fear the oppressive and crushing forces, if I do not plot and manage and manipulate my path, joining: academic, creative, & writing, and emotional & living & loving: writing makes me a small god." Unless she could control this power, she writes further, she had no doubt that these creative forces would crush her, turning to "destruction and waste."

In "Elm," one of her last poems, she wrote about her feelings of abandonment by her husband and the terror welling up inside her at the prospect of going on alone. The second stanza reads:

> *I am terrified by this dark thing*
> *That sleeps in me;*
> *All day I feel its soft, feathery turnings, its malignity.*

The next few months, the last ones of her life, were also the most prolific of her life. In a normal year, she might write twenty, or perhaps thirty, poems, but in these few months she produced more than fifty. In the three-week period from the middle of January to when she died on February 11, 1963, Plath produced a new poem each day, arguably the best work of her career. She operated at maximum height, without a net. As she began the progressive descent into madness, her tenuous grip on reality began slipping away. She became reclusive, erratic, delusional, and increasingly strange. The nanny taking care of the children reported that Plath attacked her physically, and so she abruptly quit. Her doctor, John Horder, was so concerned for her safety that he hired a nurse to watch over her.

Hughes had moved out by this time and was living with Assia, who was pregnant with his child. Plath was so depressed that she didn't seem to care. She commented in a letter to her mother that she knew Ted wanted her to kill herself so she would finally be out of his hair. Her only concern seemed to be the children. Who would take care of them after she was gone? she said aloud to a neighbor. What would happen after she died?

It was clear that Plath was not thinking very rationally during these last days of her life. She had gone to the trouble to prepare sandwiches and drinks for the children on this last night, forgetting that little Nicholas was only a year old and could hardly feed himself. The next morning, when the nurse, Myra Norris, showed up to check on things, she heard the children crying inside the house, cold, hungry, afraid.

Plath left no message for her husband, observed Jillian Becker, a neighbor and friend, who occasionally took care of the children, "but she left him her poetry, knowing that he would understand those last poems as suicide notes, not apologetic but accusatory." Most of those who knew her best agreed that she killed herself not only out of despair but also out of anger toward the man who had left her alone.

Seeking Explanations—and Blame

Decades later, there is still considerable speculation about what exactly drove Sylvia Plath mad—and ultimately killed her. There are whole books and Web sites devoted to the subject, with rather passionate—if discrepant—views. Her husband, Ted Hughes, maintained consistently that it was her addiction to sleeping pills that unhinged her. Some blamed her death on "black magic," because the couple had been delving into the occult for many years. Many people blamed Assia, Ted's lover, who "stole" his affections from Plath and sabotaged their marriage.

Ted and Assia continued to live together after Plath died, although it was far from a peaceful household. Assia became haunted by Plath's death, as if she was followed by a ghost. She could find no peace, feeling terribly guilty about her role in Sylvia Plath's tragic death. In March 1969, after four years together, Assia moved a mattress into the kitchen, carefully sealed the doors and windows, and dissolved sleeping pills in a glass of water, which she fed to their four-year-old daughter, Shura. Assia swallowed the rest of the pills, turned on the gas stove, and crawled onto the bed. She killed herself, and their four-year-old daughter, exactly the same way that Plath had done—by gas from the kitchen stove.

Far more people blame Hughes as the culprit for driving Plath crazy, with his insensitivity, manipulations, and philandering. During the first years after Sylvia Plath's death, her gravestone was repeatedly defaced by visitors who crossed out her married name: Sylvia Plath ~~Hughes~~. Many Plath fans are still enraged at the very mention of his name.

It was only after his death in 1998 that Hughes's own views on the matter emerged, as he had maintained a stubborn silence for over thirty-five years, refusing to talk about his wife or even to grant an interview. From reviewing his notes, journals, and unpublished works, it is apparent that he also accepted major responsibility for

what happened. He acknowledged that he had made "insane decisions" and had been both unpredictable and unreliable. Perhaps the
accumulative effect of having Assia kill herself (and their child), in
exact imitation of Sylvia, forced him to finally examine his own role
in the tragedies. In the beginning, he may have blamed Plath's reliance
on drugs, and on her own instability, but there is little doubt that he
realized he had helped push her over the edge. In a letter to Sylvia,
composed as a series of poems several years after her death, Ted
Hughes wrote:

> *You were the jailer of your murderer—*
> *which imprisoned you.*
> *And since I was your nurse and your protector*
> *your sentence was mine too.*

A number of psychiatrists who treated Plath during her lifetime
presented their own theories to account for her mental illness. They
blamed Plath's cold, withholding, tyrannical father, who died when
she was a child, before she had a chance to work through the anger
she felt toward him. Others blamed Plath's mother, who she felt was
so demanding. It is notable that during Sylvia Plath's last months, during the summer of 1962, she built a bonfire and then proceeded to
burn over a thousand of their letters in front of her mother's eyes. This
was her way of getting back at her mother and expressing her rage.
This was especially hurtful, Plath's mother later disclosed, because she
had intended to publish their correspondence, which had endured
over the previous ten years. As a further expression of rage toward her
mother, Sylvia built another fire in front of her mother and casually
tossed into the flames the only copy of her second novel, which she
had been writing, a sequel to *The Bell Jar.*

Although these are compelling explanations, certainly for psychoanalysts who explore the impact of early childhood experience on the
development of mental illness, there is a far simpler but no less compelling explanation for Plath's gifts, and her madness. With two gifted,
creative, and intellectually accomplished parents, it is no surprise that
she would have been born and nurtured to become a great poet, even
while still in elementary school. Even more closely linked to genetic history is mental illness, especially bipolar disorder and major depression.

Sylvia Plath's father, Otto, suffered from depression throughout most of his life, and he functionally committed suicide by refusing medical attention for a curable diabetic condition. Plath later admitted that her father willed himself to die. There were other such currents running throughout the Plath family: Otto's mother, Sylvia's grandmother, also suffered depression so severe that she had to be hospitalized. Otto's sisters, as well, seemed to have inherited the condition, so it was not totally surprising that the propensity would have been passed on to another generation.

Sylvia Plath's incredible creative talent and her debilitating depression were both inherited and nurtured in her family. One was inseparable from the other. In a sense, both the creative talent and the mental illness influenced each other, for better and for worse.

One developmental psychologist has offered the provocative theory that rather than the depression only affecting her poetry, perhaps it was also the other way around: the writing itself exacerbated the mental illness as a consequence of her extreme emotional investment. Plath cared so much about the quality of her artistic achievement, as well as how it was received. She had once admitted in her journal, "I felt if I didn't write nobody would accept me as a human being." It is no wonder, then, that each rejection letter from a magazine or publisher wounded her so grievously.

In a scientific investigation of the observed phenomenon that writers in general, poets in particular, and female poets most of all, suffer extraordinary rates of mental illness, one psychologist dubbed this "The Sylvia Plath Effect." Poets have the highest rates of attempted self-destruction (26 percent compared with 14 percent for other artists and 1 percent for the normal population). They also have the highest incidence of mental illness—according to a study of a thousand distinguished creators.

Other experts believe that the reason why poets like Plath are so prone to madness is because of an external locus of control. More than other artists (and even other writers), they often subscribe to the belief that their creativity emanates from a muse or divine inspiration. As a result, they are helpless and powerless when the words don't flow, unable to conjure the magic needed to produce great works.

Plath wrote a journal entry in 1958, during her brief teaching stint at Smith, berating herself for the loss of creativity, beseeching some external force to restore her gift:

Paralysis still with me. It is as if my mind stopped and let the phenom-
ena of nature-shiny green rosebugs and orange toadstools & screaking
woodpeckers—roll over me like a juggernaut—as if I had to plunge to the
bottom of non-existence, of absolute fear, before I can rise again. . . . I
can't take things as they come, or make *them come as I choose. Will this*
pass like a sickness?

In Plath's case, she was even more susceptible to helpless depression
than other artists and poets because of her strong beliefs in the occult
and spirit world. As mentioned earlier, Plath and Hughes dabbled in
the occult, even using a Ouija board, before undertaking new paths.
Plath engaged in highly personal, self-reflective expression. Most of
her poems, especially during the later years, were written directly
about her daily struggles. Al Alvarez, a friend of Plath and Hughes, as
well as the poetry editor for the *Observer* of London, wrote her obit-
uary, which read, in part:

But it was only recently that the particular intensity of her genius found
its perfect expression. For the last few months she had been writing con-
tinuously, almost as though possessed. In those last poems she was systematically probing that narrow, violent area between the viable and the
impossible, between experience which can be transmuted into poetry and
that which is overwhelming.

It was Plath's fearlessness—and perhaps desperation—that made
her creations so powerful and unique but that also subjected her to
greater vulnerability to critics. She could not help but take any negative comments about her later poetry or autobiographical novel personally because she had invested so much of herself in the material.

It is well-known that parachutists, mercenaries, and stunt drivers
are engaged in dangerous professions. It is far less appreciated just how
risky writing poetry can be, especially for those like Plath who were
already easily wounded, who experienced a lot of the stressors at high
intensity, and who had such a total commitment to their art.

Al Alvarez believed that Plath's brilliance did not lie in her technical skills but rather in her willingness to explore her inner world, "going
down into the cellars and confronting her demons. The bravery and
curious artistic detachment with which she went about her task were
astonishing—heartbreaking, too, when you remember how lonely she

was." In the end, Alvarez no longer believed that any poems—or any art—were truly worth the kind of price that his friend paid.

Not Quite the End of the Story

Just as Plath was strongly affected by Virginia Woolf's brilliant career, as well as her tragic end, so too did the vicious cycle continue after Plath's death. Anne Sexton was so distraught by her friend's suicide, that she, too, began to lose all hope. She mourned her friend's death and also began to feel despair for her own future. Sexton was hospitalized repeatedly for a variety of symptoms: hysteria, mania, depression, insomnia, eating disorders. She sought comfort in alcohol and in a drawn-out destructive affair with her psychiatrist during the time when her marriage began to unravel.

"Sylvia's death disturbs me," Sexton confessed in an interview. They had talked together about their mutual problems and had made a contract with each other to endure for the sake of their art. But after Plath killed herself, Sexton found her own suicidal fantasies increase in frequency and intensity.

In a poem she wrote to honor her friend, "Sylvia's Death," Sexton's own pent-up grief and anguish leaked out as she admitted her own longing for release. Plath's suicide was the beginning of the end for Sexton as well, and yet, just as with her fellow poet, the quality and quantity of her creative work reached a new level of excellence before her death. Sexton attained a level of fame and status during her lifetime that Plath was never able to enjoy. Still, it was not enough. After her marriage dissolved, just like Sylvia's, she sank deeper into depression, isolation, and agitation. Less than a decade after her friend's suicide, Sexton made herself a large drink of vodka, went into the garage, where she started the car, climbed inside, and asphyxiated while listening to the radio. Another charismatic poet ended her own life in madness.

The Plath Legacy

In her final act of self-destruction, Sylvia Plath gained the attention—and recognition—that she so desperately desired. Her suicide and its implicit madness attracted not only public sympathy but also the attention of critics who had previously responded with mostly positive but restrained enthusiasm.

Immediately after her death, Plath's collection of poetry, *Ariel,* sold over five thousand copies in England alone, most of them purchased not by fans of poetry but rather by those, according to biographer Edward Butscher, "who apparently felt compelled to possess the last will and testament of a frustrated kindred spirit, or who wished to certify their own normalcy by comparing their sensibilities to those of a 'mad woman.'" In the end, it was Plath's madness, as much as her creativity, that garnered so much attention and devotion.

She is now generally regarded as one of the greatest poets of the last century, fearless in her willingness to bare her soul and reveal herself so transparently in the beautiful images she created—first of the natural world, and later about the internal conflicts in which we all struggle.

In truth, nothing ever felt good enough for Plath, no matter how many awards, scholarships, or laurels she received. She compared herself to others—her husband, Ted Hughes, for instance, who had been chosen by Queen Elizabeth as Poet Laureate. Whereas Hughes had published numerous volumes of his poems, both in the United Kingdom and America, Plath could not manage to get her novel published in the United States, much less her poetry in outlets other than popular magazines like *The New Yorker* or *Mademoiselle.* It was only after her death that her second volume of poetry, *Ariel,* was published, as well as her novel, *The Bell Jar,* which was finally released under her own name and published in her own country.

Plath had known her whole life that she was different from others, not only with respect to her extraordinary talent but also with respect to her emotional volatility. She considered herself beyond help, beyond redemption. She was a hopeless case, biding her time, trying to churn out as much poetry as she could before she couldn't stand it any longer.

Plath has become a cult figure who still enjoys both a loyal and dedicated following and also new generations of admiring readers of her poetry. Her novel, *The Bell Jar,* has become required reading in many schools and colleges. She has been regarded as among the first feminist poets, an inspiration to other young women (and men) who struggle against their own demons, not to mention the forces of patriarchal oppression, which kept her so insecure and vulnerable. Yet it is this same fragility and oversensitivity that make her art so unique and so powerful. One cannot read her poems, short stories, or *The Bell Jar,* without being so touched by the author's complete openness to her experience. Plath has become the poet with whom depressed, potentially suicidal readers most identify. Her poems evoke raw emotion and yet reassure those in despair that they are not alone.

Sylvia Plath's art is inseparable from her emotional struggles. There are few writers who sought more courageously to excise the relentless grip of depression through creative expression. As great a wordsmith and crafted poet as Plath was, there is little doubt that she would never have attained such greatness if she had chosen to stick with poems about spiders, flowers, and melons rather than her own inner experiences—and excruciating pain. It was her so-called madness, her manic depression or bipolar disorder, that stamped its indelible influence on her writer's voice. Without the pain, there would have been so much less for her to say.

CHAPTER THREE

Judy Garland

Under the Rainbow

J udy Garland was locked in the bathroom, lying on the floor, refusing to respond to any of the desperate calls from her hotel bedroom.

"Mama," her daughter Liza Minnelli screamed through the door. "Mama, are you OK in there?" She banged louder, knowing that something was seriously wrong. Liza was certainly the only kid she knew who had to travel with a stomach pump in case she had to save her mother from another drug overdose, which was occurring with frequent regularity. More than once, she'd had to crawl through the window of a bathroom like this in order to revive her mother's unconscious body, lying in a pool of vomit.

It was the early sixties. Judy's career was on the skids. Again. She was losing her voice. No producer would agree to work with her after the Metro-Goldwyn-Mayer studio canceled her contract. She had tried television next, but *The Judy Garland Show* was being creamed in the ratings by *Bonanza*. It was then considered the most expensive production mistake in the history of television. Her third marriage, to Sid Luft, was failing. Her mood swings had become so extreme that she was even frightening herself, because she had no idea who would emerge next: the lethargic, depressed victim; the agitated, enraged screamer; or the charming actress eager to please.

Even the usual drugs she consumed were not working any longer, handfuls of them, including prescription pain killers, tranquilizers, amphetamines, and anything else she could get her hands on. When washing them down with wine still gave her no release, she began using heroin and morphine as well.

This time, the bathroom scene was a false alarm. Judy staggered to the door, groggy and disoriented, wondering what the fuss was all about. Liza could only shake her head in frustration. She was just a teenager, trying to make her way in the world, and here she was, the primary caregiver, the one person in the world who was most responsible for keeping her mother alive.

Who Was Judy Garland, Really?

Judy Garland's life resembled absolutely nothing you have ever heard before. She was the ultimate, temperamental thoroughbred. Few people have ever been born with more pure artistic talent that realized itself so early in life. With these gifts, however, came a sensitivity and vulnerability that had to be nurtured if she were to survive. Instead she was subjected to constant manipulation, exploitation, and abusive medication by unscrupulous adults determined to keep her going way beyond normal human endurance. Already needy, insecure, and unstable, she developed chronic, incapacitating anxiety that could never be controlled even with all the pills she consumed—Seconal, Tuinal, Demerol, Ritalin, heroin, morphine—pills to lift her up, pills to bring her down, and most of all, pills to numb the pain.

Had Judy Garland not been started by her mother and professional managers on highly addictive, dangerous drugs when she was nine years old, perhaps she might have had the chance for a more normal childhood and the opportunity to mature in healthy ways. Instead she learned from the earliest age to reduce any discomfort or provide any needed boost through chemical means. She was a commodity to most of those around her: a meal ticket to her mother and later her producers, directors, and husbands. So they took advantage of a vulnerable, needy, and sensitive child to enjoy the maximum benefit from their property.

Judy Garland may very well be the greatest entertainer who ever lived. She wasn't just a singer with the best instrumental voice of her generation (or perhaps *any* generation). She wasn't only a dancer who could hold her own with costars like Fred Astaire and Gene Kelly. She was also a great actress who worked with the biggest names in Hollywood: Spencer Tracy, Burt Lancaster, Richard Widmark, Mickey Rooney, Maximilian Schell, Montgomery Clift, to mention a few. She used her childlike vulnerability to draw the audience into her heart and wide eyes of amazement—as if she, too, was stunned by the magic. She didn't just sing *to* an audience, she sang *with* them in a way that they felt transported over the rainbow.

In a career that began when she was two years old and lasted forty-five more years, Judy Garland made thirty-two movies, earning Academy Award nominations for her role in both a musical (*A Star is Born*) and a dramatic performance (*Judgment at Nuremberg*). Her films *Meet Me in St. Louis, Easter Parade, The Pirate, Babes in Arms,* and others she made with Mickey Rooney when she was barely a teenager rank as among the best musicals ever. Then there was *The Wizard of Oz,* often regarded as the best film (and certainly most watched) ever made.

Her work as an actress would have qualified her for immortality alone. Although *The Judy Garland Show,* offered late in her career, would meet stiff competition, her TV specials in the late fifties and early sixties attracted the largest audiences in the history of CBS. Her live concert in 1961, *Judy at Carnegie Hall,* became the fastest-selling record album of the era, winning five Grammy Awards. In the thousand concerts she gave all over the world, from the London Palladium to the Palace Theatre on Broadway, record-breaking sellout crowds waited months for tickets.

Her personal life, the subject of tabloids during the time (and long after), only added to her legend. She was the original diva, a superstar who lived with the relentless pressure of sustaining a superhuman level of performance and who sought constantly for the reassuring reward of applause and the love of her audience. The same talent that allowed her to reach such lofty heights of creative and artistic expression, however, was also her scourge. She never stopped being an actress, even when the cameras weren't running. She played roles—often deceptive—that compromised her relationships. In order to keep up her performance, alleviate her anxiety, and achieve some kind of happiness, however transient, she lied to her friends, coworkers, even to her doctors and psychiatrists, about her problems and ailments, making it impossible for them to help her. Worse still, she believed her own lies after a while, no longer able to separate the actress from the person. For years, she had been able to pretend that her husband, Vincente Minnelli, was only "artistic" in his manner, even though everyone else knew he preferred the companionship of men. There came a point when she could no longer indulge the fantasy that they were anything other than friends, roommates, and coparents of their daughter; they had never really been lovers.

Garland created fantasy worlds for her fans and inhabited them herself. When reality intruded, she closed her eyes, clicked her heels three times, and wished herself back to Kansas—or rather to the small town in Minnesota where she spent her earliest years—the only time she ever remembered being happy. When the illusions, fantasies, and denial failed her, she used more and more drugs to prolong the dreams and deaden the pain.

Judy Garland's art, her amazing talent to act out different roles, dance to whatever tunes her directors orchestrated, or seduce others through the powerful vibrato of her voice, also enhanced her madness. She was so used to taking direction, from age three onward, that she was virtually incapable of making sound, mature decisions.

If Garland was literally born and bred to perform on stage, it was this same extraordinary talent that would eventually destroy her; it was the madness that took her art to unprecedented levels. She was absolutely wild, impulsive, uninhibited, reckless—all the qualities of a self-destructive personality—but also the features that made her stage presence so transcendent. Audiences got the sense that this was someone who was putting *everything* into her performance, inviting them to join her with an equal level of passion. When she would sit on the end of the stage, dangle her feet over the edge, and begin belting out "Over the Rainbow," people would begin sobbing for their own lost dreams.

Judy Garland was not a controlled method actor. She would turn on a switch and the electricity would flow—sparks flying everywhere, circuits shorting, blowing out the transformer on occasion. Her performances may have seemed effortless with her photographic memory for scripts and reluctance to ever rehearse, but that was because she wanted to put every piece of herself into a line, a song, or a dance. She could only do that by letting herself go completely. Director George Cukor was thoroughly blown away by her power to hit the perfect dramatic nuance of any scene, usually on the first take. Judy told him, only half kidding, that it wasn't really acting on her part because she was so used to dramatic roles in her life. But whatever admiration Cukor ever felt for Garland's talent was counteracted by his firsthand frustrations with her self-indulgences and erratic behavior, which were so disruptive to his set.

Early Life

Judy Garland's parents, Frank and Ethel Gumm, were vaudeville entertainers, who traveled small towns in the rural Midwest and settled for a time in Grand Rapids, Minnesota, in 1914, where they set up their own permanent stage show in the New Grand Theatre. Prior to purchasing the building and refurbishing it, Frank would travel across the country to sing, sometimes visiting as many as twenty-eight states in a single trip, while Ethel would pursue her own musical career as a pianist.

The Gumms made the Grand Theatre their family business, Ethel playing the piano, as she had done for the silent movies of the time, and Frank singing. When their first two daughters were born, they also joined the act, performing as the Gumm Sisters to appreciative crowds. There was little else to do in this town during the long, cold Minnesota winters.

When Frances, the third daughter, was born in 1922, she was immediately nicknamed "Baby" and quickly became the center of her father's world. Frank would disappear for long periods of time on occasion, but when he returned, it was always to hold Baby on his lap and sing her favorite songs.

Little Frances was perched on her father's lap during one of the Gumm Sisters' performances, when she started bouncing up and down and whispering excitedly that she too wanted to go up on stage and sing with her sisters. "Can I do that, Daddy?" the little girl pleaded. "Can I, can I, pleeease, can I?"

Frank could deny his youngest child nothing, so eventually he relented. A few weeks later, when the curtain rose, there stood the two Gumm Sisters, Mary Jane, aged nine, and Virginia, seven, in their accustomed positions. Standing next to them was tiny Frances, about to make her debut.

They sang a song together, to wild appreciation by the audience, followed by little Frances doing a solo of "Jingle Bells." She was so excited by the attention and the applause that she refused to leave the stage when the act was over. She had to be carried away, crying, because she wanted to go on.

Frances, "Baby," Gumm, to be known ultimately by the stage name Judy Garland, was two years old. She was already a star.

Stage Mother

Mary Jane and Virginia were talented, but Baby was born with a magical voice. By the time she was four, she was already the main attraction of the theater. The family entertainment business would have continued to flourish if Frank hadn't run into a bit of trouble. It seems that over the course of the previous years, he had indulged himself in a certain proclivity to befriend and seduce young high school boys. The family had already been run out of one town because Frank had been caught with an underage boy. Now the pattern repeated itself and the Gumms had to flee in a hurry. It was to the West, and Hollywood, that they set their sights.

Once settled in Southern California, the two older sisters eventually pursued other interests, leaving show business to their talented baby sister, while Ethel groomed Baby to be the family breadwinner. She was now six years old, a polished and charismatic entertainer, who sang like an angel. There was a purity to her voice that was innocent and yet resonant and mature.

When you think about the prototypical stage mother of a celebrity child, living vicariously through her talented daughter, Ethel surely fit the mold. In later life, Judy would refer to her as the "Wicked Witch of the West." According to one early biographer, Ethel was "the archetypal, fire-eating, greedy, ambitious, stage matron, a child-devouring monster who was always waiting in the wings." Ethel totally controlled and managed her young daughter's life, with the sole determination to make her daughter into the kind of star that she could never be. Baby, soon to be called Judy, was signed up for dance lessons with the same instructor as Shirley Temple's. Ethel trained and managed her little girl just as she would an employee. Of course, it wasn't that Judy needed that much encouragement: she *loved* performing. She *needed* to sing, to express herself as much as any artist.

During these years, and afterward, nobody ever saw Ethel hold her daughter or even hug her. She was described by neighbors and Judy's friends as cold, withholding, domineering. There was no affection between them, no displays of warmth; it was only from Daddy that Judy found any parental comfort. The problem was that although Frank struggled to maintain a low profile, before long he succumbed to his predatory sexual behavior, and his family was once again evicted from their community in the desert town of Lancaster, a few hours' drive from Los Angeles.

Ethel found them a new place closer to Los Angeles and began dragging Judy around to the Hollywood studios, auditioning her for roles and trying to break into movies. If Ethel was a taskmaster who was hard on Judy, she was just as demanding of herself. She would do whatever it took to ensure that her daughter would succeed. This included having sex with producers or doing anything else to get a break.

How was it possible that Ethel could abuse her daughter, not allow her to live a normal life, and work her like a trained seal, while Frank, who dearly loved his Baby, stood by and permitted his wife to take over such control? As with so many other instances of child abuse, one parent silently colluded, pretending that nothing untoward was going on. Besides, Frank still had his own problems, staying a few steps ahead of the law, because he was still an active pedophiliac, seducing young boys. Each of the parents colluded with the other, forming a silent agreement to overlook each other's destructive behavior.

Because Judy had such an unusual childhood and two such self-indulgent parents, it is little wonder that she would have grown up with a problem or two. But the worst part was still to come. There were times that Judy, now in elementary school, would become exhausted from all the auditions, the rehearsals, and the performances. She was trying to keep up with her schoolwork during the day (when she wasn't pulled out of school altogether), plus working well into the late hours of the evening. Her mother's solution to Judy's normal fatigue and desire to rest was to feed her amphetamines to provide strategic surges of energy. Unfortunately, this meant that after a rehearsal or performance, Judy would be so wired that she couldn't go to sleep, so her mother gave her heavy sleeping pills to counteract the pep pills. By the time Judy was nine years old, she was already dependent on uppers and downers in order to function effectively. Even more remarkable, her own mother was the one insisting that she take the drugs!

Walking the Yellow Brick Road

The Gumms' marriage unraveled in 1933, shortly after Frank had been caught giving oral sex to high school athletes. By this time, Ethel could have cared less. She was having an affair with Frank's best friend. And as far as Ethel was concerned, once her husband was gone, she could have even more control over her daughter's blossoming career.

Meanwhile Judy was now on the road constantly, auditioning for parts in various productions, attending acting and dance lessons, appearing in vaudeville productions as a singer and dancer. During these years of the early thirties, Judy was virtually isolated with her mother-coach-manager. She found solace only in the friendships with other child stars, like Mickey Rooney and the Andrews Sisters, who were on the same regional circuit. When her father was able to drop around, she also continued to find comfort in their relationship, and he remained one of the few people in her life who seemed to love her unconditionally.

Things began to settle down a little for Judy when, in 1935, after rejecting her twice before, MGM agreed to a contract for her to appear in a series of films. This meant financial stability, but more important, less travel and time away from her father, sisters, and few friends. Just when things seemed to be looking up, Judy's father was diagnosed with terminal spinal meningitis. Whatever loving influence that Frank could have had in moderating his wife's controlling behavior, Judy would now have to fend for herself. The same year that she signed the MGM contract, with no less than Louis B. Mayer, one of the most powerful men in Hollywood, Frank Gumm died. She was now alone, inconsolable in her grief, even as she was on the verge of stardom.

At this crucial turning point in Judy's career, Louis B. Mayer and his minions at MGM took over control of Judy's life and summarily dismissed her mother as an unnecessary distraction. From that point on, the studio would provide professional management and made it clear that they no longer required Ethel's amateur meddling. This was good news for Judy in one sense, in that it separated her from the toxic, controlling relationship with her mother. Ethel and her new husband (she married him soon after Frank's death, much to the children's dismay) would continue to live off Judy for several years, until a final falling-out occurred in 1952. Ethel ended up working in an airplane assembly factory for the rest of her life, making $60 per week.

Whatever relief Judy might have felt in being taken from underneath her mother's thumb was quickly replaced with even greater subservience to the assigned handlers whose sole function was to keep close watch and control over this brilliant, young talent. They employed spies and informants to report on any and all movements. They owned her and they expected total compliance to any demand. Producers, directors, even Mayer himself, repeatedly tried to seduce her. There is some question as to what actually occurred in the privacy of these offices of powerful men who were used to getting their way.

As a blossoming teenager, Garland hardly fit the stereotype of the typical starlet. She was neither adorable in the Shirley Temple mold nor glamorous in the Joan Crawford, Lena Horne, Jean Harlow, or Greta Garbo style that had been popular before her. Every day on the sets, she would see the most beautiful people in the world and feel totally inadequate. According to one interview, she described herself as "a fat little frightening pig with pigtails." She felt overweight and ugly, far too plain and ordinary. Throughout her life, she would struggle with distorted views of her body, and most of these problems began during this time, when she was told that she was an ugly duckling with a swan's voice. Louis B. Mayer would even refer to her as "the fat kid." During times when important visitors would be brought on the set, people would watch in horror as Mayer would say, "Do you see this little girl?" he'd ask. "Look what I've made her into. She used to be a hunchback."

What Garland had going for her was a wholesome image. She was the girl next door, the sweet, innocent friend with whom you can confide. She exuded innocence and purity, and she was expected to behave that way at all times, with perfect comportment. More than anything else during her childhood, the one thing that she remembered most was how MGM dictated exactly what she could eat and how much of it. No matter what she ordered in the cafeteria for lunch, the staff was instructed to only serve her chicken soup. Her eating disorder developed during this time as a form of rebellion, in which she would escape the scrutiny of her "guards" and sneak off to an ice cream parlor to gorge herself on caramel sundaes. At the same time, the studio continued her mother's habit of feeding her Benzedrine for energy, then phenobarbital, tranquilizers, and sleeping pills to bring her down. They also required her to wear corsets in an effort to shape her body into the conventional ideal.

Judy tried hard to meet every expectation, to be the good girl, the *perfect* girl, even if it took the best that chemistry had to offer in order to please her masters. She was rewarded with the break of a lifetime, the leading role in the production that many agree is the greatest movie ever made. *The Wizard of Oz* was to become Garland's artistic masterpiece and most enduring legacy. At age sixteen, she began work on the film that would not only transform her career but also the imaginations of every generation that followed.

Oz was not only the most expensive movie ever made but also the most challenging to produce. Between the spectacular stunts, special effects, complicated set designs, extreme makeup, brilliant costumes, a veteran cast of Broadway musical stars, the legion of munchkins, and a child actor with an uncontrollable urge to giggle at the most inopportune moments, the film took its toll, wearing out four different directors before it was completed.

The story of the pilgrim searching for answers from the wizard, surviving trials and tribulations along the yellow brick road, is the oldest in human history. Dorothy is in search of the Holy Grail, seeking truth, trying to find her way over the rainbow back to Kansas. It is a spiritual journey, the transformation from adolescence to adulthood, from dependence to autonomy. "If I ever go looking for my heart's desire again," Dorothy (Judy) says, "I won't look further than my own backyard."

If only Judy Garland had been permitted to follow this wisdom in her real life. Practically every day for the rest of her life, she would be asked to sing "Over the Rainbow," and each time it would bring her to tears. She would be reminded again and again that she was always a long way from home and that she would never be allowed to follow her heart.

The Wizard of Oz received both positive reviews and large crowds to see the movie upon its release. It was among the highest-grossing movies of the year, but it still lost a small fortune because of its huge production and marketing expenses. It was not until it was shown on television several years later that it ever made a profit. For Judy Garland, however, the film represented an instant boost to her career. *Gone with the Wind* eclipsed *Oz* for the Best Picture Oscar, but Judy was named best juvenile performer of the year. She was now an international star.

Love Life

The stories of Judy Garland's romances and marriages could easily fill a whole volume, and they certainly played a significant role in both her creative development and her accelerating emotional volatility. The list of her lovers is impressive indeed, from actors Tyrone Power and Spencer Tracy to composer David Rose, musician Artie Shaw, director Vincente Minnelli, and producer Joe Mankiewicz. She had brief affairs with Yul Brynner, Frank Sinatra, and Orson Welles, to mention just a few. Her choice of husbands was particularly interesting, as they often resembled her father in the form of older, gay men.

Throughout her life, and in all of her failed relationships and dysfunctional marriages, Garland was looking for someone to take care of her, someone to protect her. She believed, as did many creative women of her era (Marilyn Monroe, for example), that she needed a man to complete her. She carried on serial relationships with lovers to save herself, making some disastrous choices for partners, often picking them for different qualities—for example, their congeniality (David Rose), physical beauty (Tyrone Power), intelligence (Joseph Mankiewicz), toughness (Sid Luft), presence (Vincente Minnelli). She would be married five times: to composer Rose (1941), director Minnelli (1945), bad boy Luft (1951), actor Mark Herron (1965), and disco manager Mickey Deans (1967).

To say she searched for love in all the wrong places is still an understatement. Putting aside the spectacularly poor choices she made for husbands, Garland chose lovers who were either old enough to be her father or emotionally unavailable to her. She was adventurous sexually during a time before women were allowed such indulgences. With minimal discretion, she managed to sample the most desirable hunks that Hollywood had to offer, but usually within a context of degrading herself. In perhaps the most dramatic example of this, Garland once confessed that Frank Sinatra would only agree to allow her to perform oral sex on him. Although she laughed about this and said she worried about his tastes, it was typical of the degrading relationships she endured.

The longest of her five marriages was to Vincente Minnelli, who directed several of her films and was officially approved by MGM because they figured he could manage her at home as well. That he was flamboyantly gay—and wore more makeup than any of his female stars—seemed to be overlooked as insignificant. To Judy, he was another older man who could take care of her.

Diagnoses and Treatments

Making more than four movies each year during the forties, Garland had her share of successes, as well as disappointments. But she seemed particularly ill suited to handling the critics. Like the poets Sylvia Plath and Anne Sexton, she felt that her creative talent was bestowed by the gods and could easily disappear. When things didn't go as well as her directors or producers had hoped, they put even more pressure on her to perform at a higher level. For the first time, Garland not only struggled with bouts of depression but also incapacitating episodes of panic and anxiety. Worst of all, she developed stage fright and sometimes could not perform at all.

Chronic stress develops because of hyperarousal of the body's neurological systems to ward off perceived attacks. The combination of performance pressures, and drugs administered since she was a child, took their toll. Judy became increasingly nervous and agitated, often with little provocation. During the filming of *Girl Crazy*'s rodeo scenes, every time a gun was fired, Garland would exhibit a startled response that brought her to tears. Her fight-or-flight reflex was operating at maximum survival level. Her appetite and digestion shut down. She suffered weight loss, nervous exhaustion, and finally collapse that required hospitalization. Neither electroshock treatments, hypnosis, psychotherapy, nor more drugs seemed to help her in the least.

Her behavior was tolerated—and enabled—by almost everyone around her precisely because of her amazing gifts. People put up with her tantrums and fits, her explosions of anger, her delusions and paranoia, her drug-addled mind, fearful that she would stop performing, and the financial investment and expectations they had made would collapse and fail.

Most retrospectives and memoirs of Judy are flattering and compassionate, making excuses for her volatile and destructive behavior, but she was still a very difficult person for anyone to be around for long. More than one director had his own nervous breakdown from working with her.

Other child actors, notably Mickey Rooney and Shirley Temple, somehow managed to survive the studio treatment with their sanity intact, but Garland's temperament—overly trusting, impatient, entitled, spoiled, supremely self-centered—made her particularly impossible to deal with on an adult or responsible level. Yet it was this same vulnerability that enhanced her art. The lost little girl in the *Wizard of Oz was* Judy Garland.

Garland was one of the most notorious therapy failures in history. At one point, she was seeing psychoanalyst Ernst Simmel five times per week, and still it was not enough. She was first paired with an elderly German analyst whom she disparagingly referred to as "Herr

Doctor." They worked on her Oedipal complex, explored what her mother had done to her as a child, investigated her sexual acting out and liaisons with father figures. All of this was reasonable, and the insight may even have been interesting to her on an intellectual level, but Judy found the analyst comically out of touch and difficult to make contact with. During private moments to friends, she called him a pompous ass whom she could barely understand most of the time. She prepared for her sessions just as she would for a movie set, playing a role, making up stories, deceiving the therapist, eventually believing her own lies. She often canceled sessions at the last minute or didn't show up at all.

The various psychiatrists who treated Garland, including some of the most prominent practitioners of the day—Ernst Simmel, Robert Knight, even the great Karl Menninger—each provided only a brief consultation—and could never agree on her diagnosis. She didn't exactly appear manic-depressive, even with her volatile mood swings. Nor was she stone psychotic, as most of the time she could distinguish fantasy from reality. Yet she was far more disturbed than a mere neurotic, privileged diva, complete with a personality disorder that was both narcissistic and hysterical, and a host of psychosomatic complaints, addictions, and debilitating bouts of depression. A legitimate case could be made that the source of many of her emotional problems stemmed from the effects of chronic drug abuse, begun when she was a child and continued to the point where she was taking about forty Ritalin tablets per day, in addition to sleeping pills, tranquilizers, bottles of wine, and other medications to calm her frayed nerves. Regardless of the source of problems, she was infuriatingly self-indulgent, demanding, and often mean. Even her friends—Lana Turner, Lauren Bacall, Humphrey Bogart, Joan Crawford, Frank Sinatra— could never agree whether she was charming and fun or just a giant pain in the ass.

If there was one positive effect of therapy, it was that she finally realized more clearly what had been done to her as a child, as well as recognizing what was being done to her as an adult. This could have been a critical opportunity for Garland to finally get her act together, but the extent of her drug addictions went unrecognized. Like all addicts, she was never honest with her psychiatrists (or anyone else) about how many drugs she was using and what a devastating impact they really had on her day-to-day behavior. So the insights from therapy only intensified her pain. It is also difficult for any therapy to succeed when there are outside influences working behind the scenes to sabotage any progress. Incredibly, Mayer and the folks at MGM tried mightily to end the therapy, fearing that it might change their valuable property in ways that would compromise her financial value.

Garland's anxiety symptoms worsened. Now she was dealing with intermittent bouts of panic. Insomnia became rampant to the point that she could almost never find restful sleep until dawn. She developed tension headaches. Unfortunately, she relied on more and more drugs to deal with the symptoms.

Whatever traumas Judy Garland suffered early in life, or genetic factors that shaped her mental illness and personality, her problems now exploded into full-blown manic depression. Throughout all of these emotional problems, Judy had always been able to hold things together long enough to perform. But now she lost the one thing she could always count on. She had relied on her uncanny memory for lines, her natural acting ability, her pure talent, but now these gifts began to fail her.

During May 1949, Judy began filming what is now recognized as one of the classic Hollywood musicals, *Summer Stock*. This production represented the studio giving her one last chance, and it was ultimately to be her last film for MGM. Gene Kelly had agreed to costar, only because he wanted to help his disintegrating friend save her career. Everyone on the set was rooting for Judy, hoping that this time she could keep her act together.

When Garland appeared on the set significantly overweight, this was seen as an ominous sign. When she next began showing up late for work, or not at all, the crew and director began to become increasingly concerned. Hundreds of people were now standing around with nothing to do because Judy had disappeared. As much as he admired Garland's talent as the greatest musical performer alive, the producer, Joe Pasternak, felt that he had no choice but to go to Mayer and inform him that the production might have to be shut down. Everyone agreed that Judy was impossible to work with. Her behavior just had to improve.

The filming had limped through various stages, but there was still one last crucial number to do, the finale, in which Judy was to sing "Get Happy," a song she'd always wanted to do and one that represented an ironic counterpoint to her current condition of abject despair.

To be absolutely sure that everything would go well for this final production number, Judy was shuffled away to a sanatorium for a few weeks, where she could rest, recover, and lose fifteen pounds. The treatment appeared to be successful because she returned looking both svelte and radiant, eager to begin filming the finale. Quickly, however, it became apparent why she was looking so bubbly: the cast and crew could smell the sweet scent of paraldehyde—a hypnotic drug that is designed to act as a sedative but can sometimes have opposite effects—on her breath.

The dancers who were on stage with Judy at the time were growing even more concerned when they heard the star whispering paranoid delusions in their ears. There was one small guy, who was part of the crew, who particularly drew her attention. She was convinced that he was there to harm her, that he had tried to seduce her once before. After screaming at him to keep away from her, to stay away from her body, Judy called the poor, befuddled man over to her and then proceeded to strike him in the face with her athletic dancer's high kick. She then turned around, as if the incident never happened, and proceeded to complete the scene with extraordinary brilliance. Indeed, Judy's performance singing "Get Happy" was one of the landmarks of her movie career, filmed when she was raving mad.

Reinventing Herself

Judy Garland was fired by MGM in 1950, judged as too mentally disabled to perform. She became frantic with worry, depressed, agitated, and discouraged. She was exhibiting increasing paranoia and hallucinations, perhaps as a result of the drugs she was taking, or maybe some deeper pathology. Surely, she was crushed after being dismissed by her longtime employer. She was also accepting the reality of another failed marriage, this time with Minnelli.

Arriving home after receiving news of her suspension, she ran into the bathroom and locked the door. Minnelli tried to calm her down, but with little success. He heard her scream out, "Leave me alone. I want to die." Then he heard an ominous crash. By the time he broke down the floor, Garland was lying on the floor with blood seeping down her neck where she had tired to slit her throat. It's doubtful that her effort was serious, because it was discovered that she had not cut herself very deeply. Nevertheless, even if it was meant to get attention, Judy was clearly disturbed and out of control.

Garland's situation seemed hopeless. She was written off by the film industry. Nevertheless she demonstrated an amazing degree of resilience that would become her signature during the next twenty years. Her marriage with Minnelli may have been over, but she began to take up with a new romantic partner, Sid Luft, a much younger man, who was known for his bad temper and inclination to get into bar fights. Garland seemed to be attracted to his strength.

With Luft's support, Garland jettisoned her movie career in order to start over as a stage performer. She reinvented her public image by going back to her origins in live performance. If the major studios would not work with her, then she'd just find another venue for her creative talent. This was perhaps not a conscious choice on her part as much as it was an act of desperation.

For someone who was supposed to be so fragile, Garland certainly found inner resources to pull herself together when things appeared most bleak and hopeless. It was as if her creative spirit was keeping the madness at bay—if even for a little while—until the next project could be completed.

Garland succeeded on stage, even thrived, because she so needed the audience adoration. After performing to sellout crowds at the Palladium in London during the same year of her MGM dismissal, receiving one standing ovation after another, she rejoiced: "One thing is certain. I have found out where I belong—out there in the limelights singing for my supper."

During the next few years, Judy Garland is credited with single-handedly restoring vaudeville to Broadway with her one-woman shows. In the early fifties, she appeared before sellout crowds for months at a time, two shows per night, plus weekend matinees. Critics went wild. The public embraced Judy with complete abandon, cheering her story of redemption as well as her creative genius.

In private, however, Garland's various mental afflictions continued to plague her. There were further bouts of depression and anxiety, precipitated in part by new stressors in her life from relationships, responsibilities of parenting, and the demands of life on stage. Luft may have been able to satisfy Judy's sexual desires, because he was described as a raging heterosexual, but he was also prone to volatile mood swings himself. They produced two children together, Lorna and Joey, which created even more stress on her already overextended life.

At work, Judy became increasingly demanding, petulant, volatile, and mean. Before she would agree to show up for work, her dressing room had to be filled with cases of Blue Nun wine and Bendicks chocolates. If she did not feel she was receiving sufficient respect, she would start raging and storm off stage, leaving the crew stuck without work to complete. She threatened directors that she would kill herself if they didn't treat her properly, and more than once she made good on her promise with a serious attempt.

Every year of her life was either a disaster or a triumph—and sometimes both. She was invited to do movies again, made a brief comeback in 1954 with *A Star Is Born,* and then was exiled again from Hollywood because she was viewed as "damaged goods," too difficult to work with: she would often show up at the studio falling-down drunk, high on drugs, or so hung over that she could barely stand. This behavior persisted when she was given the opportunity to host *The Judy Garland Show,* her new career in television. At times, she was brilliant on this show, as intense and dazzling as ever, but her critical success couldn't save the show from poor ratings, a lousy time slot, and conflicts between the producer and her husband, Sid Luft, who was acting as her manager. To add to the difficulties, Garland was so dependent on drugs and alcohol that she had her dresses designed with hidden compartments where she could stash flasks of vodka to calm herself before appearances. She was also becoming increasingly ill, suffering acute hepatitis from years of abusing alcohol and barbiturates.

Judy tried to lean more heavily on her friends, on Luft, who was spending her money as fast as she could bring it in, but also on those who loved and supported her dearly. Humphrey Bogart, Noel Coward, Van Johnson, Lana Turner, and others all tried to be there for her. It is more than a little intriguing that one person she often called for support during this period in the early sixties was President John F. Kennedy, who would almost always take her calls, offering encouragement and sometimes advice on how to handle her difficulties. It's reported that their calls would usually end with Kennedy begging her to sing a few bars of "Over the Rainbow" to lift his own, depressed spirit.

Family Legacies

Judy Garland gave the greatest performance of her career—maybe the best musical performance ever—at Carnegie Hall on April 23, 1961. She was alone on stage, with no props, no costume changes, no dancers or special lighting effects. It was just Judy singing twenty-six consecutive songs to an adoring audience. Those who are still alive talk about the event as the most magical evening of their lives.

As poised, self-assured, and magical Judy appeared on stage, this was quite literally her last stand. During a time when she achieved her peak of creative artistry, her life was totally in ruins. Another disastrous marriage, to Sid Luft, had ended. All the effort she had expended to achieve financial security was wasted, because Luft had spent all the money. She didn't even have a home to return to. Her relationships with her children were precarious at best. Garland's children, Liza Minnelli, Joey and Lorna Luft, suffered terribly during this period. They were neglected, pawned off on staff, and witnesses to their mother's mercurial anger, threats, violence, and inconsistencies. In her rages, Garland smashed everything in sight and twice deliberately set the house on fire. Liza, the eldest child, was forced to grow up early and take over responsibility for running the household, supervising the staff, preventing her mother from overdosing, plus managing her own skyrocketing career. Garland's health was now perilous; she had been told by doctors that she only had a few years left to live.

"When you have lived the life I've lived," Garland wrote in the pages of an autobiography she would never complete, "when you've loved and suffered, and been madly happy and desperately sad—well, that's when you realize you'll never be able to set it all down. Maybe you'd rather die first."

That is exactly what Judy Garland sought to do, to end her life not through a single dramatic act but through the progressively slow deterioration of self-abuse. The final tragedy of her life was recognizing that her voice, one of the most perfect human musical instruments on the planet, was, by the late sixties, gone. Years of neglect, side effects from drugs (now including heroin and morphine), and just the wear and tear of putting everything into her performances had done incurable damage.

About the only high point in this end stage of Garland's life was the success of her daughter, Liza Minnelli, even though their relationship was rocky at best. During the times that Judy invited Liza to join her on stage, starting when her child was only eleven years old, it was as much to give herself time to rest between songs as it was to showcase her daughter's talents. As time passed, Liza showed that she had inherited a great deal of her mother's talent as a singer, dancer, and actress who struggled at first but eventually succeeded in forging her own brilliant career before mental illness shut down her own career. But there is a phenomenon known in the field of family therapy called *cross-generational legacies*. The general idea is that unresolved issues from one generation become passed on to the next. This can be readily seen, for instance, in the cases of child or sexual abuse, in which a parent who has been abused himself might do the same to his child.

In a cruel twist of fate, Liza repeated some of the identical patterns of her mother—*and* her grandmother, choosing a gay husband who could not be fully committed to the marriage. Even more incredible, in 1967, it was discovered that Liza's husband, Peter Allen (introduced to her by Judy), and Judy's current fourth husband, Mark Herron, were having an affair with each other! Whether this was the final straw in their relationship or not, Liza cut off all contact, resenting her mother in a similar way that Judy felt toward her own mother. The legacy continued.

In one interview she gave at the time, Garland had this to say about the breakup of her latest marriage:

> *Why should I always be rejected? All right, so I'm Judy Garland. But I've been Judy Garland forever. Luft always knew this, and Minnelli knew it, and Mark Herron knew it, although Herron married me strictly for business reasons, for purposes of his own.*

Judy ended the interview by saying that she bore none of her ex-husbands any malice, except Herron, whom she could never forgive for betraying her as he did, especially with the husband of her own daughter.

Judy Garland's story becomes sadder and sadder still. By 1968, she was abandoned by almost all of her friends, as well as her two youngest children, Joey and Lorna Luft, who had suffered more than enough neglect and abuse. Judy fell so far that she was reduced to appearing in bars for $100 per night, just trying to earn enough to feed herself. As she had all but stopped eating at this point, she only needed enough to purchase her wine and drugs. She was $4 million in debt.

On June 21, 1969, in what was called a case of "accidental self-poisoning," Judy Garland swallowed ten capsules of Seconal, a powerful barbiturate, ending her life. She was discovered locked in the bathroom of a London hotel, seated on the toilet, with her arms folded in her lap and her head bent over. She was forty-seven years old. After more than a dozen previous attempts, she finally succeeded in ending her life, whether it was a conscious or accidental act.

A part of Garland's legacy is a body of music, films, and stage performances that were considered among the most brilliant and accomplished of the twentieth century. But another part of her legacy is that she is the embodiment of the struggle to overcome suffering. She may have had her life cut short because her star burned so brightly, but in one sense she attained the absolute pinnacle of artistic achievement in spite of the obstacles she faced and the pain she suffered. She endured childhood abuse, disappointments in love and work, failed marriages, estrangements from her children, lifelong addictions, and yet she still somehow managed to rise above them. The vulnerability and authentic emotional intensity that first attracted audiences when she was a child remained as a force throughout her career. People loved her—many still weep at her memory—because she was able to move people emotionally by drawing on her own powerful feelings.

Each of her crushing disappointments, failed marriages, suicide attempts, depressive episodes, drug overdoses, emotional breakdowns, and hospitalizations were reported in lurid detail to a public that devoured every word. Her early childhood abuse and victimization at the hands of unscrupulous and predatory Hollywood moguls were well-known by fans who embraced her madness with sympathy and compassion. In one sense, that was part of her appeal: she was a fragile, broken bluebird who finally, at last, aged and defeated before her time, couldn't quite gain sufficient altitude to fly over the rainbow.

CHAPTER FOUR

Mark Rothko
Painted in Blood

D uring the turn of the twentieth century, Dvinsk,
Russia, located in what is now Latvia, was a hostile place for Jews. Half
of the town's 150,000 inhabitants were Jewish, but this community
was relegated to the lower end of the economic stratum and forbidden to own land. This was a time of *pogroms* in Russia, violent riots
against Jews that resulted in the destruction of their meager shops and
that sometimes led to their deaths.

One young boy who grew up in Dvinsk, Marcus Rothkowitz, was
haunted throughout his entire life by the recollection of being whipped
across the face by Cossacks during one of these pogroms and also witnessing the digging of a mass grave, followed by a massacre in which
all the Jews in the area were murdered and thrown in the pit. Actually,
it is not clear whether young Marcus actually saw this atrocity himself or whether it was part of his family's collective memory. Regardless, he believed with all his heart that he had been there.

Fifty years later, when Mark Rothko would become one of the
greatest living painters, a leader of Abstract Expressionism and modern art in America, the first artist of his generation to have a one-man
show at the Museum of Modern Art, his creative expressions would

reflect this early trauma. "It's tempting," one art critic writes, "to conclude that this story offers an allegorical key with which we can unlock the mystery of Rothko's later obsession with the rectangle, as if his paintings of the 1950s and 1960s transformed his memory of Jewish victimization into a space of transcendent freedom and sensual pleasure."

For those unfamiliar with Rothko's seminal work as an expressionist painter, he constructed huge canvases, blocks of muted colors designed to cover walls with floating, luminescent shapes. He intended his creations to be intimate, intense, and evocative, not merely decorations of space. "By saturating the room with the feeling of the work," Rothko once explained, "the walls are defeated and the poignancy of each single work becomes more visible." To allow maximum interpretation by viewers, he stopped framing and naming his paintings, referring to them only by numbers.

Marcus Rothkowitz, who would eventually Americanize his name to Mark Rothko at the suggestion of an art dealer, remained haunted throughout his life by several themes that would become prominent in his psyche. Although well controlled, even emotionally restricted in most of his interactions with others, Rothko was also thought to be a cerebral painter, inclined to reflect on every artistic movement before picking up a paintbrush. Yet lurking beneath this controlled exterior was a man carrying around five thousand years of cultural oppression, someone who always felt like a victim, a martyr, who tried through his art to express his own pain, as well as that of his people. Although he would never be a conventionally religious man, nor anything more than a secular Jew, it was apparent that he felt deep spiritual connections to the images he created. "The people who weep for my paintings," Rothko would later explain, "are having the same religious experience I had when I painted them."

New Immigrants

Like many of their friends and neighbors in the Jewish ghetto of Dvinsk, the Rothkowitz family could see the writing on the wall, quite literally the scribblings of anti-Semitism and hate painted over their shops and homes. Mark's father, Jacob, was both intellectually and politically active in the community. He was an educated man, a pharmacist, who had managed to attain professional status during a time when there were very strict quotas on such opportunities for Jews.

At the time that Mark was born (most likely unplanned), in 1903, his father, Jacob, and his mother, Kate, already had an intact family. His older sister, and two older brothers, were all ten years older than he was, contributing to Mark's sense of isolation. This was further magnified by his precarious health—his parents and siblings never expected the little boy to survive because he was so sick most of the time. One of his brothers, Moise, later described him as "high strung," overly sensitive, fragile, and sickly. It is peculiar that his family didn't notice that one likely source of his poor health was nutritional problems, as he was often observed eating plaster off walls to feed a calcium deficiency.

Although the Rothkowitz family enjoyed a relatively comfortable life in Latvia, Jacob knew that those days of peace were numbered because of the escalating violence against Jews. He was determined to join the great wave of immigration that was taking place in the early years of the twentieth century from Russia and Eastern Europe to the West, to the dream of America, where he had heard that Jews could live like anyone else and find peace, prosperity, and freedom from persecution. So in 1911, when Mark was eight years old, Jacob escaped Latvia with his two oldest sons, leaving Mark, his sister, and his mother behind. This abandonment was agonizing for the little boy, even though he had been reassured that his father would send for them later. He was at an age when he desperately needed the guidance of his father and older brothers; yet he was left behind.

Two years later, Jacob sent for the rest of his family as promised, but by this time, Mark felt considerable ambivalence about the forced move. Nobody had ever asked him what he wanted nor consulted him on the family's plan. First, he had resented the breakup of his family, not understanding why it was necessary to split up, then he resisted further the necessity that he would have to leave behind his familiar home in order to begin a new life in a strange country. Years later, in a magazine article focused on why he was such an angry man and artist, Rothko was to trace the roots to his forced immigration. In the interview, he stated that he "was never able to forgive transplantation to a land where I never felt entirely at home."

The Rothkowitz family might have thought they'd discovered the Promised Land, but to their youngest son, Mark, it was just another kind of misery. They ended up in Portland, Oregon, because of family who had already settled in the area and the large Jewish community that would be available for support, but to Mark they had simply exchanged one ghetto for another. Even worse, he could not speak the language of this strange, new country, nor could he figure out the peculiar customs.

There may have been no Cossacks in Portland, but there were still anti-Semitic bullies who terrorized the boy. During the first weeks of school, Mark came home bruised and battered. Even at his age, it struck him as ironic that they'd left their home to escape persecution but now he was being attacked more than ever before.

The joy of a family reunion was further compromised by the discovery that Mark's father was terminally ill with cancer of the colon. Mark had not seen his father in two years and had missed him terribly. Now, at a time when the boy was most vulnerable, when he needed his father more than ever, he experienced the most devastating loss of his life, one that would haunt him continually for the rest of his years.

After Jacob died from an agonizing progression of his illness, the family was left destitute. Back in Latvia, the family had enjoyed some status as a function of their father's profession, his political activism, and his leadership in the community. Now they were penniless without a major source of support. It was about this time that Mark Rothko traced his abandonment of religious practice and faith in God. He became an angry, alienated young man with a chip on his shoulder.

Kate was forced to keep her family afloat, and she appeared to do so through sheer force of will. She sent the older boys out to earn a living for the family and exercised total control over the goings-on within the home. She was described as "plain, direct, straightforward, she conveys no sophistication, no intellectuality, no playfulness— little, in short, with which her son the painter might connect." Mark found his mother a determined woman but also without warmth, affection, or strong feeling. In a portrait that he painted of her years later, she appears detached, cold, looking off to the side as if indifferent to the son who is capturing her spirit.

Although Mark suffered daily humiliations at school, he still managed to excel in his subjects, earning double promotions and advancing through grades ahead of his chronological age. Perhaps the most interesting aspect of these early educational years is that Mark showed little interest and received no training in art. About the only evidence of his future talent was a propensity to doodle and make drawings when he was idle or bored.

Mark entered high school around the time that America was fighting in World War I. At that time, Mark had a dedicated interest in drama, mythology, and the Greek language. And he distinguished himself well enough to earn a full scholarship to Yale. But even though he did well academically, this was not nearly the case regarding his social life, where he continued to be harassed and marginalized. He still experienced his fair share of prejudice from classmates, ridiculed that he would become a pawnbroker like other Jews from his neighborhood.

Rothko channeled his frustrations and anger into political activism, not unlike his father's crusades back in Russia. He became intensely interested in the Russian Revolution that was taking place back home, overthrowing the Czar. Likewise his interest in American politics was turning radical as he voiced opposition to the current educational and political systems. He loved to argue and debate, but as a Jew, he was not permitted to participate in the debate club. Instead he started a publication during the senior year of high school to publish his views on the problems confronting society. "If we have the power of intelligent thinking and expression," he wrote in the inaugural issue, "we shall not fall prey to the smooth tongues of politicians or self-serving economists."

By the time he moved to New Haven to attend college in 1921, he was intellectually gifted but painfully insecure. He was chubby, prematurely balding, and wore thick glasses. He also exhibited the demeanor of someone who suffered constant discrimination and oppression, instinctually ducking at the prospect of an attack.

The Jewish Problem

Yale University may have been a place of gentility and intellectual inquiry, but it was still not much more welcoming of Jews than Russia or Oregon. Among all the Ivy League schools in the East, Yale may have been the most hostile environment of all, especially for those who were not fully assimilated and insisted on advertising their differences. In language reminiscent of Nazi Germany, the dean of students referred to "the Jewish problem," resulting from increased enrollments. Jewish scholarship students like Rothko were described by administrators as crude, pushy, dishonest, clannish, and materialistic, with shabby ethics. Needless to say, with this sort of policy emanating from the leaders of his university, Rothko would continue to experience discrimination, eventually losing his scholarship when they changed their policy, deciding that there were already too many Jews on campus. That was fine with him anyway as he found the classes mostly boring and uninspiring. It was from this moment that Rothko began to have serious misgivings about the academic community that he had chosen and what it could offer him. He was just so tired of being treated like a second-class citizen when he knew he had a first-rate mind.

During the two unhappy years that Rothko spent at Yale, he tried his best to immerse himself in his studies. He had few friends, except for a few Jewish classmates who came from his old neighborhood in Portland. About the only high point for him was launching another political newspaper, this one slipped under the doorways of his elitist Yale classmates, attacking their attachments to the material world. In the newspaper, nicknamed *The Pest,* Rothko and his fellow provocateurs sought to shake up the nest of elitism through what he called *destructive criticism,* an irreverent attack on the status quo. He had always been on the outside looking in, and now he had a voice to express his resentment.

While at Yale, Rothko considered careers in law or engineering, but he still showed little interest in art. During the spring term of his sophomore year, in 1923, he decided on the courageous, or perhaps desperate, decision to drop out of school and escape what he considered the oppression of Yale. By this time, he had already lost his financial assistance, but just as trying for him were the boring classes and limited minds of his fellow students. Instead he would move to New York in order to explore the burgeoning theater, music, and art scenes. For a boy from a Jewish, immigrant family that valued education above all else, this was a radical move and one that upset his mother greatly. Perhaps this was part of the appeal of thumbing his nose at the gentile aristocracy at the same time that he broke ties with his family back home.

When Rothko first arrived in Manhattan, he spent his days walking around the city, looking for something meaningful to occupy his time—and his life. "Then one day," Rothko later explained, "I happened to wander into an art class, to meet a friend who was taking the course. All the students were sketching this nude model—and right away I decided that was the life for me."

Rothko was not only searching for something to do, but he was also searching for a way of life, a focus for his energies, and he liked the *idea* of being an artist. The lifestyle of a starving painter, or perhaps an actor, suited him. He had little need for material comforts. He had an image in mind of the kind of life he wanted to lead, one on the edge: being the underdog, the victim, on the outside, creating something important.

There were few role models for Rothko at this time. Jews didn't do this sort of thing: they got a good education and went into a proper profession, as a doctor or a lawyer or even a pharmacist like his father. This being the case, the decision to explore the world of art initiated a clear separation from his family. He had perhaps a vision of what he wanted to be, but he had absolutely no training or preparation to make this dream a reality.

Rothko would describe himself as a self-taught artist, and this is mostly the case. He did attend a few art classes for a brief period of time, but he received very little formal instruction other than his association with a mentor, Max Weber (the artist, not the economist), who quickly observed that the angry young man had natural talent. Unlike formally trained students who consulted with Weber, Rothko was not limited—or handicapped—by the prevailing conventions. He was not interested in imitating Picasso or the Impressionists but instead was trying to figure out unique ways to express himself creatively. Weber not only recognized this yearning in his apprentice, but he greatly encouraged the drive to make something new. Weber had spent time in Paris with Matisse and Picasso, so he was able to help connect the young Rothko with the Impressionists and Cubists of the past, while at the same time helping him to find his own style.

Up to this point in his life, Rothko had spent most of his life in solitude, alienated from his peers, alienated from his family. He had always been different from others, even from his own kind, and he knew it. Now he chose a profession that would isolate him even further, that would not only give him an excuse for being alone but would also make this solitude necessary while working on paintings. During these apprenticeship years, he would frequent groups of other artists, but he still followed very much his own course. He was so used to being the alien, the victim, the shabby, wandering Jew, that he had become used to his position as outsider and radical.

Depressions in the Depression

Rothko spent the next several years just as he imagined—as a starving artist. He was living on five dollars a week, trying to make a go as a painter, but finding little success. He was offered a commercial job in 1928 by a friend to illustrate *The Graphic Bible* for young people. His job was to construct the maps that would bring the text alive. Even though he finally had a source of steady income, Rothko found the work demeaning and—ultimately—frustrating when he had trouble collecting his final payment. The lawsuit that followed, dragging on many years, was the first of many legal actions that Rothko initiated during his lifetime to redress perceived injustices.

Rothko met Edith Sachar in 1932, during the height of the Depression, when she was twenty and he was nine years older. During the years since he had left Yale, Rothko had barely earned a living but could at least call himself an artist. He was teaching art part time at a progressive Jewish *yeshiva*, or school, which was attached to the Brooklyn Jewish Center. He had already produced the early signs of what would become known as his *mythological period*—depictions of early Greek and primitive symbols embedded in abstract swirls of color. If he wasn't yet anything close to being successful, he was at least doing what he loved for the first time in his life. This passion was irresistible to a young art student like Edith.

Rothko's intensity frightened the young sculptress, but she overcame her misgivings to marry him anyway, just two months after she had told him she wanted some distance. Not unlike the two poets Plath and Hughes, Mark and Edith began their married life together with a plan to support each other's art, even if it meant living in poverty: their first home was in a refurbished dog kennel.

In order to help support them, Rothko continued teaching art two days per week to the children at the yeshiva. This would be a job he would continue for the next decade. He loved the idea of helping the kids find their own form of creative self-expression. He encouraged them to forget about rules and make up whatever their hearts desired. Rothko encouraged children to talk about their dreams and fantasies, to access some memorable scene from movies they'd seen or experiences they'd had. He marveled at their spontaneity, which would ordinarily handicap older students. "Unconscious of any difficulties," he wrote in an essay on preparing future artists, "they chop their way and surmount obstacles that might turn an adult gray, and presto! Soon their ideas become visible in clearly intelligent form."

During the following few years, Rothko began working in watercolors and oils, experimenting with media and with forms. When she wasn't working on her own sculptures, Edith posed for him as his favorite model. He was trying to move away from any connection to realism, to more abstract shapes and forms that captured the strongest emotions. He began to show an early talent, not only for doing art but also for talking about it. Whenever he and Edith gathered together with friends, Rothko would hold court at length discussing in detail the qualities of Cézanne or Picasso that made their work transcendent.

Just at a time when Rothko was developing somewhat of a reputation, the Depression had strangled all possible opportunities for work. The art market collapsed, along with stocks. Few people had discretionary funds for wall decorations. When Franklin Delano Roosevelt was elected president for the first time in 1932, he launched the famous Works Progress Administration (WPA), which, among other things, included hiring starving artists to create public art. Rothko was fortunate enough to be one of the few painters who were chosen by the government to produce paintings that would hang in government and other public buildings. Imagine paying the likes of Rothko, Willem de Kooning, Jackson Pollock, and Arshile Gorky about fifty cents per hour to turn out canvases. Still, it was a great gig as long as it lasted.

The good news for Rothko was that he finally felt as if he was part of a community. He worked with some of the greatest living painters, all of them struggling in the early stages of their careers and working together to form the basis of what became "modern art" in America, a movement that was to rival the great Impressionists, the Cubists, and the other experimental artists of Europe, like Cézanne, Picasso, and Gauguin.

During this period of their lives, Mark and Edith were living in a loft in Greenwich Village, the epicenter of creative arts in North America. They were still dirt poor, but at least Rothko felt like he was making progress on his development as an artist. Between his modest teaching income and a few paintings that he managed to sell for a pittance, they were surviving. The problem, however, was that Edith felt like she was living in his shadow. She was tired of taking care of a slob who could barely dress himself. She was also worn out from his depressions and moodiness. When he started drinking, he would become even worse.

Partly as a way to assert her independence, as well as to contribute to the family income, Edith adapted her sculpting talents to begin making jewelry. Her venture was so successful that at one point she asked her husband to abandon his painting, which seemed so futile, and help with the new family business that was turning out to be far more lucrative. For a period of time in 1940, Rothko was actually forced into what he considered the humiliating job of being a salesman, forced to hawk Edith's earrings for $3.75 each—plus tax. One of the greatest artists of the twentieth century could very well have ended up as a street peddler!

The marriage couldn't stand the additional strain, and so the couple separated in 1942, primarily at Edith's initiative. She was tired of his carping and volatile mood swings. At times, she felt more like a baby-sitter than a wife.

Rather than feeling as if he had regained his freedom, Rothko became so severely depressed that he collapsed, both physically and emotionally. "He loved her very much," Morris Calden, a tenant who rented space from the Rothkos, said. "He couldn't get over the fact that she had thrown him out, and just took to his bed and he'd lay in his bed week after week and I used to come and visit him and he'd just lie there." Rothko would whine and complain constantly to his boarder that he felt totally humiliated and worn out.

Rothko apparently did not spend all his time totally idle. Always intellectually voracious, he devoured volumes by Freud, mystics, and other studies of the unconscious. He was becoming interested in the phenomenon of *automatic drawing,* in which the artist allows his unconscious to guide the creative process. By the time he crawled out of bed several months later, Rothko was creatively rejuvenated and began a series of what was to be known as his *myth paintings,* based on eternal symbols that were portrayed as Surrealist primitive creatures that seemed to float in space. He was inching one step closer to the more abstract forms that would become his trademark.

The Signature Style

During the war years of the 1940s (he was exempted from the army because of poor vision), Rothko teamed up with his friend Alfred Gottlieb to construct a manifesto for what would become the rallying cry of Abstract Expressionism. There were several main points that they made, which were sent in the form of a letter to the *New York Times:*

1. *We deny that the world has any objective appearance, the world is what the artist makes it.*

2. *And in this world the eye has no precedence over feelings and thoughts.*

3. *And reason has to take precedence over unreason, the paradox, hyperbole, hallucination.*

The man who would never acknowledge, much less ever speak about, his own inner feelings was creating a form of art that would give vent to the most primal human emotions. What his words would not— or could not—say, he would let his brushes speak.

Talk about a midlife crisis! Rothko was approaching forty, and yet within the previous few years, he had changed his name at the urging of an art dealer who felt this would make him more marketable and less Jewish sounding, then his wife left him, just as his artistic style was coalescing. As World War II was coming to an end, Mark Rothko became involved with a worshipping fan, Mell Beistle. She was drop-dead gorgeous, almost half his age, and totally entranced with this charismatic painter whom she had met at a party. They were married in March 1945 and would remain so for the next twenty-five years.

Mell was in so many ways the opposite of Edith. Whereas Rothko's first wife was often described as cold, Mell was both warm and unconditionally devoted. She would become his anchor, holding him together solidly and firmly during the coming emotional storms.

Rothko was indeed volatile in his moods, partially because of ongoing frustration that as a mature adult he was still broke and struggling for any kind of professional acceptance. It wasn't until March 1947, two years after their marriage, that he finally had his first solo exhibit at the Parsons Gallery. His paintings were selling for a few hundred dollars, and that year his income netted less than $4,000, a pitiful sum even in those days.

Writing in a letter to a friend, Clay Spohn, Rothko talked about the challenges of holding on to his sanity while at the same time struggling to uncover deeper levels of creative potential:

> *I am beginning to hate the life of a painter. One begins by sparring with his insides with one leg still in the normal world. Then you are caught up in a frenzy that brings you to the edge of madness, as far as you can go without ever coming back. The return is a series of dazed weeks during which you are only half alive.*

More than any other painter of his era, Rothko was cerebral and reflective. Any classic photo of Jackson Pollock at the time would show him in a whirl of movement, throwing paint across the canvases with wild abandon. By contrast, Rothko was often seen sitting utterly and completely still for hours upon hours staring at a blank canvas, or one in various stages of completion. He would sit immobile, chin resting on his hands, listening to Mozart or Haydn, then slowly he would rise from the chair and approach the blank canvas.

The canvas would first be primed with a mix of glue and pigments that he had manufactured himself, the old-fashioned way, with mortar and pestle. Critics began to appreciate his skill as a colorist, and he approached this task so deliberately that he would never have trusted any commercial product. Next he would use a layer of oil paint, matched perfectly with the primer, to cover all the margins of the canvas. This was crucial, because he would demand that his works remain unframed. The signature rectangles would next be created with paint glazes constructed from powdered pigments and eggs. Like a mad chemist in a laboratory, he would spend hours mixing and diluting the paints until they held the perfect consistency and luminosity. It would seem at times as if the paints themselves were alive.

Rothko would use dozens and dozens of thin coats of glaze, applied with huge five-inch brushes, the kind favored by housepainters. He would keep applying coat after coat until the shapes would seem to float off the canvas. This whole process might take three to four months in order to complete a single canvas.

The paintings no longer contained recognizable images nor even the mythological icons, but rather the stacked rectangles of color that would become his signature style. Interestingly, the more abstract the paintings became, the less inclined Rothko was to talk to journalists or critics about his work or its meaning.

Rothko joined the cadre of other abstract artists who were breaking new ground in the New York scene. Artists like Motherwell, Kline, de Kooning, Newman, Pollock, Rothko, and others would meet in one another's homes and studios or in bars, talking about their work, and they would vow their determination to turn the art world upside down. The other artists were often beguiled by Rothko's ability to talk about his art, as well as critique that of others, but they were also taken aback by the depth of his despair. Robert Motherwell, the youngest and most prolific painter in the group, commented that Rothko seemed "clinically depressed." Keep in mind that even among a group of complex and flamboyant artists, Rothko still stood out as a troubled man. He did not drink quite as much as Pollock, nor was he given to eccentric excess like Picasso, but in the depression department he put everyone else to shame.

Unlike Plath, or Woolf, or Hemingway, Rothko did not seem to have inherited his mood disorder directly from the family line, but few data are actually available about the history of mental illness among his ancestors. Perhaps during the terrible days of suffering in Latvia, it was considered normal to be depressed; *everyone* suffered traumatic stress, and so anyone who appeared more distraught than usual was not given much notice. We also cannot easily point to any one of the early traumas of his childhood—his isolation, alienation, victimization, forcible dislocation, loss of his father—as the sole cause of his emotional troubles. Nor can we ascribe his moodiness solely to a self-protective, pessimistic cognitive style: he always expected disaster around the corner so that he would never be disappointed. It would seem that a combination of all of these factors (and others) contributed, in part, to Rothko's troubles. He was certainly a maverick, a radical, who enjoyed pushing the limits of the status quo. This same quality that allowed him to co-invent a completely new style of expressionist art made him insufferable and miserable as a human being.

Plagued by Success

Mark Rothko had felt like an outsider his whole life—as an immigrant, a Jew, and an artist. He was so used to being a starving, unrecognized, struggling artist that this role became who he was. He ridiculed any artists who "sold out" and went for commercial success, despising the business end of the art world. He cared nothing about clothes, possessions, or even where he lived. All he lived for was to paint.

In the new decade of the fifties, Rothko was now the father of his first child, Kate. He had an adoring wife, who made every effort to care for him in the best way she could. His home life was stable. He was now earning a reasonable if unstable income from the sale of his paintings. Most important, he had just invented what would become known as *a Rothko*. His painting *Number 10*, produced in 1950, featured three rectangles, stacked vertically, in blocks of blue, yellow and greenish-beige (all his colors are difficult to describe with words). Some viewers might dismiss the painting as nothing but pretty, decorative squares, but a closer, longer look for a period of time reveals that the forms actually come alive.

"Filled with deep yellow," writes Rothko biographer James Breslin, about how the painting affects him, "the surface of the rectangle constantly fluctuates as varying densities of paint change the hue from golden to a dark orange where a brownish-red area beneath, still visible as a fringe around the yellow, pushes through to create mystery shadowy presences that form and dissolve . . ." Such is the mysterious effect of a Rothko on the discerning eye.

Discussions about the underlying meanings of Rothko's paintings could easily fill a graduate-level art course. One explanation that has

particular psychological resonance was best described by his friend Al
Jensen, who said that Rothko's rectangles resembled the mass grave he
had seen (or claimed to have seen) as a child in Latvia. "He said he'd
always been haunted by the image of that grave, and that in some profound way it was locked into his painting."

After spending many years teaching art to children, beginning in
1951 he "graduated" to offering classes at Brooklyn College for the next
three years. Despite this job, and some continuing sales of his paintings,
he became increasingly difficult to get along with, except of course with
his wife, Mell, who continued to offer support. His antisocial behavior
rivaled that of his friend and fellow painter Jackson Pollock, although
whereas Pollock might very well show up at a party falling-down drunk,
Rothko was more prone to uncomfortable, prolonged silences that
would erupt into volcanic displays of rage. One time, while standing in
the lobby of the Whitney Museum and seeing an art critic he didn't
much like, he put his fist through a plate glass window. Fellow artist
Motherwell referred to him as "Ivan the Terrible."

Around 1957, when his income tripled from the preceding year,
Rothko's paintings suddenly began to turn dark. No longer did he
favor the vibrant, primary colors of yellows and reds and bright or-
anges. Instead he was growing increasingly attracted to blacks, grays,
dark browns, and blues. Paintings that once radiated light now seemed
to hold it within.

The art market was beginning to really take off during the end of the
fifties, and abstract expressionists were becoming the rage. A Rothko
that might have sold for $1,000 in 1955 was worth five times that much
by 1960 and thirty times that much five years later (In 2004, a Rothko
painting set a record at Sotheby's by selling for over $17 million.)

In addition to his increasing financial success, Rothko was experiencing (but not necessarily enjoying) critical acclaim. He was even
called by Art News's Thomas Hess the "leader of postwar modern art."
As much as he yearned for acceptance, approval, endorsement from
the art establishment, he was not really comfortable with being in any
position except the underdog. He remained depressed and angry despite any level of success that he achieved during his lifetime.

Declining Health

By the 1960s, as he was approaching his own sixth decade, Rothko's
mental health declined as steadily as his physical condition. Always a
heavy drinker, he was observed now as almost always holding a drink

in one hand and a cigarette in the other. Elaine de Kooning, wife of Willem de Kooning, once visited his studio at ten in the morning and was offered a cocktail. When she politely declined, saying she hadn't had breakfast yet, Rothko responded cheerily that neither had he, admitting that he usually limited himself to one drink each hour, ensuring that he was always a little tipsy from the moment he awakened until the time he went to sleep.

Mell Rothko was saddled with the responsibility of taking care of two children: her daughter *and* her erratic husband. Whether this is what drove her to drink herself or she just wanted to keep her husband company, Mell also became an alcoholic, but one who was less able to control herself.

If their health and personal lives were in a sad state of decline, their financial and professional status made them increasingly well-off. During the early 1960s, Rothko was acclaimed by many critics and patrons as the greatest living American artist. He was offered several huge commissions, one to design a series of murals for the Seagram Building and another to do the same at the Four Seasons restaurant. It was the latter, in particular, that drove him crazy trying to reconcile the creation of art with its placement in the most decadent setting imaginable.

"I accepted this assignment as a challenge with malicious intent." Rothko said, "I hope to paint something that will ruin the appetite of every son of a bitch who ever eats in this room."

The more success Rothko attained, the more he began to hate himself and everything the art world stood for. He felt like he was no longer producing great works of art to explore the deeper limits of his own creativity; he was doing it to sell paintings. He was also repeating himself, each new canvas an application of the same basic technique, the same applications of layers, the same basic forms. But by that time, a Rothko painting was so recognized the world over that even if he had wanted to change his style, he would not have been allowed to do so.

Some critics would claim that by 1960, Rothko had lost his stuff. He was no longer a maverick, a trailblazer, a spokesperson for a new movement in art. He was a bitter old man who was past his prime and couldn't accept that the new generation of pop artists—the Andy Warhols and Roy Lichtensteins—were displacing him.

In 1961, during his one-man exhibit at the Museum of Modern Art, Rothko's health problems worsened considerably. He had gained considerable weight during the preceding years of affluence. He had high blood pressure. He complained of blurred vision. He had insomnia.

Soon he would develop an aneurysm and gout. On top of these physical problems, his depressions lasted longer and occurred more frequently. He became so claustrophobic that he would not set foot on an airplane or any closed space.

Despite Rothko's declining health and continuing depression, Mell gave birth to their second child, nicknamed "Topher," in August 1963. But Rothko would insist that his real children were his paintings. He had difficulty letting them go. Not content to merely sell them, he would interview potential buyers and collectors to determine if they were worthy of owning one of his paintings, if they would take good enough care of them and hang them in a proper setting. When Jean Kennedy, sister of the president, and her brother-in-law Sargent Shriver visited the studio one day to consider a purchase, Rothko booted them out because they had the audacity to ask if they could take a painting home on conditional approval. Rothko had never liked art dealers and critics; now he found it almost intolerable to deal with customers.

Failures and Despair

By the end of the sixties, Rothko could no longer work productively. He tried to put in a few hours each morning, as usual, but he realized the extent to which he was repeating himself, painting the same thing over and over again. Even worse, he felt his life's work was being commercialized, that he was being sold out by agents and art dealers who were making a fortune on his legacy.

In addition, his twenty-five-year marriage to Mell was beginning to fall apart. They had begun arguing constantly, and now she was fighting back instead of simply accepting his rages passively. In addition, he had become less dependent on her, needed her less, because he had taken a lover. Mell knew about the relationship but tried to ignore it as much as possible. Then, to add to their misery, in April 1968 Rothko suffered an aneurysm as the result of advanced arteriosclerosis and hypertension; both conditions were related to the chronic abuse he had subjected his body to throughout his life. In addition, he was diagnosed with cirrhosis of the liver from all the alcohol he had consumed over the years. He also developed impotence, probably as a side effect of the medications he was taking—and this was the worst assault of all as far as he was concerned.

Even had Rothko wanted to paint, his doctors warned him that he was not physically well enough for the exertions of creating his large canvases, as some of his paintings were regularly over ten feet high. He was instructed that he should not even raise his arms above his head.

At a time when things seemed at their absolute worst, when Rothko could have been forgiven for choosing retirement, he attempted one last effort to save himself through creative expression. In constant physical pain, suffering from debilitating depression, loneliness, estrangement from his wife and children, he chose to begin working again in a different medium. If he could not paint in oils on large canvases that required ladders, then he would use acrylics on rolls of paper arranged at eye level. Instead of producing paintings measuring ten by twenty feet, he would reduce the scale to something that was literally within his reach.

The paintings that Rothko created at this point were similar in form to his signature style: stacked, floating rectangles. But with an assistant to cut, prepare, and stretch the paper, as well as to help mix the pigments, the artist found that he could actually work at blazing speed. In the past, it had taken him as long as several months to complete an oil painting, but working with acrylics that dried much faster, he could work on a dozen of them at the same time. Those he didn't like, he could simply tear up. Rothko could have thrown in the towel and spent his retirement years at his cottage in Cape Cod living off the millions of dollars that would soon come pouring in if he decided to unload his inventory of work that he had been hoarding for years. Although Rothko threw himself back into work, this final binge of creative expression would not last long—he was slowly being devoured by the progressive mental illness that was robbing him of his sanity. The acrylic period represented only one last gasp before he surrendered.

By the beginning of 1969, Rothko separated from his wife. He did so by simply walking out of their home two days after New Year's Eve. He didn't bother to tell Mell what he was doing or where he was going, nor did he even pack a bag—he just walked out the door and moved into his studio. Whenever he needed a clean shirt he would sneak back into the house and tuck a clean one under his coat.

Rothko's behavior not only became more bizarre, but it also became increasingly desperate, as he tried reaching out to others for support. He ruminated constantly about his reputation. He was obsessed with death. He became so needy, dependent, and fearful of abandonment that he began calling friends constantly, sometimes a dozen or more times each day, railing and ranting about his fears and delusions—despite the fact that he had never been so admired and respected for his work or so financially secure. Several of his friends actually disconnected their phones so he could no longer call them and disrupt their sleep.

With few people left to turn to, Rothko continued to reach out to his various doctors. He began calling and visiting his friend and internist, Dr. Albert Grokist, several times each week, complaining about a variety of ailments—hypertension, gout, swollen joints, leg aches, back pain, heart problems, fears of cancer. Grokist prescribed tranquilizers, which were augmented by Rothko's high intake of alcohol.

When Grokist was out of town, Rothko sought the care of another physician, who directly contradicted the advice that Rothko had received before. Then Rothko visited a psychiatrist friend, Bruce Ruddick, who later disclosed that the artist was depressed and "heartbroken." Although Ruddick refused to treat his friend, he did agree to speak with him on occasion, during which time Rothko confessed his terrible losses—of love, creativity, productivity, health, and even privacy. "He felt that depth of his suffering he was going through," Ruddick revealed, "was debilitating him as a creative person. He didn't say it stopped him, but it was draining him. He did not feel he had the élan, the vitality, and the energy."

When Ruddick tried to refer Rothko to another therapist, one who was not also his friend, Rothko became enraged. Instead he sought the assistance of a controversial psychiatrist, Nathan Kline, who had no faith whatsoever in psychotherapy but was a passionate advocate of psychopharmacology. This suited Rothko just fine because he had absolutely no interest in stirring up the past. In very brief consultations, Kline would construct a stew of various psychoactive ingredients, combining tranquilizers with antidepressants. Rothko left their first meeting with a prescription for Sinequan and Valium.

When both Kline and Grokist were out of town, Rothko went to see still another doctor, who was unaware that his patient had other prescriptions from other doctors, so he prescribed a different antidepressant, one that conflicted with Kline's choice. Several days later, Rothko turned up at a cardiologist's office, overmedicated and disoriented. Again, without consulting any colleagues who were already treating the patient, the doctor canceled the current regimen, issued his own, and referred Rothko to still another psychiatrist because he thought Kline was a quack.

When Grokist, the internist, returned to town, he was angry that Kline and others had been meddling in his case without the least consideration to inform him of what they were doing. Subsequently, each of these medical professionals continued to pursue his own agenda without considering what else was going on. The conflict escalated into arguments and threats between the doctors, each blaming the other for being incompetent. The real tragedy in all of this was that despite all their bickering, these doctors appeared to miss their patient's chronic suicidal depression, hypochondria, and alcoholism.

To be fair, Rothko was not the most cooperative patient. When a doctor would not do what he wanted (or what he hoped for), he would simply search for another one. He refused to comply with whatever medical advice he was given, refusing to exercise or watch his diet, continuing to smoke like a chimney and drink himself silly.

"I don't think he trusted anybody," Grokist later reflected. "And it went back to his mother and father starting with them. He had zero trust in his parents, and that led to this extended, protracted distrust of the outside world."

Final Canvas

On the morning of February 25, 1970, Oliver Steindecker arrived at the studio to find his boss and mentor lying on the floor, face up, in a pool of blood. Rothko's arms were flayed open at his side, almost in the pose of a crucifixion.

Based on reports by the investigating detective and the medical examiner, as well as interviews with the witnesses, it was determined that Mark Rothko, at age sixty-seven, had killed himself with a determination that left little doubt about his true intentions. Rothko had once confided to another of his assistants that if he could ever find the courage to do himself in, it would not be one of those "accidental" deaths like his friend and fellow painter Jackson Pollock, who died in a car crash while drunk.

Consequently, during the evening of the twenty-fourth, Rothko methodically plotted his final act. He swallowed a large dose of Sinequan from his pharmaceutical stash. While waiting for the drugs to provide a welcome numbing, he carefully prepared the scene so as to minimize any mess during cleanup. It was almost as if he were preparing to create one of his monstrous canvases of black and gray, where "the dark is always on top." In his latest work, the heavy black rectangles were usually pressing down on the gray or blue, as if squeezing the life out of them.

Once the drugs began to take effect, Rothko took off his shoes and pants, folding them carefully and placing them over the back of the chair. This struck observers as particularly out of character for him because he was typically slovenly. It led some to speculate that he must have been murdered, because Rothko would never in his right mind have taken such care.

Wearing only his underwear and socks, he walked up to the sink and turned on the water, which was still running when his body was discovered the next morning. Perhaps he thought he would give the cleanup crew a head start, or maybe he just forgot to turn off the faucet. In any case, he stood at the sink and took a double-sided razor blade, wrapped with Kleenex so he would not injure his fingers. Paddy Lapin, the detective on the scene, noted that this was a common and peculiar phenomenon. People who were about to slash their arteries, he said, were unduly concerned about not cutting their fingers in the process.

Rothko first made a small cut on his forearm, as if to test his resolve. Then with deliberate care, he made two long cuts just inside the crook of his arm, each about two inches long and an inch deep, severing the brachial arteries in such a way that blood drained quickly from his system. He had obviously done his homework and had discovered that this was a much more certain way of doing the job, rather than the more-common slashes near the wrists, where the arteries are narrower. After making the cuts, he removed his eyeglasses, which he would have needed to complete the procedure up to this point, and placed them on the counter, perhaps concerned that they might break.

It would have taken less than a few minutes before Rothko became light-headed from the loss of blood. He finally collapsed on the floor, landing on his back with his arms outstretched, never even trying (or able) to break the fall. His blood formed a pool, six feet by eight feet, almost a rectangle—and about the size of one of his canvases. It was as if his last canvas was painted in his own blood.

CHAPTER FIVE

Ernest Hemingway
Living Up to His Legend

Ⅰt was an early summer morning in the Boulder Mountains of Idaho. The large two-story home in Ketchum, close to the ski resort of Sun Valley, offered panoramic views of surrounding hills and the backdrop of the snow-dappled peaks. It was secluded in the woods on seventeen acres, overlooking the Big Wood River, the perfect hideaway for a writer looking for solitude.

The house was furnished with the trophies of a big game hunter—kudu, impala, and gazelle heads mounted on the walls. There was a painting of a bullfight on one wall, the bull obviously losing the battle, and another small drawing by Picasso, given to the author by the artist. In front of the large picture window in one of the bedrooms, overlooking the mountains, was a desk and typewriter. This is where the writer completed his last book, *A Moveable Feast*.

On this morning of July 2, 1961, Ernest Hemingway was a man in excruciating pain. He was suffering from hypertension and hepatitis. His body was emaciated; he looked gaunt. On top of his physical maladies, he was hearing voices. He suffered delusions, obsessions, and hallucinations, convinced he was being persecuted and under surveillance by the FBI. He could no longer sleep. He was impotent, a terrible blow to his masculinity. The shock treatments he had received to treat his depression had destroyed his memory. He could no longer write, the one thing that still gave him pleasure and kept him alive. He complained to his editor and friend, A. E. Hotchner, about how clueless the doctors were about his world and what made him tick: "They should make all psychiatrists take a course in creative writing so they'd know about writers."

When Hotchner became seriously concerned about Hemingway's threats of doing himself in, just as his father had, Hemingway thought for a moment and then told Hotchner with chilling clarity: "What do you think happens to a man going on sixty-two when he realizes that he can never write the books and stories he promised himself? Or do any of the other things he promised himself in the good days?"

Hemingway awoke early, before six, as was his custom. His wife, Mary, had been up to get a glass of water and heard him moving around. She had been thinking about the night before, when they got home from dinner. She had been singing one of his favorite Italian folk songs, when Hemingway joined in the chorus. The last words he spoke to her before they went to bed were, "Good night, my kitten." Mary smiled at this endearment, then turned over and tried to get back to sleep.

Hemingway had indeed been up for some time, thinking, ruminating, plotting, planning. He put a bathrobe on over his pajamas and shuffled down the stairs into the basement, where the hunter's guns were locked in a storage room. Mary had warned the doctors not to release her husband from the hospital because she knew he was still quite crazy. He kept muttering to himself—and to anyone else who could overhear—that his phone and house were bugged and that he was being followed. Just a few weeks earlier, Mary found him holding a shotgun, lovingly caressing it. This frightened her to the point that she put all of his weapons under a padlock. She put the key on the windowsill, not thinking he would make the connection. But he did.

Hemingway went down in the basement and unlocked the door where the guns were stored. He selected a favorite shotgun, the most reliable of the bunch, a twelve-gauge double-barreled Boss, and loaded it with two shells. Then he walked back upstairs to the foyer, a place where he knew Mary would find him immediately. He carefully placed the barrel of the gun inside his mouth, reached down with his hand, and pulled the trigger. Most of his head was blown off during the blast: his hair, teeth, scalp, and face plastered on the ceiling and walls.

When Mary heard the explosion, she hurried down the stairs to find a pile of clothes and blood on the floor. She actually had to step over parts of his head in order to reach him.

The Hemingway Legend

Anyone who knew Ernest Hemingway was not surprised by the manner in which he took his own life. He was a mythic figure, larger than life itself, so much the embodiment of all that is masculine and heroic that even Hemingway believed in his own legend. He always *played* Papa Hemingway, stayed with the persona and public image of macho adventurist and reckless sensation seeker, "lover of danger, of the bullfight, of flying, of the wartime front lines; the friend of brave men, heroes, fighters, hunters, and matadors."

By almost anyone's account, Ernest Hemingway is one of America's greatest writers and one of the most legendary figures of the twentieth century. He was awarded both the Pulitzer Prize (in 1953) and the Nobel Prize for literature (in 1954). He was the author of the classic books *The Sun Also Rises* (1926), *For Whom the Bell Tolls* (1940), and *The Old Man and the Sea* (1952). From these dates, it can be seen that his writing career spanned four decades and remained consistently acclaimed throughout his life.

Hemingway lived a dozen lives, not content to write about anything he hadn't experienced directly. He was an ambulance driver for the Red Cross during World War I, where he was wounded and decorated for acts of bravery. He was a war correspondent during the Spanish Civil War and World War II. He was a big-game hunter in Africa and a sports fisherman in Cuba and the Florida Keys. He was a brawler and a boxer, an aficionado of bullfights. When he was awarded the Nobel Prize, *Time* magazine put the announcement under "Heroes" rather than "Books," proclaiming him "a globe-trotting expert on bullfights, booze, women, wars, big game hunting, deep sea fishing, and courage." He was also an expatriate writer living in Paris along with the greatest writers of his generation: F. Scott Fitzgerald, Gertrude Stein, Ezra Pound, and James Joyce.

A Family Legacy

Ernest Hemingway came from a long, distinguished line of suicides. One of his earliest memories was of a story, told by his father, Ed, about Ernest's namesake—Ernest Hall, his grandfather, who had suffered painful wounds during the Civil War. Hall tried to end his own life by shooting himself with a revolver, but he was foiled by his son, Ed, who had secretly removed the bullets. Young Ernest, at age six when he heard the tale, thought this was the cruelest thing he'd ever heard.

Ed may have objected to his father's suicide attempt, but that did not stop him from blowing his own brains out with that very same .32 caliber Union pistol when debts and poor health got the best of him. Hemingway could never really decide after that if his father was a coward or if he had special courage.

Hemingway was never the same after his father's tragic death, but this was only the beginning of a family legacy that would continue throughout five generations—to some extent, because of his own self-destructive actions. Hemingway's sister Ursula killed herself in 1966, five years after her brother Ernest's death. She died by drug overdose after she had developed cancer and severe depression. Hemingway's brother, Leicester, who modeled himself after Ernest in every way possible, including his appearance with the trademark beard, killed himself in 1982, after becoming depressed and sick with diabetes. Leicester never really recovered from his brother's and sister's suicides.

Continuing into the subsequent generation, Ernest Hemingway's youngest son, Gregory, developed clear indications of manic depression and alcoholism similar to that of his father. He suffered seven nervous breakdowns during his lifetime and underwent ninety-seven shock treatments to cure his illness. He died in rather mysterious circumstances in a jail cell, possibly a suicide, after being picked up for walking around the streets naked, carrying a black cocktail dress across his arm. At the time, Gregory was a transsexual who had undergone a sex change operation. "I never got over a sense of responsibility for my father's death," Gregory wrote in his memoir. "The recollection of it sometimes made me act in strange ways." He was referring to the embarrassment his sexual orientation had caused his father, because Hemingway had known about the cross-dressing since the early seventies. It seemed to be a particular affront to hypermasculine Hemingway that his son would act like a woman. Unbeknownst to most people was that Hemingway had his own unresolved issues related to this matter. He had often dressed as a girl while a youngster, and he struggled with his own latent homosexual urges.

Hemingway's other son, Patrick, also had severe problems with mental illness, having been treated with electroconvulsive shock treatments like his brother Gregory and his father. He eventually suffered a head trauma that sent him over the edge into a psychotic state from which he never recovered.

Only Hemingway's son Jack managed to escape the fate of his brothers and father. He suffered his fair share of tragedies: he was wounded and captured in World War II, his wife died of cancer, and his infant daughter died as well. Still he endured as the only living legacy of the Hemingway name. Unfortunately, one of his daughters, Margaux, also inherited the family depression. The actress, and grand-daughter to Ernest Hemingway, killed herself by drug overdose in 1996 at the age of forty-one.

If ever there was a case made for the phenomenon that mental ill-ness and suicide run in families, it would appear that Hemingway rep-resents a classic example. Like those of writer Virginia Woolf, poet Alfred Lord Tennyson, composer Robert Schumann, and artist Vin-cent van Gogh, the Hemingway genes seemed to pass on not only the gift of creativity but also the plague of madness. (See illustration of family genogram.)

Unhappy Childhood

Ernest Hemingway was born in the summer of 1899 in the upper-middle-class suburb of Oak Park, Illinois, just outside Chicago. His father, Ed, was a physician and sportsman, deeply religious and com-mitted to the Protestant work ethic of hard work, self-reliance, phys-ical fitness, and respect for the outdoors. Ed was reported to have delivered over three thousand babies during his years of practice, in-cluding every one of his own children, which numbered six in all. Ernest was the second oldest, one year younger than his sister Mar-celline and three years older than his next sister, Ursula. He also had two other younger sisters, Madelaine and Carol, and a brother, Leices-ter, who was born in 1915 when Ernest was already a teenager.

If Ed taught his son to hunt and fish, then his mother, Grace, in-troduced him to music and literature. She had once been a profes-sional singer and by this time earned extra income for the family by giving vocal, cello, and piano lessons. She also dominated and con-trolled her husband, which Ernest found abhorrent and emasculat-ing. Ed was prone to debilitating depressions, quite serious ones when Ernest was four, and then again when he was nine. During these episodes, he would disappear for long periods, often on extended fish-ing trips, alone, as his form of therapy. It was at the end of one of these retreats, in 1909, that he wrote Grace a letter telling her how to cash

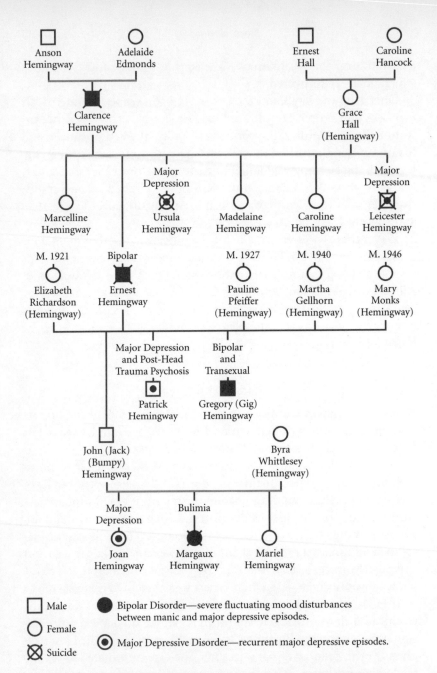

Ernest Hemingway's Intergenerational Legacy of Mental Illness.

Note: This genogram, a graphical device used by family therapists to plot multigenerational patterns in families, clearly illustrates the multitude of emotional disorders that have plagued the ancestors of Ernest Hemingway. Note, in particular, how the history of depression can be traced back through the family line and how it appears to have been passed on from one generation to the next.

in his insurance policies and disguise the cause of his death if he should meet an untimely end. It is apparent that through most of his adult life he thought about killing himself and must have talked about this with his son.

In his autobiographical *Nick Adams* stories, there is a conversation between father and son while they are in a rowboat. The boy asks why a man that they knew had killed himself.

> "He couldn't stand things, I guess" the father replied simply.
> "Do many people kill themselves?" the boy asks.
> "Not very many, Nick."
> "Was dying hard?"
> "No, I think it's pretty easy, Nick. It all depends."

Hemingway thought about this re-created conversation a lot while growing up. He obviously knew his father was depressed, sometimes dysfunctional. As much joy as Ed derived from his outdoor activities, and from his obstetric practice, there was always a layer of despair just underneath the surface.

Precious little is known about Hemingway's early years, other than the way he was coddled by his mother and dressed as a girl. It must have been an interesting contradiction of parental influences that while his father taught him to be a man, learning to hunt and fish and be a sportsman, his mother insisted on dressing him in the clothes identical to his sister Marcelline, complete with pink frocks, crocheted bonnets, flowered hats, ruffled skirts, and patent leather Mary Jane shoes. She also styled his hair in a girl's pageboy so that he would more closely resemble his sister as a twin. This occurred until he was at least six years old, at least according to existing photographs of Ernest and his sister Marcelline.

Hemingway claimed that he had led a normal and enjoyable life as a kid, but later he was to say that an unhappy childhood was a pre-requisite for a writer and that he certainly qualified. Throughout school, he showed an interest in sports, especially boxing and football, but was also active on the school newspaper and debate team. He en-joyed studying literature and developed an early talent for making up and telling stories. This is one reason why it has always been difficult to distinguish between the legends of his youth and what really oc-curred in his life.

Although Hemingway's school record would have qualified him for admission to college, either at Oberlin, his father's alma mater, or at the University of Illinois, by the time he graduated from high school in 1917, America was smack in the middle of a world war. He intended to enlist and fight in the tradition of the Hemingway warriors, who had distinguished themselves during the Confederate insurrection.

Ed would not allow his son to enlist, considering him still too young, but he did arrange for his son to obtain a job with the *Kansas City Star* as a cub reporter. This early training taught the young writer some important lessons that he was to follow for the rest of his career—to write short sentences, short paragraphs, and aim for precision and clarity.

After serving several months of his apprenticeship, Hemingway again tried to enlist but was turned down because of poor vision. His backup plan involved volunteering to drive an ambulance, and for that he was accepted. It is interesting that his eyesight was considered too poor to shoot a gun but not too poor to drive a vehicle under hazardous conditions. Nevertheless he was just grateful to get into the war so he could fight the Germans any way he was allowed.

In July 1918, Hemingway was wounded in action when an artillery shell exploded nearby. Although he suffered multiple pieces of shrapnel in his leg and hip, he managed to rescue several Italian soldiers who were more seriously hurt. For this he received a medal of valor. The experience was critical in another respect in that the young volunteer felt proud that he had demonstrated courage while under enemy fire. Even the pain was a fine teacher. He later remarked that you "have to be hurt like hell before you can write seriously." This would be the motto of his life, constantly testing the limits of what he could get away with and using the experiences to tell a story.

The incident was also significant in that it became the first of many stories that he would embellish and exaggerate as time went on. Although in truth, Hemingway was a noncombatant passing out chocolate to the troops when he was injured, he would often say that he had been wounded while part of an elite attack unit. Throughout his life, if Hemingway was ever challenged with the facts about one of his lies, he would defend his right as an author to make up whatever he wanted: "It is not unnatural that the best writers are liars. A major part of their trade is to lie or invent and they will lie when they are drunk, or to themselves, or to strangers. They often lie unconsciously and tend to remember their lies with deep remorse." This sort of justification for self-deceit made it only that much more difficult for Hemingway to live up to the standards of his own legend.

One thing that is certain about Hemingway's experiences in the war is that during the two years of recuperation that followed, from 1918 to 1920, he suffered spells of major depression. He could only sleep with the lights on, afraid of the dark, and sometimes insisted that his sister Ursula sleep with him to keep him company. He received several painful operations on his leg at this time, and he had a very close brush with death, but the emotional struggles were also related to problems with his mother, as he was trying to break free from her controlling influence. She considered her son to be lazy, wasteful, corrupt, and disrespectful, and she told him so in no uncertain terms. This wounded him even more deeply than the shrapnel in his leg.

The experiences of being wounded in battle, of having suffered a disappointing love affair in Europe, of fighting with his mother, would find their way into stories he was writing at the time of his convalescence. This would become the pattern throughout his life: almost everyone he met and everything he lived would end up in his books. For example, his recovery from his physical and psychological wounds became the basis for one of his most memorable stories of this era: "Big Two-Hearted River."

Paris Years

At just about the time that Hemingway broke contact with his mother, he met a woman eight years his senior and married her in 1921. Hemingway would insist that Elizabeth (nicknamed Hadley) was nothing like his mother, but it was more than coincidence that Hadley, like Grace, was a musician, as well as being an older woman. If Hemingway could never control his mother, he sought to do so with this surrogate.

Upon the advice of fellow writer Sherwood Anderson, the Hemingways decided to move to Paris, where there was a rich and exciting scene for up-and-coming young writers. The Hemingways would live and work there for the next seven years, until 1928, during which time Hemingway would befriend the likes of Henry James, T. S. Eliot, F. Scott Fitzgerald, Pablo Picasso, James Joyce, John Dos Passos, Ezra Pound, Gertrude Stein, and dozens of other writers and artists who liked to hang out in the cafés and bars. It was Stein, the matriarch of the bunch, who encouraged Hemingway to write sparse, simple, compressed sentences, filled with deep meaning. He had been developing this unique style since he first wrote for the high school newspaper, and this has become his trademark.

Hemingway has been accused of writing only simple, declarative sentences, seemingly averse to using adjectives and active verbs, but this belies the complexity of his craft, even this early in his career. In the story "Big Two-Hearted River," written a few years previously, there is one passage toward the end that showcases the command he had of language and the creative flexibility he employed to bring the narrative alive. Nick Adams, the protagonist, comes upon a river, where he spies something that catches his attention:

As the shadow of the kingfisher moved up the stream, a big trout shot upstream in a long angle, only his shadow marking the angle, then lost his shadow as he came through the surface of the water, caught the sun, and then, as he went back into the stream and under the surface, his shadow seemed to float down the stream with the current, unresisting, to his post under the bridge where he tightened facing up into the current.

Note that this is just one sentence and *not* the fabled three- and four-word terse constructions for which he was known. This is one reason why the greatest writers of his generation considered him to be the most accomplished of the lot.

Two particular incidents during this time spelled doom for his marriage. The first was Hemingway's rather peculiar belief that his sexual potency and creative ability were directly related. (This would play a significant role in his suicide years later.) He was convinced that having orgasms would drain away his ability to write: "I have to ease off on making love when writing hard," he disclosed in a letter to a friend, "as the two things are run by the same motor."

Not only was Hemingway sexually unavailable to his wife a good amount of the time, but he was emotionally and physically absent as well. He would write all day and then sleep all night, leaving little time for any companionship or intimacy between them. If this was not enough of a strain on their relationship, a final straw occurred during an unfortunate incident in which Hadley had been carrying all of her husband's unfinished manuscripts in a suitcase on a train. When she went to check on the baggage, the suitcase had disappeared. This struck Hemingway as such a betrayal or act of negligence that he could never forgive her. As far as he was concerned, she could no longer be trusted.

Whether it was because he was restraining himself sexually, or he was just feeling increasingly confident in his writing style, Hemingway had by then refined his technique, which unleashed a burst of creativity. He also enjoyed the benefit of mentors, like short story writer Sherwood Anderson, novelist James Joyce, and poet Ezra Pound, who recognized the young writer's creative genius and helped him to develop it. All he needed were subjects to write about, and with his lust for new adventures, there was no shortage. By 1923, he had become enamored with bullfights, a passion that would remain for the rest of his life. His novel *Death in the Afternoon,* completed ten years later, would immortalize his fascination with the sport.

Hemingway's life, from this point forward, reads like an adventure tale in which he is the heroic protagonist. As mentioned earlier, although some of the installments of the saga were indeed based on myth, a good part of his story is true. With an appointment as foreign correspondent for the *Toronto Star Weekly,* Hemingway had a license to roam the world and report on whatever interested him most. During the next few years of the early twenties, he covered the Greek-Turkish War, the French occupation of Germany, the bullfights of Spain, skiing in the Alps, and his beloved fishing. But he was never content to simply be a spectator; he insisted on getting in on the action whenever he could.

Hemingway fancied himself a boxer, but most of the time he was just a bully. He was a hulking and muscular fighter, six feet tall and weighing over two hundred pounds, yet he would often initiate fights with smaller, weaker opponents, those he could beat. This is another example of where the personal legend departs from the reality: he was known as a brawler, but he was inclined to brutalize and humiliate others who assaulted his sense of masculinity. The man who was dressed as a girl as a child, who demonstrated consistent homophobia throughout his life, felt the need to continually prove to himself—and others—that he was a real man. During the next years, he would routinely assault anyone who offended him—Ward Price, an English reporter who wore a monocle that Hemingway found offensive, writer Robert McAlmon for spreading malicious gossip, poet Wallace Stevens, and publisher Joseph Knapp. It wasn't just that Hemingway had a bad temper but that he needed to let everyone know that he was the most macho guy in the room. In his own terms, he considered that all his altercations were about defending his honor, a theme that would run strongly throughout all his books.

When his wife, Hadley, became pregnant with their child in 1923, a situation about which Hemingway was less than pleased, he was forced to alter his plans to pursue writing fiction as his full-time career.

They returned to Toronto for a brief period of time, where their son, Jack, was born, and then they came back to Paris so Hemingway could take up where he'd left off.

By this time, breaches had developed in the relationships among the group of artists and writers. Gertrude Stein and Hemingway were no longer speaking and would savage one another in their future books. Hemingway made fun of Sherwood Anderson in *The Torrents of Spring*, ridiculed John Dos Passos in *To Have and Have Not*, attacked Sinclair Lewis in *Across the River and into the Trees*, and went after Stein every chance he got. His competitive nature not only to be the best but also to crush everyone else, whether in the boxing ring, a bar fight, or literary circles, led him to treat the arena of writing as another war.

Hemingway may have been a fluent and prolific writer, but the creative process was agonizing and exhausting for him. There were mornings in which he would labor for hours just to construct a single paragraph that met his exacting standards. He dismissed contemporaries like Thomas Wolfe and Sinclair Lewis as hacks, because he felt they were sloppy and not in his league. In one of his most famous quotes about the nature of writing, Hemingway considered that what he eliminated was just as important as what he included: "The most essential gift for a good writer is a built-in, shock-proof, shit detector." He elaborated further on his minimalist style: "I always try to write on the principle of the iceberg. There is seven-eighths of it underwater for every part that shows. Anything you know you can eliminate and it only strengthens your iceberg."

We now so take Hemingway's writing for granted after seventy-five years of popularity that it is difficult to appreciate just how novel and creative his work was at the time. Most editors didn't appreciate his sparse, unusual style, nor did they particularly like the subjects he chose to write about. Yet when his first collection of stories, *In Our Time*, was published in 1925, he enjoyed instant celebrity and acclaim. D. H. Lawrence and F. Scott Fitzgerald pronounced the book important and original. Interestingly, Hemingway's parents both despised the book, as well as everything their son wrote thereafter, calling his writing vile, filthy, morbid, and shameful. When they were sent copies of his first book by the publisher, they promptly returned them with a note saying that they were horrified.

Rather than feeling discouraged by his parents' rejection on the grounds that their Puritanical religious and moral values were compromised, Hemingway seemed to draw strength and resolve from the criticism.

Conflicts with Friends and Family

Paris became less attractive as a place to live once Hemingway's marriage to Hadley dissolved and his friendships fractured. Don Stewart was a fellow writer and friend at the time, with whom Hemingway went to Pamplona, Spain, to run with the bulls. When Stewart was injured by the stampede, Hemingway was credited in the papers as saving his life, a complete falsehood. But soon afterward, Hemingway turned on his friend just as he had on so many others in their group of writers.

"The minute he began to love you," Stewart explained, "or the minute he began to have some sort of obligation to you of love or friendship or something, that is when he had to kill you. Then you were too close to something he was protecting. He, one-by-one, knocked off the best friendships he ever had."

Stewart is referring first to Gertrude Stein, then to F. Scott Fitzgerald and Sherwood Anderson. Several years later, Hemingway would break with his closest writer-friend, John Dos Passos, in a bitter feud that lasted decades, in which they took turns attacking each other in their books. Over the next several years of the twenties in Paris, Hemingway chased away most of his friends. Then, in 1926, he had an affair with another correspondent, Pauline Pfeiffer, who was to become his next wife. For a while, he juggled both relationships—Hadley and Pauline—with each woman knowing about the other, until finally Hadley bowed out with some dignity.

If Hemingway was fighting with his friends and feuding with his parents, he was also a challenge for his editor, Max Perkins, at Scribner. Perkins was actually similar to Hemingway's father, Ed, in that he held certain moralistic and rather Puritanical beliefs that were offended by Hemingway's coarse language and blunt manner. Perkins was too intimidated to approach the writer directly about the matter, but he wrote himself a note in his calendar that said, "shit piss fuck bitch." This was a reminder to discuss the problem during their next scheduled editorial meeting. When the boss himself, Charles Scribner, walked into Perkins's office and noticed the note, he said to his editor that he must be exhausted and overworked and urged him to take some time off.

Perkins was hardly the only one who treaded lightly around the volatile writer who was prone to rages. Hemingway himself would suffer the consequences of his recklessness and irrational responses: throughout his life, he would be accident-prone, almost dying a half dozen times in plane crashes, car accidents, hunting accidents, and various expeditions.

When Pauline, his new wife, became pregnant with another son (Patrick) in 1927, Hemingway figured it was time to leave Paris and relocate somewhere closer to her family and where he could pursue his pastimes of hunting and fishing. They settled on the most remote outpost of the American continent: Key West, at the very end of the Florida Keys. He would spend the next decade there completing a series of books that would cement his reputation as the greatest living writer: *A Farewell to Arms, Death in the Afternoon, Green Hills of Africa,* and *To Have and Have Not.*

In December 1928, Hemingway received a telegram that would change his life forever: his father had killed himself. Ed used his father's own .32 Smith and Wesson Civil War revolver. This was the same pistol that Ed's father had tried to use to take his own life when Ed was a child. Ed had been physically sick, financially troubled, and seriously depressed. He saw suicide as the only way out.

Hemingway was furious at his father's cowardly action. He asked his mother to send him the gun that had been used in the suicide and then proceeded to throw it in a lake. It felt to him as if he was burying the last remnant of his father as he watched the gun sink to the bottom. If only this single action could have banished ongoing thoughts about his father's death, but the image of the suicide continued to plague him until he replicated the same act when he was just a few years older than his father had been.

A third son (Gregory) was born in 1931, but Hemingway admitted he had trouble being around little kids. Once they got old enough for him to teach them to hunt and fish, he'd be a good father, but for the most part he ignored the boys when they were young. By the time Gregory was born, Pauline confessed that she felt even stronger than her husband as far as her aversion to infants. She had enough to do trying to keep her husband happy and so felt little compunction to show much attention or love toward her children. She later admitted to Gregory when he was older that she flat out couldn't stand being around kids before the age of six.

During the thirties, when his reputation was well established, and he was earning enough money to support his mother and siblings, Hemingway declared himself the head of his family, replacing his father. He liked everyone to call him "Papa," and he ruled with an iron hand that was not unlike Ed. When his youngest sister, Carol, made plans to marry a man she met in college, Hemingway absolutely forbade the union, insisting that her fiancé was not good enough. Carol ignored her brother's directive and married the man anyway. Afterward, Hemingway wrote his sister off forever. He never spoke to her again and told anyone who asked about her that she was dead.

If Carol suffered complete ostracism and withdrawal of his support, Papa Hemingway's other siblings experienced varying degrees of the same thing if they ever dared to defy him. He described his sister Marcelline as a "bitch complete with handles." His relationship with his brother, Leicester, was not much better. Only his sister Ursula escaped his wrath, mostly because she lived far away in Hawaii.

Becoming Papa

It would seem to many biographers that Hemingway's descent into madness was a phenomenon that occurred later in his life, largely the result of the various physical maladies that plagued him. It is apparent, however, that the writer not only struggled with a number of emotional problems since early childhood, but as he began to gain stature in his thirties, he started manifesting a number of alarming symptoms. His explosive temper tantrums grew more frequent and violent. His depressions lasted for longer periods of time and became more crippling. He also developed a number of obsessions and compulsions that seemed to help him maintain an illusion of control over his life. One need only have a cursory knowledge of his writing to realize his preoccupation with death. His first published story, written in high school, ends with a suicide. Five of his seven novels end in tragic death.

Even more than his preoccupation with death and suicide was his propensity for compulsive counting and list making. He would count the words he had written in a day and keep track of the number of birds he shot and the number of fish he caught. In itself, this would not be so unusual, but the appearance of these behaviors accompanied periods of insomnia, impotence, and writer's block. Like many writers, Hemingway was terrified that he would lose his powers of creativity.

Another interesting aspect of his mental health that has received intense scrutiny by scholars and psychoanalysts, even the subject of a whole book, was his hair fetish. From the earliest age, he became fixated on hair as a source of endless stimulation and arousal. In all his writings, he paid particular attention to describing the hair of the women in his stories. From hundreds of examples of Hemingway's writings, one psychoanalyst identifies "The Last Good Country," from the Nick Adams stories, as evidence of Hemingway's obsession with haircutting, hair dying, and sexual transformation. In one passage, typical of the writer's attention to the subject, the female protagonist is described in this way:

> Her hair was cropped as short as a boy's. It was cut with no compromises. It was brushed back, heavy as always, but the sides were cut short and the ears that grew close to her head were clear and the tawny line of her hair was cropped close to her head. . . . She turned her head and lifted her breasts and said, "Kiss me please."

Hemingway not only thought about, fantasized about, obsessed about, wrote about, hair—its length and color and texture and smell and tactile sensation, how it felt, tickled, moved, shimmered—but his fetishes later extended to other objects, such as feet, cats, and certain words. He was clearly a kinky guy, sexually aroused by associations developed early in childhood. Psychoanalysts have had a field day examining him from every possible angle, including his latent homosexuality, Oedipal complex, post-traumatic stress disorder, death wish, bipolar disorder, self-image problems, narcissism, personality disorder, spousal abuse, and sexual inadequacy. He has been quite literally one of the most frequently and thoroughly analyzed persons in history, largely as a result of his stature, plus the sheer variety of dysfunctional symptoms he presented.

Rather than overly pathologizing the man, diagnosing and cataloging all his symptoms, it seems far more useful to focus on those aspects of his mental and emotional (dys)functioning that most influence his creative process. All of the factors just mentioned help explain why he was so tough for others to be around and why his wives and children struggled so much to contain him.

During the early thirties, when he was planning his first hunting trip to Africa, Hemingway found it difficult to recruit any companions. As many friends as he was purported to have (and who claimed him as a friend), none would agree to join him on the adventure because of fears that he would be too difficult to get along with. "Papa," as he now liked to be called, was controlling and domineering. Eventually, he persuaded a new local friend living in Key West to join him.

By the middle of the thirties, when he was past the midpoint of his life, Hemingway began to take an interest in his sons, who were now thirteen (Jack), eight (Patrick), and five (Gregory). By then, they were old enough to hunt and fish with their father, and this is what he lived for. In later years, his sons would talk about this as the best times they had together. As long as they were obedient, respectful, and did *exactly* what Papa said, things were fine. Once the boys entered adolescence and demonstrated the slightest sign of rebellion, Papa jumped all over them. He tried to dominate his sons—he *needed* to dominate them— long past the point where it did any of them any good. This did not bode well for ongoing, healthy relationships as the boys matured.

Papa could not remain isolated in the Florida Keys for long; he thrived on adventures far more than structured hunting trips could allow. During World War I, he had been frustrated by his noncombatant role; it was humiliating not to be allowed to carry a weapon because he was working for the Red Cross. When the Spanish Civil War began in 1936, he *had* to be part of the action.

Just as in the previous war, where he had fallen in love with another woman, divorced his wife, and moved on to the next marriage, the pattern repeated itself once again. His next lover (and future wife), Martha Gellhorn, was thirteen years younger than Pauline. She shared his interest in the Spanish conflict and was an avowed anti-Fascist. She encouraged Hemingway to go to Spain and report on what was going on. Hemingway needed a break from his staid life, so it seemed like a perfect opportunity not only to explore a new relationship with his lover but also to access more creative energy in his writing.

Most of Hemingway's colleagues and fellow correspondents reporting on the war remember him as generous and helpful during this time. As a celebrity, he was entitled to access and privileges not afforded the rest, and he used this position to assist his friends, as well as to lobby on behalf of the Loyalists. He was hardly an objective journalist on the scene, and this passion is what led to the final breach with his friend John Dos Passos, who was more sympathetic to the Fascists. As in most civil wars, there were no good guys and bad guys; both sides were committing atrocities. Unfortunately, after the dispute with Dos Passos, Hemingway lost his last friend who was a writer or artist. For the rest of his life, he would hang out only with sportsmen, soldiers, celebrities, and fans, but never with other creative men and women. He just couldn't seem to handle the competition.

The Loyalists lost the Spanish Civil War, but Hemingway at least came back with the material he needed to write one of his greatest and best-selling novels, *For Whom the Bell Tolls*, published in 1940. This is about the same time that he left Pauline for good. His creative energy seemed to thrive on adversity. He felt terribly guilty and conflicted about his second marriage ending and the secret affair he had been carrying on. And all this took place within the backdrop of a war in which he had watched his friends die, placed his own life in jeopardy, and had his cause defeated. Rather than become dispirited by these tragic events, he drew creative inspiration from them.

Hemingway and Martha began their new life in Cuba, a place where they could start over and where he could enjoy some anonymity. After the excitement of the previous years in Spain, he longed for some peace and relaxation. It is also to his credit that Papa wanted to escape his legend and spend time among people who would not become intimidated by his reputation or celebrity status. His friends in the coming years would be Cuban aristocrats but also fishermen very much like Santiago from *The Old Man and the Sea*. They were sometimes seedy characters and hard drinkers, men whom his new wife found frightening.

This third marriage was doomed from the beginning. Ernest and Martha Hemingway seemed to do well together when they were in the midst of war, first in Spain in 1936, and then in China during the first years of World War II. In between these times, they fought constantly. Martha did not enjoy sex (at least with Hemingway and her previous husband), which felt to him like a personal assault on his masculinity. Rather than being the compliant wife like Hadley and Pauline, Martha fought back against her oppressor. She was sick of his lies and tall tales. Worst of all was his drinking. Hemingway had always been a heavy drinker, but by this time he was a raging alcoholic. One time, when Leicester, Hemingway's younger brother, came to visit, he counted Papa drinking seventeen Scotch and sodas in a single day. Like Mark Rothko, Hemingway often started drinking as soon as he awoke and continued drinking until he fell into bed. Like other noted writers— Sinclair Lewis, Eugene O'Neill, Scott Fitzgerald, Hart Crane, John Steinbeck, Virginia Woolf, John O'Hara, Edgar Allan Poe, Upton Sinclair, William Faulkner, Truman Capote—Hemingway, according to biographer Jeffrey Meyers, "found liquor an instant relief from the oppressive strain of writing as well as an anodyne for the even greater torments of creative sterility."

Hemingway tried to restrict himself to only three or four drinks before dinner but could never manage to do so. He needed the alcohol the way so many other American writers needed it. They used it as a muse, as well as a crutch, during those times when the words would not come. For Hemingway, he had so many other demons that he was trying to pacify: the ways he had treated his friends and children, guilt over his failed marriages, close brushes with death, pain from his various wounds and accidents, and always at the brink of his consciousness, his grandfather's pistol lying at the bottom of the lake.

Going After Still Bigger Game

The conflicts between Martha and Ernest Hemingway escalated with the start of the war. They screamed at each other in public settings. In a story that she wrote about him after their marriage ended, Martha described him as impotent, depressed, unable to write, and on the verge of losing his mind. Part of this resentment may have come from jealousy. She was tired of living in the shadow of his fame and yearned for recognition in her own literary career. On his part, Hemingway discouraged if not sabotaged his wife's plans; he needed and demanded all her attention.

During the early years of the war, Hemingway wanted to stay put in Cuba. He didn't feel like traveling all the way to the front in Europe, only to have to operate under so many rules that confined the role of a journalist. Instead (as incredible as this may sound), he launched his own spy network in Havana, recruiting operatives and gathering intelligence about German activities in the vicinity. This drove J. Edgar Hoover, director of the FBI, and an even more megalomaniacal control freak, crazy. He sent FBI agents down to Cuba, suspicious of Hemingway's activities and his previous affiliation with the Socialist Loyalists in Spain. The FBI not only opened a file on Hemingway but also began following him to see what he was really up to. The amateur "man in Havana" now had to look over his shoulder not only for potential Nazi spies but also for Hoover's "G-men."

Hemingway loved the intrigue of being a spymaster. There is some evidence that he did some good with these efforts. Even if the information he gathered about potential enemies in the area was less than reliable, he probably discouraged the Germans from expanding their surveillance activities further. Hoover eventually forbade him from continuing this illegal and unsanctioned espionage, so Hemingway changed "outfits" from intelligence to the navy.

There were quite a few German submarines operating in the waters south of Florida, and Cuba was a good base. Hemingway decided next to outfit his fishing boat, the Pilar, as a sub hunter to patrol the waters. He recruited a crew of locals who were familiar with machine guns, as well as a jai alai player whose job would be to lob small homemade bombs if they could entice any submarines to approach them. The plan was to use themselves as bait, attract subs in the area to investigate, and then sink them when they came close. Unfortunately, all they ever caught were fish, but that did not deter Hemingway and his buddies from going out on patrol together, drinking, fishing, and keeping an eye on the local territory. They may not have actually sunk any enemy boats, but they did report sightings to the authorities, which allowed them to track and restrict their freedom of movement.

In 1944, Hemingway decided to join the war more actively and made plans to head for France and the Siegfried Line, a defense system built by the Germans. This would give him an excuse to get away from Martha, as they were driving themselves (and everyone else) crazy, and also get him more directly into the action. He wasn't writing much in those days anyway, so he hoped another adventure, hunting bigger game (first subs, then humans), would get his creative juices flowing. This had always worked for him before.

An auspicious sign that the previous template of his life would be continued was that upon arriving in Europe, he immediately fell in love with Mary Welsh, who would soon become his fourth wife. Mary had been married twice before and was introduced to her future husband by writer Irwin Shaw, the author of *Bury the Dead* and *The Young Lions.* Hemingway hated Shaw because he was seen as a competitor writing about war and also because he had slept with Mary. Nevertheless Hemingway must have been grateful that he now had his next wife lined up before he extricated himself from his marriage to Martha.

Like each of his previous wives, Mary, also a writer, idolized Hemingway. She also knew what she was getting into when she was subjected to his drunken binges, as well as emotional and physical abuse. Early in their relationship, he threw a photograph of her latest ex-husband into the toilet of their room at the Ritz Hotel in Paris and blew it away with a machine gun, causing flooding that was difficult to explain to the management.

War brought out the best in Hemingway, and this, the biggest one of all, really activated his spirit. The seven months from June to December 1944, he was to describe as the happiest time of his life, totally in his element. He loved the thrill of combat and freely admitted that he enjoyed killing things, whether birds, lions, or more dangerous game, like humans, as enemy combatants.

Hemingway did indeed try to live up to his legend during his stint on the front. Although it was totally illegal, because he was a registered journalist, he carried weapons and fought bravely in several important battles. He killed his share of Germans and suffered causalities among his squad on several occasions. It is interesting to note that he was also reckless and deliberately exposed himself to danger, taunting the enemy to target him. He either believed himself invulnerable to harm (he rarely bothered to duck during incoming artillery barrages because he claimed a shell was not a threat if he could hear it coming) or he welcomed death. His companions could never quite decide if he was truly courageous or just stupid and insane.

Of course, Hemingway exaggerated his exploits, claiming that he had been among the first to liberate Paris or that he led forces into battle, but there were still plenty of witnesses who testified that he was indeed someone they'd want on their side when things were most precarious. One intelligence officer and future ambassador to Germany, David Bruce, provided clear corroboration that Hemingway had often been in the thick of things: "I entertain a great admiration for [Hemingway], not only as an artist and friend, but as a cool, resourceful, imaginative, military tactician and strategist. . . . He was a born leader of men, and, in spite of his strong independence of character, impressed me as a highly disciplined individual."

Hemingway returned to Cuba as a war hero, adding to his already legendary reputation as a fearless warrior. He also brought with him a new wife, one who would stick with him, through all the trials and tribulations that would follow, for the next seventeen years until his death.

Rising Fame, Declining Health

Hemingway's sons liked Mary very much. They were well aware of the sort of abuse that their father had inflicted on their mothers, so they appreciated Mary's patience and stability, hoping it would take some pressure off them. Jack, the eldest, was doing well in his life, having served in the war with distinction and afterward working as a stockbroker. Patrick, the middle son, was having terrible problems that resulted in a complete nervous breakdown and hospitalization. He was diagnosed as paranoid schizophrenic and would remain troubled for the rest of his life. Gregory, the youngest, as mentioned earlier in the story, had gender identity issues. Of all the boys, he suffered the most from his father's wrath and disapproval.

Hemingway's own health had taken some serious hits from all of his war wounds, hunting and fishing accidents, car and plane crashes, as well as his alcohol abuse. For someone with a hair fetish, it was especially demoralizing to find he was losing his hair and what he had left was turning gray. Yet as his condition deteriorated, he began boasting more than ever. In a letter to his publisher, Charles Scribner, he wrote with glee that he had finally been able to overcome his superstition related to sexual and creative potency: "To celebrate my fiftieth birthday," he wrote, "I fucked three times, shot ten straight at pigeons (very fast ones) [clay pigeons] at the club, drank with five friends a case of Piper Heidsieck Brut and looked at the ocean for big fish all afternoon."

Because most of his Cuban *compañeros* were usually drunk when they heard his stories, it didn't seem to bother him much. His celebrity status as "Papa," the godfather of literature, brought all the famous people of his era to his doorstep—Trygve Lie, secretary-general of the United Nations; philosopher Jean-Paul Sartre; actors Gary Cooper, Marlene Dietrich, Ingrid Bergman, and Ava Gardner.

Hemingway experienced another creative renaissance in his fifties with the writing of *Islands in the Stream* (never completed and published after his death) and perhaps his most famous and best-selling book, *The Old Man and the Sea,* based on his years in Cuba. This occurred immediately after a series of deaths that floored him. His first grandson (by Jack) died. Then his mother passed away at age seventy-nine. Next his father-in-law was diagnosed with cancer, followed by the death of Pauline, the mother of his two younger sons. A trusted maid in his house killed herself that year, a woman that he had been trying to help recover from a previous suicide attempt. Then, perhaps must devastating of all, Charles Scribner, one of his oldest friends and confidantes, as well as his publisher, died suddenly. Nineteen fifty-one was a hellish year, yet a productive one for him. This is all the more remarkable for someone who was obsessed with death. He seems to have been able to compartmentalize the tragedies long enough to complete his books.

To add to Hemingway's problems, once Pauline died, Gregory went off the deep end. Hemingway had already lost Patrick to mental illness, and now his youngest son began to act more strangely, with his drug problems, mental instability, and eventually overt transsexualism, which he pretended to keep hidden from his homophobic father.

The good news was that the critics loved *The Old Man and the Sea,* and this sustained Hemingway during difficult times. *Life Magazine* published the book in its entirety, and it sold over five million copies in two days. The book itself was a best-seller for most of the year. It was awarded a Pulitzer Prize, then made into a movie. Papa had all the acclaim he could ever want. Well, almost.

It was while returning to Africa in January 1954, to regain some of his youthful identity as the great, white hunter, that Hemingway suffered not one, but *two* different plane crashes. In the first, he suffered a sprained shoulder, but in the second, far-more-serious wreck, he was actually reported dead in the world's newspapers. He suffered a fractured skull, dislocated shoulder, ruptured spleen and kidney, compressed vertebrae, vision and hearing loss, and internal bleeding. He would remain in pain for the rest of his life.

Hemingway had the privilege of reading his own obituaries once he returned home. He was also forbidden to drink alcohol during his recovery, so the one crutch that he had been able to depend on his whole life to control his spells of depression was now denied him. Even with the warnings of what continued drinking would do to his injured kidneys and liver, he could not stop himself even if it meant a premature death.

Just as his health continued to decline, his fame leaped still another notch when he was awarded the Nobel Prize in 1954.

Like Father, Like Son

By the late fifties, Hemingway had become worn out by the heat, humidity, and hurricanes of Cuba. The political situation was also becoming dicey, and he sensed that the Batista regime would soon fall. Although he was sympathetic to Castro, just as he had been toward the Spanish Socialists, he was a loyal American, who, in the end, decided to honor his government's decision to boycott the new revolutionary. Still, in the months after Castro came into power, he and Hemingway enjoyed a friendship, a situation that did not exactly further endear him to J. Edgar Hoover.

Ernest and Mary Hemingway had found a new home in Idaho, a locale in which the change in scenery might do the couple some good—or so Mary had hoped. Hemingway was then infatuated with an eighteen-year-old girl, Valerie Danby-Smith, an apprentice reporter who had been sent to interview him but had completely made a mess of things. Hemingway was immediately taken with her youth, her spunk, and her innocence. It is more than a little interesting that he had attempted to prove his masculinity while in his twenties by choosing wives who were significantly older; once he was sixty, he became attracted to teenagers.

The sad part of this tale is that Mary was well aware that he was chasing after the girl right under her nose. Hemingway pretended that she was his secretary and assistant, but anyone in the vicinity could see the lustful way that he looked at Valerie. Perhaps in some ways, Mary welcomed a younger pair of hands, and body, to reduce the burden of taking care of Papa, who was becoming more and more difficult, if that was even imaginable. Observers noted that he treated his wife like a dog.

It was while he was convalescing and reflecting on the obituaries written about him that Hemingway first seriously considered writing his memoirs. He had recently uncovered a trunk full of materials and documents from his Paris years, when he had been creative and vital and when his writing had been at its absolute best. In *A Movable Feast*, his slightly fictionalized autobiography, Hemingway sought to tell his own story, in his own words. He was tired of critics and psychiatrists always trying to make sense of him. He was trying to save himself in the only way he knew how—by digging into the depths of his own life through creative writing. Although written during a time when he had significantly deteriorated mentally and physically, the book is regarded as his single best piece of nonfiction work.

Once the book was done, Hemingway was literally spent; he had nothing left to give. His body was giving out on him and his mind was no longer reliable. When he was examined by doctors at the end of 1960, he was told that he had developed a form of diabetes that would leave him blind and impotent within the next few years. For a writer and imagined lover, this was a death sentence.

The delusions of being followed and persecuted by the FBI were by that time based, in part, in reality. Hoover *did* have it in for him after twenty years of Hemingway's defiance. There *was* a special agent assigned to his case who was following him and monitoring his activities. But what started out as reasonable suspicion had by that time spun out of control. Hemingway was convinced that his rooms were bugged, as were his phones. He believed there was a plot to assassinate him.

Mary became so concerned that she felt there was no choice but to have him hospitalized. He was disintegrating before her eyes. Because there was no possibility he would agree to visit a psychiatric facility, Hemingway was sent to the Mayo Clinic in Minnesota, supposedly for treatment of his hypertension. Once he was admitted, however, the doctors decided to attack his mental illness with a vengeance. They decided that electroconvulsive shock treatment was the ticket, just as doctors would recommend for poets Sylvia Plath and Robert Lowell (with equally disastrous results).

When his son Patrick suffered his first nervous breakdown, Hemingway had witnessed the terrifying procedure and so was understandably reluctant. Nevertheless he was administered a dozen treatments that left him even more paranoid, delusional, and depressed, with the added side effect that his memory had been wiped clean. When the results were less desirable than expected, they subjected him to another course of ten more shock sessions. He felt like a drooling imbecile but told the doctors anything they wanted to hear, just to let him out of the prison and torture chamber.

Mary realized how sick her husband really was and begged the doctors not to release him. They felt they had done all they could; the rest was up to him. By the time they wheeled him out of Mayo, he had lost seventy-five pounds from his normal weight when he was healthy. He could think about nothing other than the guns locked in the basement and his grandfather's pistol that he had thrown in the lake.

Not Happily Ever After

Mary screamed as she stepped over her husband's body to reach the door. She was breathing hard, concentrating on trying not to faint. George Brown, a boxer and sparring partner of Papa's from the old days, was staying in the guest house and he raced over, guessing that the worst had finally happened. When he called Don Anderson, another friend and former guide for Hemingway, all he said was, "Papa's finally got the job done." Don knew immediately what he meant.

Anderson came over to help Brown clean up the mess. They wanted to make sure that Papa's reputation was preserved and decided on the official story that appeared in the papers the next day: the great author had accidentally killed himself while cleaning his shotgun.

The house may have been thoroughly cleaned of Hemingway's brilliant brain, but the mess was only to become far worse in the coming weeks. First, the truth leaked out that it had indeed been a suicide (anyone who knew him in his later years could have believed nothing else). Then his last will and testament was read, announcing that he'd completely disinherited his sons, leaving them nothing.

Jack, Patrick, and Gregory showed up at the funeral, all of them bitter about not only how they had been treated by his last wishes but especially the way their father had bullied them when he was alive. Most of the attendees, Mary included, felt nothing but relief.

Hemingway's suicidal act—passed on from his grandfather, to his father, to himself, to his brother and sister, to his sons, and finally to his granddaughter—presents one of the most tragic family legacies on record. In a strange footnote to the story, Gregory, the youngest and most damaged son, married his father's girlfriend, Valerie. They hardly lived happily ever after.

CHAPTER SIX

Virginia Woolf
A Great Lake of Melancholy

I n 1929, Virginia Woolf was at the height of her acclaim. Credited with practically reinventing the novel and modern fiction, she had also distinguished herself as a brilliant essayist and literary critic, as well as author of some of the most important books of her era, including *To the Lighthouse* and *Mrs. Dalloway.* She had developed a unique style of writing that employed both stream of consciousness and *moments of being:* vivid descriptions of particular states of experience in which the reader could practically see, hear, taste, smell, and feel what was going on at the time. Along with Marcel Proust and James Joyce, she is credited with redefining the novel as a subjective experience.

Most of Woolf's works were painfully autobiographical, based largely on her own turbulent emotional struggles. She is also acknowledged as being among the first feminist writers, one who took up the point of view of women and their plight. Finally, along with her husband, Leonard, she launched Hogarth Press, which, ironically for someone so averse to looking at her own unresolved issues, published the works of the most notable archaeologist of the mind, Sigmund Freud, as well as T. S. Eliot, Katherine Mansfield, Maxim Gorky, and others.

In March 1929, Woolf had been confined to bed for weeks because of another incapacitating depression. Bed rest seemed always to be the recommended cure by her doctors, one that she found not only worthless but a complete waste of time when she could be writing. But according to the orders of her husband, Leonard, and the doctors, she was permitted to do nothing but remain in bed. There were times when she lay there quietly, staring at the walls, watching the changes of light, the shimmering of shapes and images that formed themselves into faces. The doctors called these hallucinations, but she found them interesting, very interesting.

On March 28, she wrote in her diary for the first time in months, quite uncharacteristic for her as she had been journaling since she was a child and would eventually produce five published volumes of her most private thoughts. For some time, she had been unable to write even if she had been permitted to do so. She was working on the novel *A Room of One's Own* but was stuck for an ending. Then, while lying in bed in this dreamy, disoriented state, all at once she was flooded with perfect clarity on exactly how things would come to a conclusion. By the time she retrieved her diary, the words came pouring out of her in a steady stream. She was to call this a *fertile illness*.

A few days after this incident, Woolf wrote in a letter to her friend Ethel Smyth, "As an experience, madness is terrific I can assure you, and not to be sniffed at; and in its lava I still find most of the things I write about. It shoots out of one everything shaped, final, not in mere driblets, as sanity does."

These manic states would sometimes result in hallucinations and delusions, or at the very least, all her senses intensified. "I've had some very curious visions in this room too," she noted in her diary, "lying in bed, mad, & seeing the sunlight quivering like gold water, on the wall. I've heard the voices of the dead here. And felt, through it all, exquisitely happy."

In June of the same year, the tide turned in the opposite direction, from the ecstatic creativity of her mania to the total depths of her depression. She began to doubt her ability to write, even during a time when she was lauded as one of the greatest authors of her generation. She described herself as living at the precarious edge of a "great lake of melancholy." Whatever stable ground she might have ever felt, at any moment she could be pitched into the sea and drowned in an instant.

"Lord, how deep it is. . . . Directly I stop working I feel that I am sinking down, down. And as usual, I feel that if I sink further I shall reach the truth."

Woolf believed that there was a kind of nobility, a truth, in her pain. Yes, she suffered terribly, beyond what anyone could endure, but she also believed that it was this same anguish that made it possible for her to create great fiction.

Of all the writers and artists who ever lived, there was nobody whose madness and creativity were so intertwined. Virginia Woolf understood this clearly about her own process. She knew that she was unstable but also realized that it was these same waves of disturbance that allowed her to access levels of her own inventiveness that would not otherwise have been possible. Woolf wrote fiction, but it was solidly based on her own experiences. She wrote about incest, and abuse, and damaged families. She wrote about her own life.

Multiple Causes

There has been more written about Virginia Woolf's mental condition than about everyone else in this book combined. There have been dozens of biographies, hundreds of scholarly articles, plus essays and films, that have explored her madness and the effects on her work. Psychoanalysts have devoted complete journals to discussing her childhood. Psychologists and psychiatrists continue to debate her diagnosis, as if figuring out whether she was manic-depressive or schizophrenic would unlock the mysteries of her creative spirit.

There are also as many theories about the causes of her mental illness as there are literary criticism of her work. Her depressions and manic episodes have been attributed to (1) the genetic inheritance of her illness, (2) the function of her neurobiology, (3) the trauma of childhood sexual abuse, (4) the subsequent dissociation that occurred after the trauma, (5) the result of her defective personality, (6) separation-individuation issues related to her mother, (7) the abandonment of her husband, who was coping with his own depression at the time. Even Sigmund Freud was blamed by some analysts, because of the ways his books stirred up early childhood traumas that had been effectively repressed. Suffice it to say that a lot of very bright, learned people have some rather strong (but often contradictory) opinions about the subject.

Regardless of the debate as to the causes of her mental illness, what remains clear is that Woolf was not only one of the most creative women and writers who ever lived but also one who faced unimaginable obstacles and challenges to survive. Her whole life can be chronologically sequenced according to the devastating psychotic breakdowns she suffered before her final surrender.

The first, at age thirteen, occurred after the death of her mother, an accumulative effect of childhood trauma.

The second, at age twenty-two, took place after the death of her father.

The third, at age thirty-one, was perhaps the most incapacitating of all, beginning immediately after her marriage and honeymoon. There was a relapse a year later. Each of these breakdowns lasted anywhere from a month to as long as six months, during which time she would exhibit symptoms of raving mania or depressive stupor so severe that she couldn't speak, much less write a complete sentence.

Woolf's story is particularly instructive because therapists who treat childhood sexual abuse and traumas rarely find out how things turn out in adulthood; the children disappear and are never heard from again. From Woolf, however, we have a long and distinguished narrative history based on her autobiographical novels, her journals and letters, and the analyses by the legion of psychobiographers who have attempted to make sense of her life.

A Circus of Family Dysfunction

At six years of age, Virginia appeared to live within the perfect upper-class London family. Her mother, Julia Duckworth, was part of a publishing empire that had been in the book business for generations. Her father, Sir Leslie Stephen, was a well-regarded literary critic who associated with the greatest authors in Britain, including Henry James; Alfred, Lord Tennyson; and William Thackeray (whose daughter Sir Leslie married as his first wife).

For a child who showed such early interest in reading and writing, Virginia lived in her own heaven, a home filled with books. "Think how I was brought up!" she wrote to a friend. "No school; mooning about alone among my father's books; never any chance to pick up all that goes on in schools—throwing balls; ragging; slang; vulgarities; scenes; jealousies!" An ideal life indeed.

Virginia had been born into this distinguished literary family in 1882, when her father was fifty. She was one of four children from his second marriage to Julia Duckworth, combined with Duckworth's own three children from her first marriage. To add to the complexity of this blended family, Sir Leslie also had a daughter from his first marriage to Minnie Thackeray. As a result, there was a household full of children in the blended family, which included Leslie's daughter, Laura, who was twelve years old at the time Virginia was born, and the

Duckworths from Julia's first marriage—Gerald, the same age as Laura; Stella, thirteen years older than Virginia; and George, fourteen years older. In addition, Virginia's own natural siblings included Vanessa and Thoby, who were two and three years older respectively. Finally, there was the baby of the family, Adrian, who was born just a year after Virginia. So there were a total of eight kids, ranging from infancy to adolescence, more than enough to fill a home school.

Any illusion that this was a happy, well-adjusted family would have been completely demolished by a glimpse at the family tree, which featured a history of mental illness going back several generations and clearly manifesting disturbing symptoms in the current crop. There was enough mental illness in this family, past and present, to keep a psychiatric hospital in business. (See illustration of family genogram.)

Even under optimal conditions, a family composed of children from three different sets of parents would have presented some interesting challenges. Among the Stephens, however, there were so many other undercurrents and problems to face. Julia, the mother, was melancholic if not clinically depressed. Sir Leslie was subject to cyclical emotional breakdowns—called *cyclothymia*—that were considered customary among his ancestors; both his father and brother were severely depressed. He suffered numerous episodes of mental collapse throughout his life that were both unpredictable and frightening to the children.

Among the children, the eldest daughter, Laura, was "intellectually challenged," as we might say politely, and as was probably framed in similar language in Victorian times. She most likely suffered from *Asperger's Syndrome,* a kind of autism that renders a child mute and antisocial. Her parents considered her uncooperative and stubborn and so attempted to discipline her cruelly, without success. Because of her bizarre behavior, she was kept a prisoner in the attic throughout much of her childhood before being sent off to an asylum.

The two older Duckworth boys, Gerald and George, had learning problems and trouble passing their exams. Adrian and Thoby also had difficulties, a peculiar phenomenon in such a literate, privileged family. Stella, perhaps the most wounded of all, was a victim of abuse and was treated more like a servant than an equal family member. Virginia's cousin James Stephen, the son of her father's brother, was so violent and crazy that he was known to burst into the house in a mad rage and forcibly assault and rape Stella, who tried to hide from him. During one manic episode that occurred when Virginia was just eight, James entered the home in an uncontrolled rage, hunted down Stella,

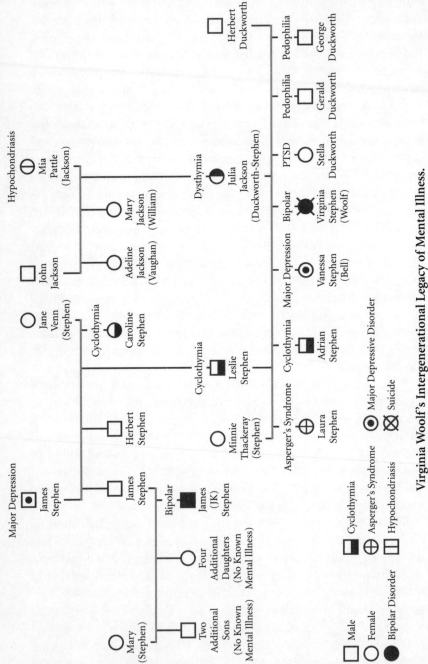

Virginia Woolf's Intergenerational Legacy of Mental Illness.

Note: This genogram for Virginia Woolf's family illustrates the history of mental illness throughout four generations, especially in the paternal line. Note, as well, the prevalence of emotional problems among each of Virginia Woolf's siblings.

and then raped her. Before he was eventually institutionalized, there were a few notable authorities who believed that he was actually Jack the Ripper, who was murdering so many young women in the streets of London at the time.

This suspicion was based on a number of similarities that police observed between the notes sent to Scotland Yard by The Ripper and the violent writings of James Stephen. Whether this theory was true or not, Virginia and the other younger children must have wondered whether the madman who sometimes ran loose in their house assaulting Stella was the same killer stalking the streets. There is some evidence that James, who Virginia described as a "tormented bull," once abducted her for a period of time and sexually assaulted her as well.

It has taken whole books (and many of them at that) to describe all the weird goings-on at Hyde Park Gate, the Stephens estate. For now, let us agree that there were many, many family secrets that caused great harm to the children, most of whom struggled with the lingering effects for the rest of their lives.

Personal Trauma

Little Virginia was to experience one of the most damaging secrets in the family about the time when she was six years old. She had just barely recovered from whooping cough. Spasms would wrack her body for hours, followed by intense pain that would leave her wasted. This went on for six weeks and it almost killed her. She still felt weak and disoriented from the illness and had not yet regained her strength, when she was playing quietly in the hallway of her house. Virginia had always been a quiet and obedient child, afraid that if she acted up in any way, she might become confined to the attic like her sister Laura. Even at such a young age, she liked to wander in her father's extensive library and spend endless hours reading.

During one afternoon when she had been playing in the hallway of the house, her stepbrother Gerald, age nineteen at the time, invited her to join him in a game. Gerald scared her a little, the way he looked at her sometimes, but he was her brother and she was afraid to disobey him. He enjoyed a special relationship with his mother, who worshipped him and thought he could do no wrong.

Gerald insisted that Virginia approach him and she did so wearily. She could tell that something was not quite right, the way he was whispering to her and gesturing for her to come closer. She looked over her shoulder and noticed that they were completely alone.

There was a ledge in the hall, just outside the dining room door, a mirror on the opposite wall. The ledge was usually used for stacking dishes, or holding plates of food before they were served. On this day, the ledge was empty.

Gerald reached over and lifted his little sister up onto the ledge, holding her tightly by the waist. She was frightened to be up there. Maybe she could fall if he let go of her. And it hurt, the way he was holding her. Out of the corner of her eye, she could look over his shoulder and see their reflection in the mirror. He looked so big compared to her, even though she was almost at eye level with him.

Gerald next reached under Virginia's dress, stroking her stomach and legs. "I can remember the feel of his hand going under my clothes," she was later to confess to a friend, "going firmly and steadily lower and lower. I remember how I hoped that he would stop; how I stiffened and wriggled as his hand approached my private parts. But it did not stop. His hand explored my private parts too."

There were at least two aspects of this first experience of sexual abuse that stuck with Virginia Woolf throughout her life. The first is a recurrent vision of seeing herself in the mirror during the assault and forever being haunted by that image. She could never after look at herself in the mirror without feeling some horror. Why didn't she fight back? Why did she allow him to touch her like that?

The second lingering effect was the eating disorder that developed after her abuse experiences. It has been theorized that the origins of this problem developed as a consequence of the association she developed between the scene of the first abuse, sitting on the pantry shelf where food was stored. It is far more likely that the struggles she had with food in later life were related to issues of self-control, perfectionism, and depression. They frequently centered around anxieties about how her books would be received.

This experience of molestation could have been more than enough to compromise the sanity of any human being, but it was only a small fraction of the chaos, conflict, and perversity that went on in this upper-crust English family.

The Creative Spirit and the Love of Writing

One might have the impression from the foregoing family history that Virginia Woolf grew up to be a raving lunatic, but this was far from the case. Based on all of the evidence from letters, diaries, and testimonies of her many friends, colleagues, and family members, she was described as someone who was witty, brilliant, stimulating, and an absolute joy to be around. Certainly, she was viewed as vulnerable, eccentric, and unpredictable at times, but during the periods when she was relatively free of her extreme mood swings, she was not only incredibly productive but also charming and fun company. It was hardly pity alone that kept Leonard Woolf so devoted to her throughout the years of their turbulent marriage. He worshipped her even though she was completely unresponsive to him sexually and romantically. He admired and respected her, enjoyed her company, and thrived on her intellect and kindness to the point that he could not have imagined living with anyone else.

How was it possible for someone so disturbed to also be so creative and prolific? Virginia Woolf suffered depressions that were so severe, manic episodes so florid, and psychotic hallucinations so pervasive, that she often operated only in her own inner world. She struggled with a lifelong eating disorder, relationship problems, sexual ambivalence, pathological insecurities, plus the subsequent consequences of all these disorders. It was a wonder that she could get out of bed many mornings, much less produce a body of work that is among the most important of the twentieth century.

Ultimately, what saved Virginia Woolf—or at least allowed her to live a fruitful and productive life—was her creative spirit and love of writing. She had discovered during her childhood years that reading books and writing about her experiences would not only earn the approval of her parents but also help her to make sense of others' behavior, as well as her own inner world. When she began her diaries during early adolescence, she described the ways she used dissociation to bury the traumas she had suffered. Creating an alternative identity, Miss Jan, she told of riding her new bicycle for the first time and how uncomfortable the experience was for "Miss Jan." Rather than dealing with her own negative feelings, she had invented a way to use fictional characters to express her fears and play out the unresolved dramas of her life. This would become the trademark for all of the books that would follow.

Virginia Woolf happened to survive as long as she did precisely because she was a writer. From the time she first learned to read, she began writing, imitating her father and trying to earn his approval. What began as a means to save herself from being locked in the attic like her sister Laura developed into a coping mechanism to work through her emotional pain and make sense of the confusing things (molestation, violence, cruelty, neglect, craziness) that were happening around her, and to her. She learned early in life that writing was one of the few ways she could moderate her own moods, not to mention create something useful from the anguish.

Woolf's diaries are chock-full of entries throughout the years that testify to how she used writing to prevent or minimize anticipated breakdowns. She could feel the beginnings of a manic or depressive episode by the headaches or insomnia that would signal impending doom.

"I want to stabilize myself," she wrote, and then a few years later wrote this: "Odd how the creative power at once brings the whole universe to order." It was the writing, and the long spells she spent incapacitated by her madness, that taught her to live in her imagination and use it as a fertile source for the stories that would pour forth upon her recovery.

Lest we romanticize the power of mental illness as a creative inspiration, it is also important to realize that there were many instances in Woolf's life in which she was so incapacitated by depression that she could literally not get out of bed for months. Writing, or even productive thinking, was out of the question during times that all she could imagine were ways that she could end her life. For a writer, whose whole existence revolved around her ability to create, these depressions were especially devastating:

> I know the feeling now, when I can't spin a sentence, & sit mumbling & turning; & nothing flits by my brain which is a blank window. So I shut my studio door, & go to bed, stuffing my ears with rubber; & there I lie a day or two. And what leagues I travel in the time! Such "sensations" spread over my spine & head directly I give them the chance; such an exaggerated tiredness; such anguishes & despairs; & heavenly relief & rest; & then misery again. Never was anyone so tossed up & down by the body as I am, I think.

And never has a writer suffered so in order to pursue her creative art.

A Small World Inside a Big World

Let's pick up Virginia's story about the time she was eight years old (in 1890). Both her parents were clinically depressed. Sir Leslie was more than eccentric—he was so neurotic and given to spells of gloom that he would disappear for weeks at a time and then return with manic energy and new resolve. By contrast, Julia was more melancholic. In today's language, she would be called *dysthymic,* meaning that she had a chronic, low-grade depressive personality. There is not a single photograph of her that survives that ever shows her smiling. Perhaps one good reason for this was her being saddled with the responsibility for running a household that contained so much conflict and illness, not to mention that she had little time to recover from her pregnancies before another child was born.

Virginia Woolf's childhood had its horrors but also its privileges and opportunities, as well as some joys. Their family home at Hyde Park Gate was a Victorian structure six stories high, with more than seven servants to take care of their needs. It was a dark and gloomy mansion, filled with its share of perversity and disturbances, but the summers were spent at the Cornish seaside, where Virginia retained many happy memories. In describing the sound of the waves, she wrote of "lying and hearing this splash and seeing this light, and feeling, it is almost impossible that I should be here; of feeling the purest ecstasy I can conceive." It turned out that she would experience many such ecstatic moments in later life, many of them unfortunately activated by manic episodes rather than by the sounds of the sea.

Virginia's first major emotional breakdown occurred when she was thirteen, soon after her mother died of influenza, or perhaps from the stress and nervous exhaustion of trying to keep her family from falling apart. Virginia's grief response can best be described as more than a little strange, as she began giggling at the sight of her mother's body and reported hallucinations of seeing a man sitting on the bed with her.

Leslie was so distraught by the death of his wife that he completely fell apart. He wandered the house at night, unable to sleep, moaning and sobbing and crying, frightening the children terribly. Virginia started to withdraw during this time, to spend more time alone, locked in her room. At one point, she refused to leave the house. She stopped eating and could not sleep, the first of many such episodes in which her basic biological functioning would be disrupted by madness. Even more distressing to her, she began to lose the ability to hold a thought; she could neither read nor write.

Stella, the eldest daughter (Laura was still confined in the attic), took over the responsibilities of female head of the household—in more ways than one. Not only was she expected to take care of all the children but also to offer comfort and companionship to her father. In what can only be imagined as the most bizarre and horrifying spectacle, Stella became her father's lover, a replacement for his wife. Poor Stella not only had to put up with being stalked and raped by a madman (if not the actual Jack the Ripper) but also had to serve as her father's replacement wife. One can only imagine what Virginia and the other children (not to mention London society) thought of Sir Leslie running about town with his daughter on his arm.

Stella eventually escaped the clutches of this incestuous relationship by marrying in 1897 (Virginia was then fifteen). Stella's happiness would be short-lived. Immediately upon returning from her honeymoon, she was stricken with appendicitis, which was misdiagnosed and mistreated by the doctors. She died soon thereafter. This was not only a tragedy for her but also for Virginia, who now lost her second mother in less than two years.

Virginia and her sister Vanessa were both subjected to sexual advances by their stepbrother Gerald Duckworth. He was inclined to fondle each one of the sisters any time they were alone or the situation presented itself. One time, Virginia was bent over, studying her Greek lessons, when Gerald sneaked up behind her and stuck his hand under her pants. These ambushes became a frequent occurrence, eventually progressing to the point where he joined one or both sisters in bed at night. Virginia described herself and Vanessa as "Greek slaves," subject to the sexual domination of their brothers.

In some ways, their mutual sexual assaults brought the two sisters closer together. By this time, Vanessa, at age seventeen, was saddled with stepping into the role of head of household, but she didn't have to worry about her father molesting her because George had narrowed the focus of his amour to Vanessa alone, taking her as his lover. She would accompany George to all the social functions and serve as his companion. Invitations came to the house addressed to "Mr. Duckworth and Miss Stephen," as if everyone understood their arrangement.

As if this were not perverse enough, Vanessa and Virginia also began to sleep together, first in comfort, and then as lovers. About their relationship, Virginia Woolf would write in her diary, "Coming and going, we formed our private nucleus. . . . And therefore we made together a small world inside the big world."

An Unusual Honeymoon

The next major blow occurred when Virginia's father died of bowel cancer in 1904. (Another tragedy would soon follow in which her most trusted and beloved brother, Thoby, would die of typhoid fever at twenty-six.) At first, she seemed to take the loss in stride, but within months she launched into a manic state that became so crazed, it took three nurses to keep her under control. She remained totally psychotic for several months afterward, spewing unintelligible torrents of abuse and anger, mostly directed toward Vanessa. She heard voices speaking to her. Birds sang to her, but in Greek. She believed that King Edward was stalking her, hiding out beneath her window and taunting her when nobody else was around. Once she became so distraught that she launched herself out the window in a misguided attempt at suicide (the room was on the first floor).

In 1906, when Virginia Woolf was twenty-four years old, Vanessa finally escaped from the draconian intimacy of her relationship to her half-brother George Duckworth by getting married. Vanessa's marriage felt to Virginia like another loss—of her sister but also of her only confidante, who understood what they both had lived through together. They had been living together their whole lives (by this time, they were in their mid-twenties), and this meant that Virginia would now have to live in a "small world" by herself, kept company only by her imagination.

It is interesting to note that when Virginia met Vanessa's new husband, Clive Bell, she chose to confess to him about the incest experiences that she and Vanessa had both suffered. If that didn't scare him off, she next seduced him as a way to get back at her sister, who she felt had betrayed her. This would be one of the few (if only) voluntary sexual experiences with a man that Virginia Woolf would have in her lifetime.

During the next years, until 1912, when Virginia Woolf was thirty, she was busy establishing herself in a literary career. She met Leonard Woolf, a kind and gentle man who shared her passion for writing and literature, but who was far beneath her on the social scale. Whereas Virginia came from an aristocratic, upper-class family, Leonard was Jewish and had been a scholarship student at Cambridge University. They had met through Virginia's brother Thoby, who had been part of a group with Leonard called The Apostles, which included Bertrand Russell, E. M. Forster, and John Maynard Keynes. This would eventually evolve into the Bloomsbury Group, a gathering of writers and thinkers who would meet on a regular basis and discuss the issues of the day.

Leonard was so besotted by Virginia that he seemed to have blinders on that allowed him to ignore her emotional instability. He knew about her previous "spells" but decided that he was just what she needed in order to remain stable; he believed he could save her and was so committed to the relationship that he put aside his own career to support her. From Virginia's perspective, she enjoyed the mild scandal of being associated with a Jew. But far more than that, she sensed that Leonard was safe and trusting in the same way her sister Vanessa had been.

Virginia warned her fiancé that she felt little physical attraction to him and was not interested in sex in the least, but he seemed to believe he could change her mind. Their honeymoon would be a disaster: Virginia was completely unresponsive and vowed that she would never allow him to have sex with her. For reasons that are still not completely clear, for a man who was unabashedly heterosexual and passionate, he decided to accept their agreement and live together as loving companions. They would kiss, hold hands, and snuggle, even repeatedly avow their mutual love, but they would never consummate their marriage.

Soon after the honeymoon, Virginia had her worst breakdown of all. She had just finished the last draft of her book *The Voyage Out,* and in a pattern that would repeat itself after the completion of every project, she began to be wracked with doubt and insecurities. It would become Leonard's job, after each book was done, to reassure her repeatedly that her work was indeed important and well written.

Virginia continued to obsess about how her novel would be received. Whether that was the cause of her mental deterioration, or just an exacerbating factor, is difficult to determine. What is known is that she became acutely paranoid, believing that there were plots against her and that she was being watched by spies. She could no longer sleep at all without the aid of pills. She stopped eating. What is called a *flight of ideas* became manifest in her speech. Leonard described what this was like:

> She talked almost without stopping for two or three days, paying no attention to anyone in the room or anything said to her. For about a day what she said was coherent; the sentences meant something, though it was nearly all wildly insane. Then gradually it became completely incoherent, a mere jumble of dissociated words. After another day the stream of words diminished and finally she fell into a coma.

Once, when Virginia was in a manic state, Leonard was exposed to a part of his wife that seemed bewildering and terrifying. She was excitable; at times, even violently agitated. She was also actively hallucinating, claiming that her dead mother came to visit her. Leonard did his best to cope with the outbursts, but rather than feeling discouraged by the state of his new wife, he redoubled his efforts to care for her.

Upon her recovery, Leonard may have felt both relieved and concerned about future recurrences, but Virginia was intrigued, if not elated, by the creative energy that had been generated by the experience. During both her manic and depressive states, she discovered that germinating within her were "truths" about herself and her writing.

> *Curious how all one's fibres seem to expand & fill with air when anxiety is taken off; curious also to me the intensity of my own feelings: I think imagination, the picture making power, decks up feelings with all kinds of scenes; so that one goes on thinking, instead of localizing the event. All very mysterious.*

The inner world that Woolf inhabited, no matter how terrifying at times to herself and others, inspired her to create in ways that would not have otherwise been possible. She was certainly afraid of her own insanity, and the possibility of relapses, but also amazed at what could result from such episodes. Madness was her muse.

The Milk Diet and Other Cures

During the next years of Virginia Woolf's life, Leonard consulted psychiatrists and other doctors about his wife's condition. The general consensus was that the best that he could do was look carefully for early signs of the illness and then insist on complete bed rest until the spells passed over. Another favored remedy was the "milk cure," in which Virginia was required to drink up to four or five pints of milk each day. This was supposed to help her relax and to calm the inner demons. One outcome for certain is that she was inclined to gain weight when on this program.

Leonard had been encouraged to find some sort of occupational therapy for Virginia, something to keep her occupied. It was reasoned that the busier she was, the less likely she would be to have another breakdown. It was with this idea in mind that Leonard returned home one day in March 1917 and plopped a hand-operated printing press on the kitchen table. He thought it would be an interesting diversion for Virginia, as well as for himself, if they could produce a few booklets containing their own short stories and poetry. They decided to call their publishing enterprise Hogarth Press, after the large Georgian house that they lived in.

It turned out that Leonard's plan was a brilliant one, at least for a while. Virginia became thoroughly engaged in their new publishing enterprise, involved in every facet of the typesetting, printing, bookbinding, and distribution, not to mention the writing and production of several manuscripts. Hogarth Press would become not only the outlet for the Woolfs to produce and distribute their own works in future years but also one of the most esteemed publishing houses in the world.

A Torrid Affair

By 1920, as Virginia was approaching forty, she and Leonard had settled into a platonic relationship in which he no longer attempted to climb into her bed and risk rejection. This task was made all that more difficult by Virginia's insistence in sleeping in a narrow "virginal" bed that left no room for a visitor. She may not have welcomed a man's sexual advances (and it is certainly easy to see why, given her history), but she still felt a strong sexual longing that could more safely be directed toward women. During the previous years, she had found herself with crushes on several women—feelings that seemed based on intellectual and emotional attraction as much as physical needs. She eventually began a rather torrid affair with Vita Sackville-West, an aristocrat and artist.

From entries in both their diaries, as well as their lengthy correspondence over the next fifteen years, Virginia Woolf and Vita Sackville-West carried on a romantic relationship all the while they remained married to their husbands, who both knew about their liaison but chose not (or were not able) to put a stop to it. For Leonard's part, he was willing to be with Virginia on any terms.

Whatever peace Virginia and Leonard enjoyed during the mid-1920s, it was not to last indefinitely. Glasses of milk, the affair with Vita, work in her writing and publishing, bed rest, were not enough to stem the tide of madness that took her over again. Many of Woolf's biographers look for specific causes and precipitators of her episodes of acute mental illness, but with her family history it is rather clear that her condition was genetically influenced and biologically based, even if it may have been exacerbated by early traumas and current stressors.

For example, she tried to kill herself with an overdose of a barbiturate while returning from a visit to see Vita. It is likely that an argument had developed between Virginia and Leonard on the return trip over his jealousy toward their relationship. But the intensity of Virginia's response certainly must be taken in the context of her psychological legacy and biochemical predisposition.

Another daily source of stress and exhaustion was their publishing company, which rapidly became quite a big operation. What began as a kind of therapy had become another burden for Virginia. Hogarth Press was so successful by 1925 that it had published twenty-five books. Virginia was now not only trying to maintain her own writing but also acting as acquisitions editor for the publishing company. There was also considerable physical labor involved, because she and Leonard had been trying to run the whole operation on their own, without any assistants or employees. This now became impossible.

Leonard had been enthusiastic about taking on the Sigmund Freud project, having the psychiatrist's complete collection translated and published in English. At first, Virginia was scornful about the Viennese doctor's work. She found it useless to spend one's time reflecting on the past and ridiculed what she considered his weird manner. Several years later, she would change her mind and begin studying his work with enthusiasm (after all, he was her compatriot in valuing the power of the unconscious in creative endeavors), but for now she simply felt overwhelmed by all the responsibility.

Leonard's job was to be the pillar of strength in their relationship, the guardian who would watch over his fragile wife, but he had his own problems to deal with as well. Leonard had also been prone to bouts of depression throughout his life, as well as constant trembling, especially of his hands. He claimed that the tremors were the result of an inherited disorder, but it is just as likely that it was a symptom of his own nervousness.

The next decade was an incredibly productive one for Virginia Woolf, in spite of her setbacks and emotional challenges. She had structured her life (with Leonard's assistance) so that she began writing as soon as she awoke (after a pint of milk). Her classic novels *Mrs. Dalloway* (1925), *To the Lighthouse* (1927), *Orlando* (1928), *A Room of One's Own* (1929), and *The Waves* (1931) were all produced during this era, in addition to an impressive body of literary criticism, poetry, plays, and political and social commentary.

The Waves is perhaps considered her masterpiece, the most complex, lyrical, and haunting of her books, concerned with the inner life of six characters, each of them a part of herself and all of them struggling to make sense of their experiences. It begins:

> *The sun had not yet risen. The sea was indistinguishable from the sky, except that the sea was slightly creased as if a cloth had wrinkles in it. Gradually as the sky whitened a dark line lay on the horizon dividing the sea from the sky and the grey cloth became barred with thick strokes moving, one after another, beneath the surface, following each other, pursuing each other, perpetually.*

As she put the finishing touches on the last words of the story, she wrote in her diary that she experienced incredible "intensity & intoxication that I seemed only to stumble after my own voice, or almost, after some sort of speaker (as when I was mad). I was almost afraid, remembering the voices that used to fly ahead." This book was to be her most autobiographical and personal novel but grew to be something far deeper, as she attempted to excavate her own unconsciousness just as Freud had been attempting to do with his patients. In the history of fiction writing, it has been most influential in moving beyond the narrative form to a work that is far more metaphorical and that accesses not only the unconscious feelings of the writer but also the reader.

Writing in her diary about the creative process that she had unlocked during the writing of the book, she remarked about how the metaphors and images seemed to emerge of their own accord:

> *What interested me in the last stage was the freedom and boldness with which my imagination picked up, used and tossed aside all the images, symbols which I had prepared. I am sure that this is the right way of using them—not in set pieces, as I had tried at first, coherently, but simply as images, never making them work out; only suggest. Thus I hope to have kept the sound of the sea and the birds, dawn and garden subconsciously present, doing their work under ground.*

Who else, but someone with considerable experience on the other side of reality, could have invented such a way of writing? It is through this method that one psychoanalyst and Woolf scholar concluded that "she challenges us to believe in our own voices sufficiently that we can imagine surviving the encounter with the incredible and terrible richness of our own inner beings." Unfortunately, Woolf was not to survive this inner conflict much longer.

War

During the decade of the 1930s, Virginia Woolf was one of the most famous writers of her day. Her books were best-sellers both in England and the United States. She was a celebrity and a star, a spokesperson for the cause of women.

Woolf remained at the height of her creative powers even after completing *The Waves* in 1931. Once the Woolfs were able to pass on the administration of Hogarth Press to a surrogate who ran the business, Virginia was freed from the additional pressures. This was a time of a very active social life for her, attending literary groups, becoming involved politically, speaking before audiences, even telling the story of her early childhood traumas publicly. She had her ups and downs, but they lasted days at a time rather than the months of dysfunction that had occurred earlier in her life.

It was during this decade before the war that Woolf became more active in speaking out on behalf of women's rights. In her book *Three Guineas,* published in 1938, she explored the plight of women and their oppression. She lauded the value of women's unique contributions and asserted that the creative process can only take place by fusing the best qualities of both genders.

Leonard and Virginia had always been politically active, not just as writers but as community activists. When Hitler invaded Europe and began to directly threaten Britain, they both became highly agitated. For Virginia, her concerns may have been partially the result of personal convictions against violence, but for Leonard, as a Jew, he knew that if the Germans conquered Great Britain, which seemed a distinct possibility at the time, his days were numbered. As the bombing of London increased, even as the offices of Hogarth Press were destroyed, they talked of a suicide pact to end their lives before the Nazis could take them. They stockpiled lethal doses of morphine to prepare for Armageddon.

As news of the war began to worsen and Hitler's invasion seemed more likely, the Woolfs became even more despondent. Leonard had always been Virginia's source of strength, the loving companion who kept her grounded, who nursed her during the turbulent times, her soul mate and trusted critic, the only person she could truly count on. Virginia had been dependent on her husband but also resentful and angry at the ways he tried to control and dominate her.

As Virginia began to grow more depressed and agitated, at times eerily silent, the anxiety became contagious. Leonard's hand tremors became more acute. He began keeping a closer eye on his wife, concerned about her welfare, but this felt to her like he was smothering her. She felt paranoid, with some justification, that he was always watching her (which he was). Leonard, too, could barely keep up his own spirits, much less bolster those of Virginia. One can only imagine how bleak that house must have been with the two of them in a depressive hopelessness trying to comfort each other.

The Last Two Weeks

Even during a time when Virginia Woolf was literally losing her mind, she still exercised the discipline to continue writing in her diary and in correspondence to her husband and several friends. It is both fascinating and horrifying to follow her progressive descent into madness. It is like watching one of the greatest creative intellects of the century lose its luminescence, and then, finally, blink out.

Tuesday, March 18, 1941

Virginia went out for a long walk and didn't return for some time, even when there had been a rain shower. By the time she showed up hours later, she appeared disheveled and disoriented.

"Where have you been?" Leonard asked anxiously. "I've been waiting for . . . " He left the thought unfinished. He knew she hated it when he let her know how worried he was.

Virginia shrugged, as if it were of no importance at all. "I just fell, slipped in a ditch," she said in a voice without inflection or tone. There is some evidence from notes available that she had tried to drown herself in the river near the house but for some reason could not complete the job.

Leonard waited but there was no further explanation. He examined his wife as if seeing her for the first time. She looked emaciated, absolutely skeletal, because she had not been eating lately. He thought about saying something to her, perhaps offering to make her something for a meal, but he knew that would just make her more upset.

Friday, March 21, 1941

Virginia met with her friend and physician, Octavia Wilberforce, a week earlier when she had stopped by to visit. Immediately, the doctor could sense something was wrong. Virginia seemed depressed and when confronted about this admitted that she felt useless. She had just finished writing her book *Between the Acts* but felt neither relief nor pride, just disappointment and despair.

Octavia tried to reassure Virginia that she was indeed important, that the things she had written were significant and influential. Virginia just shook her head with impatience. She quickly changed the subject and complained that even after all these years, she felt burdened with grief for her father, and yet was also terribly resentful. She had not been allowed to have a proper childhood. Her innocence had been stolen from her. All she had learned to do was to hide inside herself. This might be an excellent tool for a writer, but it was hardly adaptive for someone struggling to stay in contact with the world. When the conversation ended, Octavia felt uneasy and concerned.

Sunday, March 23, 1941

Leonard was relieved to observe that Virginia seemed to be feeling better. She looked, well, almost normal again. She was writing in her diary. She appeared chatty, commenting on the weather. Yet she was good at hiding the way she was feeling from her husband, who was watching her like a hawk, refusing to let her out of his sight. Even though all seemed to be going well as far as he was concerned, Virginia wrote the following letter to her sister Vanessa Bell:

> *I feel I have gone too far this time to come back again. I am certain now that I am going mad again. It is just as it was the first time, I am always hearing voices, and I know I shan't get over it now.*
>
> *All I want to say is that Leonard has been so astonishingly good, every day, always; I can't imagine that anyone could have done more for me than he has. We have been perfectly happy until the last few weeks, when this horror began. Will you assure him of this? I feel he has so much to do that he will go on, better without me, and you will help him.*
>
> *I can hardly think clearly any more. . . .*
>
> *I have fought against it, but I can't any longer.*

Wednesday, March 26, 1941

Virginia appeared worse than she ever had before. Leonard had seen her before when she was in a bad way, when she was raving, but at this moment she looked, well, . . . *dangerous* was the word that came immediately to mind.

In actuality, she was desperate beyond anything she had ever experienced before. Her thoughts raced so fast that she could neither grasp nor understand them. She could feel the madness coming on but felt absolutely powerless to do anything about it. It felt as if someone or something else was in control of her now.

Leonard could see that she was slipping away, but he couldn't figure out what to do. He remembered almost thirty years ago, when they had first gotten married, and she had tried to kill herself. She had told him then that there was nothing wrong but he knew she was lying. If he asked her right now what she was feeling, he was convinced she would lie to him again. Gently, he asked if she'd be willing to see a doctor.

Virginia shook her head, twice, leaving no doubt about her opinion on such matters. "No doctors," she said, in a voice that could barely be heard. "I don't need a doctor. There's nothing they can do."

Against her wishes, Leonard called Octavia to return and examine his wife. She agreed to come the next day.

Thursday, March 27, 1941

When Octavia showed up, it was obvious that her patient was not going to be cooperative when she announced formally that "it was *quite* unnecessary for you to have come."

Octavia tried to question Virginia about her condition, her symptoms, but she received only minimal answers or none at all. It seemed as if Virginia was now closed off from the outside world, almost completely unresponsive.

There are times when caring is not enough. As well intentioned and persistent as Octavia was, the more she pushed, the more Virginia seemed to retreat. Octavia begged her friend to trust her, to tell her what was going on, but Virginia just remained silent and stared off into space. Her expression may have been blank, but inside she was seething at the intrusion. Why couldn't Octavia just leave her alone? Octavia was just like her husband, always meddling, always pushing. Why couldn't everyone just go away and leave her be?

When Octavia and Leonard spoke in whispered tones later, they both agreed that Virginia seemed on the verge of a major breakdown. They debated on the best course of action—whether bed rest would be enough this time or whether they needed to send her to a sanatorium.

Friday, March 28, 1941

Leonard tried to keep Virginia's mind off her condition by getting her involved in tasks around the house. He gave her a duster and instructed her to give his study a quick go-over. She performed the task with robotic movements, then put the duster down, and walked out of the room.

Leonard noticed Virginia writing something at her table when he went to do some work at his own desk. As soon as he left the room, Virginia stood from the table, retrieved her coat and walking stick, and walked with calm deliberation out the door. She proceeded at a brisk pace through the garden. It was a gorgeous day—cool but clear.

Virginia followed the muddy path as it led into the brush. Several times, she lost her balance in the high weeds and boulders that were buried beneath them. As she walked, she scooped up rocks, seeming not to care about their color or shape as much as their size. The hefty ones, she shoved in the pockets of her woolen coat.

As she approached the river bank in her gum boots, she slipped a little in the mud, then regained her balance, stepping into the eddies of the water. She could feel the current against her legs, advancing one step at a time as her boots filled with water. Her legs felt leaden, weighed down by the water and a lifetime of carrying so much pain. She found it interesting that she could no longer feel the chill from the air or even the frigid water. Keeping her posture erect, she waded further into the current, until it carried her downstream, of its own volition.

A few hours later, Leonard noticed two letters sitting on the fireplace mantel. One was addressed to him, the other to Vanessa. As he reached for the one with his own name, his initial curiosity turned immediately to horror; before he even opened the envelope, he knew what it would say.

Dearest,

I feel certain that I am going mad again: I feel we can't go through another of those terrible times. And I shan't recover this time. I begin to hear voices, and can't concentrate. So I am doing what seems the best to do. You have given me the greatest possible happiness. You have been in every way all that anyone could be. I don't think two people could have been happier till this terrible disease came. I can't fight it any longer, I know that I am spoiling your life, that without me you could work. And you will I know. You see I can't even write this properly. I can't read. What I want to say is that I owe all the happiness of my life to you. You have been entirely patient with me and incredibly good. I want to say that—everybody knows it. If anybody could have saved me it would have been you. Everything has gone from me but the certainty of your goodness. I can't go on spoiling your life any longer.

I don't think that two people could have been happier than we have been.
V.

The note had been written several days earlier, on March 18. Without thought, he ran out of the house and headed to the river. He sensed immediately that that was where she would have gone. He walked along the bank, searching for a sign of her but found only her walking stick lying in the mud. Her body would not be discovered for three more weeks, quite close to where Leonard stood peering out into the water.

A bit later, when struggling to make sense of what had happened, of where his wife had gone, and what he would now do without her, he found another note sitting on her writing table. It is what she had been working on when he had last seen her, and it repeated the same messages that had been contained in the earlier one. It was as if she had forgotten that she had already said the same things or that she wanted to make sure that the husband she left behind felt reassured that none of this was his fault.

Leonard Woolf—who had been so devoted to his wife for thirty years that he had elected to surrender his own sexual needs, his career, and his own mental health—did not feel sufficiently reassured by Virginia's pleas. He remarried but remained celibate for the rest of his life, until he died at age eighty-eight. He never forgave himself for not taking better care of his precious love.

CHAPTER SEVEN

Charles Mingus
Musical Hallucinations

Several months after Charlie "Bird" Parker was released from the Bellevue Psychiatric Unit after attempting suicide, he tried to make one last attempt at a comeback. He was broke, disoriented, and almost friendless. Nevertheless he managed to get himself a booking at a famous jazz club, appropriately named Birdland, for two nights only, March 4 and 5, 1955. He called in some favors, assembling a band of the best musicians he could find, including Bud Powell, a brilliant pianist who was repeatedly hospitalized for mental illness; Art Blakey on drums; Kenny Dorham on trumpet; and on bass, Charles Mingus. Even by the standard of the day, this was indeed an impressive group of musicians.

There was a big crowd in attendance for the first performance on Friday night, eager to hear the much-hoped-for comeback of Charlie Parker. Unfortunately, they were to be sorely disappointed. By the time Bird showed up, a half hour late, the band was already well into the set. To make matters far worse, Bud Powell was drunk and incoherent; the others were doing their best to cover for him.

Just about the time that Bird was to take the stage, Powell collapsed over the piano, either passed out or dead—at first nobody was sure which. Bird then stalked off to the dressing room, deciding to wait until the next set. Mingus and the others, not sure what to do next, started to carry Powell away, but he regained consciousness and insisted he be allowed to return to his instrument. Given Powell's propensity toward violence, Mingus thought it best to back off.

Bird now appeared to be unaware of what had been going on in his absence. He had downed a few shots of whiskey, so he was feeling no pain himself. He directed the band to play "Hallucination," a new composition that seemed an appropriate choice, given the circumstances. Unfortunately, Powell had other ideas in mind. When the band struck up the first notes, Powell launched into a completely different tune and started banging away on the keys with a fury. This brought the others to an abrupt halt.

"There was no love and no joy in the playing of these men," writes one of Parker's biographers. "Instead evil forces were being set loose in the room."

Powell and Parker started screaming at each other, arguing in front of the astonished audience, until the pianist staggered off the stage muttering to himself and swearing up a storm at Parker and the others. Parker, in turn, began yelling into the microphone, demanding that Powell return. When there was no response, he became even more strident and angry.

People started leaving the club, shaking their heads in wonderment at the chaos taking place on stage. It was at this point that Mingus grabbed the mike and announced, "Ladies and gentlemen, please don't associate me with any of this. This is not jazz. These are sick people." Then he packed up his bass and left the scene too.

Bird sat alone on stage watching the last of the crowd and musicians file out. When the place was finally empty, Bird walked to Mingus standing in front of the club and said, "I'm goin' some place where I ain't ever goin' to bother nobody. Not any more."

With that, he disappeared around the corner. Within a week, Bird was dead of complications from years of abusing drugs and alcohol.

Mingus could only shake his head at how far his friend and mentor had fallen. It scared him, because he knew that they shared a lot more than their love of music. Mingus had felt such reverence for Bird that he had even named a song in honor of him: "If Charlie Parker Was a Gunslinger, There'd Be a Whole Lot of Dead Copycats." As Mingus left the club, walking in the other direction, he made a vow to himself that he'd never let himself get to the point of Bird's collapse.

Sure, they had a lot in common, he admitted to himself. Mingus also had a ferocious temper. Reluctantly, he admitted that he also had his share of mental problems. But no way would he ever let himself go like that. He figured that as long as he stayed away from heroin, kept the drinking under control, and just concentrated on the music, he'd be fine.

A Culture of Madness

Charles Mingus was arguably the greatest bass player who ever lived. He was also one of the most innovative jazz composers, along with Parker and Duke Ellington. He was also just as wild, violent, abusive, angry, and utterly unpredictable as Bird; and in the years to come after that night in 1955, he would eclipse his mentor in the sheer drama and audacity of his antics. To understand his story, it is important to understand the context of Mingus's experience growing up African American during a time when his people were forbidden to pursue careers in classical music (his first love). When he entered the jazz scene as a young man, there was a whole other code of conduct, one without many rules, and one that tolerated almost any level of madness in the pursuit of creative music.

Why do jazz musicians, even more than artists and poets, suffer such a high incidence of mental illness? On stage that night in New York were three of the most creative jazz players and composers in the world: Bud Powell, Charlie Parker, and Charles Mingus, and all three of them spent considerable time on psychiatric wards, crippled by madness.

Everyone who knew Mingus loved to tell stories about him—about the time he became so angry during one of his concerts in Philadelphia that he punched out one of his musicians on stage. And this was after attempting to slam down the piano lid on the pianist's fingers. About the time he smashed his $2,000 bass at the foot of a fan because he was annoyed with the man's behavior. By unanimous agreement, Mingus was a wild man, a glutton, a bully, and a genius. He worked with not only the greatest musicians of his day—Charlie Parker, Billie Holiday, Miles Davis, Louis Armstrong, Dizzy Gillespie, and Lionel Hampton—but also choreographer Alvin Ailey, director John Cassavetes, artists Willem de Kooning and Franz Kline, and folk singer Joni Mitchell. He had the distinction of being the only musician who was ever personally fired by Duke Ellington (but that's another story). He engaged in fruitful dialogues about race with Allen Ginsberg, Jack

Kerouac, Ken Kesey, Timothy Leary, Martin Luther King, some of the most influential minds of the sixties.

Mingus was single-handedly responsible for moving the bass from the back of the orchestra to a prominent position up front. Besides having the fastest, most sure hands on the bass, he was an accomplished pianist, who could play that instrument with equal fluency. His music compositions were unique and creative. His innovations—blending blues, gospel, bebop, Latin, and modern classical—foreshadowed the *free jazz* movement. He combined the perfect harmonies of Duke Ellington with the dissonance of classical composer Igor Stravinsky, to produce a constant shifting of harmonics, tempos, and tones. And on top of everything else, he was an accomplished writer: he not only wrote a best-selling autobiography, *Beneath the Underdog,* but he also won a Grammy Award for writing the liner notes to his album *Let My Children Hear Music.*

In the very first paragraph of his book, Mingus launched into the war that went on within him. He confessed to being three different people: the creative artist, the madman, and the mediator between the two.

> One man stands forever in the middle, unconcerned, unmoved, watching, waiting to be allowed to express what he sees to the other two. The second man is like a frightened animal that attacks for fear of being attacked. Then there's an over-loving gentle person who lets people into the uttermost sacred temple of his being and he'll take insults and be trusting and sign contracts without reading them and get talked down to working cheap or for nothing, and when he realizes what's been done to him he feels like killing and destroying everything around him including himself for being so stupid. But he can't—he goes back inside himself.

Charles Mingus was a bitter man, an angry man, a crazy man, a genius on the string bass. There's never been anyone like him, and there never will again. Yet in one sad and significant way, Mingus was representative of a culture that was operating in New York during the forties and fifties. It was a time when creative musicians and artists were permitted almost any indulgence, as long as it enhanced their work.

In a sampling of forty jazz musicians from the years 1945 to 1960, one psychiatrist collected the life histories of the most famous trumpet players (Dizzy Gillespie, Miles Davis), saxophone players (John Coltrane, Stan Getz, Charlie Parker), bass players (Charles Mingus, Ray Brown), drummers (Kenny Clarke, Art Blakey), pianists (Thelonious Monk, Bud

Powell), and others. What he found was staggering: 30 percent suffered major depression (compared with less than 3 percent of the general population), another 5 percent had major anxiety disorders, 10 percent were schizophrenic, 50 percent were addicted to heroin, and 25 percent abused alcohol. It was rare to find almost any jazz musician in those days who was not either an addict or crazy (or both).

Based on the study, the researcher concluded that in spite of the spectacularly high incidence of mental illness among jazz players, they still appeared to be able to overcome their disabilities (most of the time) to produce superior creative work. Mingus was certainly no exception.

Finding Solace in Music

Charles Mingus would claim in later years that he killed his mother, but like many of his legends, that was a considerable exaggeration: at the time he was only three months old. Baby Charles, born on April 22, 1922, was headed West on a train from a border town near Nogales, Arizona, and Mexico. He was accompanied by his two older sisters, as well as his father, Charles Senior, and his ailing mother, Harriet. His father had just retired from the army after serving twenty-seven years as a sergeant, and he was taking his family to Los Angeles to start a new life.

A few months after their arrival, Harriet died of a heart ailment, most likely unrelated—despite her son's eventual guilt—to having given birth to her son. Baby (as Mingus would be called by his family) was considerably more light-skinned than his two older sisters, as he had inherited his mother's mixed blood (Chinese, English, perhaps even Mexican and Indian), and this set him apart from the others. The color of your skin was everything in those days; it determined where you could live and how far you could go. Within the African American community, as well, status was often measured by the relative lightness of pigmentation. But for Baby Charles, the unique tint of his skin, often described as more yellow than black or white, set him apart in ways that would haunt him. It would be the same with his musical compositions, which, like his complexion, would defy classification.

Mingus's father remarried soon after they settled near the Watts area of Los Angeles. He had been a noncommissioned officer in the Quartermaster Corps, used to being in charge. Anything less than immediate compliance from his children would be met by violent beatings. But his cruelty wasn't confined to mere physical intimidation. He'd also rely on a wide assortment of psychological tortures that he had perfected in the army. For example, when his son got himself in a bit of trouble in school one day (he was caught looking up girls' dresses), Senior humiliated him by shaving the boy's head.

Writing about the abuse he suffered years later in a dissociated third person, Mingus reported, "The beatings at dawn went on for months [after the school incident] and it got so sometimes they didn't even wake my boy. Daddy would beat on his body but the child was no longer inside, he was out with me waiting till the agony was over."

It turned out for young Charles that his father's wrath was the least of his problems growing up in South Central Los Angeles during his childhood in the late 1920s and early 1930s. There were gangs of blacks, whites, Mexicans, and other groups roaming the neighborhoods, and they loved to pick on someone who stood out. Charles suffered abuse from the whites who treated him as a "nigger," from the blacks because he was too white, and from almost everyone else because of his distinctive appearance: not only was he light-skinned, but he was also bowlegged with a tendency to walk pigeon-toed. He suffered his beatings as best he could but seethed inside, vowing revenge.

As befitting a family searching for middle-class respectability, Charles's father insisted that all the children take music lessons. Between his father's salary from the postal service and his military pension, the Minguses enjoyed some degree of comfort. They used part of their discretionary income to provide lessons for the two girls to play violin and piano, and Charles was told to play the trombone, which, a few weeks later, he exchanged for a cello. It was the one bright spot in Charles's life as an eight-year-old: he could escape the beatings from his father and the neighborhood gangs by finding solace in music.

Uncontrolled Fury

Charles's task of avoiding conflict on his way to school was made that much more difficult now that he had to lug a huge cello case on his back. With his awkward gait, he could never run fast anyway; he was an easy target. It was a matter of survival that he would have to learn to defend himself in some way and so he devoted himself to learning how to fight with the same passion he brought to playing the cello.

Charles's father was just about the scariest guy in the neighborhood—if anyone could teach Charles how to fight, it would be him. One day, with more than a little trepidation, he approached the ex-sergeant.

"Daddy," he said, "can you teach me to fight?"

Senior looked up from the paper and examined his son thoughtfully, then he slowly nodded his head. "Come here, boy," he said.

Charles approached cautiously, then before he could react or even comprehend what was happening, his father head-butted him in the face, sending him flying across the room. "That's your first lesson, son," he said with a grin. There weren't any more lessons from Dad after that.

Charles was already prone to a certain wildness, showing evidence of the same kind of violent temper he observed in his father. But his anger and frustrations continued to build. He was neither athletic nor imposing in any way. About the only weapon he had to protect himself was unpredictable rage.

Meanwhile, on the music front, Charles had what he described as incompetent and racist music teachers in school. They believed it wasn't right for a Negro boy to play classical music. But he still devoted himself to mastering the cello as best he could. He studied Debussy and Bach, and he especially enjoyed Stravinsky, who was the first classical composer to use elements of jazz.

About the time he entered high school, Charles had finally made a few friends, Britt Woodman (who would someday play trombone for Miles Davis) and Buddy Collette (a saxophonist who would form his own quintet with the legendary Chico Hamilton). The three African American boys formed a union of sorts, committed to music, but also to watching one another's backs. It remained one of the mysteries of Charles's childhood that he would lash out at everyone else around him, except Britt and Buddy. He just seemed so grateful to be accepted by someone, especially peers who shared his love of music. It was actually his friend Buddy who first suggested that Charles give up the cello and take up the bass. Buddy emphasized an obvious point that Charles already understood very well—that no black man would ever be allowed to play classical music in an orchestra and especially to ever earn any money doing it. By this point, at age fourteen, Charles and his friends had already decided they wanted to be professional musicians, so the only avenue open to them was "Negro jazz."

Buddy, a few years older than Charles, already had his own band and desperately needed someone to play the string bass. He figured that because his friend already knew how to play the cello, another large stringed instrument, the switch would not be that difficult. Charles was game, mostly because he loved the idea of being in a band with his friends.

It was his other friend, Britt Woodman, who noticed the big changes in Charles once he took up the bass. It was as if he had finally discovered his soul mate in that structure of wood and strings. "He got over being bowlegged once he got his bass," Woodman recalled. "All of a sudden, he was growing out of all his complexes."

Another difference, which Woodman reluctantly took credit (and blame) for, was teaching Charles how to fight. Mingus's father had never followed up on that first lesson, so Britt set up a punching bag in the garage and started drilling his friend. "Charles," he told him, "these cats are picking on you every day, so we'll show you the one-two punch." Charles learned it well, but with uncontrolled fury. Once he gained height and weight, as well as confidence on the bass, he started picking fights with anyone and everyone. He was one scary dude.

Charles's experiment with the string bass was love at first sight, but his first efforts were both awkward and as uncontrolled as his fistfights. He worked as hard as he could on the bass, trying to make adjustments from the lyrical cello to a new instrument that was used mostly for keeping the beat in the background. Surely, he reasoned even during these early years, the bass could have a prominent voice of its own. Charles had absolutely no intention of ever being hidden at the back of an orchestra being drowned out by the horns and drums.

By Charles's senior year in high school, his father had decided that the boy would follow him into the postal service. It was steady work with a lot of security. He decided it was time for Charles to take the postal exam. Charles had good reason to expect the worst when he approached his father and announced that he didn't show up for the exam.

Surprisingly, rather than exploding in rage, Senior asked Charles what he intended to do. When Charles looked his father straight in the eyes and told him he planned to be a musician, his father nodded thoughtfully, but instead of head-butting him, he asked what they needed to do to make this happen. His attitude was always if you were going to do something, you might as well do it right. Charles was stunned but regained his composure enough to say that he needed a good bass and some lessons. Senior replied that they would find him the best teacher available.

Moods of Innovation

Lloyd Reese, Charles's new music teacher, was both a college graduate from the University of Southern California and a musician employed by Warner Brothers Studio. Remarkably, he was also black, the first role model that Charles had ever met who had completely crossed over into the white world. Also impressive to Charles was the way that Reese was so knowledgeable about music theory and so versatile in all types of music. They studied the classical composers more deeply, especially Beethoven, Debussy, Ravel, and Schoenberg. But they also played the music of Benny Goodman and Duke Ellington.

The theory was one thing, but Charles yearned for more technical instruction on his instrument. He vowed that he would be the greatest bass player who ever lived and was determined to make that happen through sheer force of will. He practiced on his bass relentlessly under the guidance of another mentor, Red Callender, who was only a few years older but far more experienced. Mingus was particularly intrigued with the way that Red played melodies on the bass as well as keeping time—not easy to do.

"Mingus knew little about the bass," Callender recalled, "but even then he knew what he aspired to be: the world's greatest bass player. He practiced seventeen hours a day."

At eighteen years of age, Mingus was already developing a reputation, not only for being hotheaded but also for his innovation on the bass. He was invited to join another band with his friends, headed by Floyd Ray, that was the opening act for Sammy Davis Jr. They played clubs around the L.A. area during 1939, just as the war was heating up in Europe.

It was during this time that Mingus met one of the most important mentors in his life while playing a gig in San Francisco—Farwell Taylor, a painter who was fifteen years his senior. Taylor was one of the organizers of the underground *beat culture* that was developing in California, salons that attracted the most innovative minds around. Taylor subscribed to Hindu beliefs and began to teach them to Mingus, especially preaching greater acceptance of people regardless of their faith. The Hindu philosophy and its mysticism, combined with his own Native American roots, helped Mingus make sense of the musical hallucinations he was now hearing constantly in his head. Instead of being visited by voices, he could frequently hear melodies, riffs, and sometimes whole pieces of music. He started to write down the compositions that emerged, spending hours on the piano to give them form.

Because Taylor was the superintendent of the Casbah Apartments in the ritzy Nob Hill area of San Francisco, he was entitled to live in the penthouse, where he would throw parties for the intellectual superstars of the era. During the time Mingus stayed with his friend and mentor on occasional trips to San Francisco, he had the opportunity to meet the likes of Ernest Hemingway, Eleanor Roosevelt, and jazz singer Billie Holiday, whose band he would join one day. Taylor also introduced Mingus to a world of books, which he devoured, reading Freud, Dostoyevsky, Homer, and Rilke. They talked late into the night, along with visitors, about ideas and Hindu practice.

Nevertheless whatever philosophy or meditative practice Taylor introduced to Mingus, it didn't appear to stick. His volatile mood swings were as explosive as ever. He continued to lash out at people who disappointed him or who he believed slighted him in some way. He was becoming known as much for his mercurial personality as for his music. But within the world of jazz, where drugs and eccentricity were so common, there was tremendous tolerance for strange behavior. Mingus even came to think of his temper as an asset, a way to distinguish himself in a crowded field of up-and-coming musicians.

During the time of the early forties, Mingus adopted another hero: the great actor, writer, and director Orson Welles, who had just completed his masterpiece, *Citizen Kane.* For the rest of his life, Mingus would take on the dress, manner, even the bulk, of Welles. Although he would never have the pleasure to actually work with the great actor, Mingus still adopted the posture and distinctive cigars of his hero. He believed that men of their creative genius were entitled to certain eccentric latitude in their behavior; it was considered the privilege of their gifts.

Mingus managed to get himself out of the war by putting on a show at the induction center, either acting crazy or simply giving vent to his underlying madness. In case that display didn't work, he also inserted sugar under his fingernails to produce a diabetic urine test. When others of his generation were shipped off to Japan or Europe, he stayed behind and was able to get bookings because of the shortage of musicians around.

Mingus got hired as the only black player in several big band–era orchestras, playing the bass with such distinction that people began to notice. This is especially unusual as the instrument was basically stuck way in the back to keep time along with the drums. He signed on with Duke Ellington's, Alvino Rey's, and Louis Armstrong's bands, playing their music and even joining them in the recording studio. He was becoming known as a virtuoso on an instrument that until then everyone had taken for granted.

As much as he admired the jazz masters, Mingus had other things in mind for his music. He loved the mellow melodies and brassy horns of the jazz scene. He worshipped Ellington and later Parker. But he could hear other music inside his own head, sounds that were quite unlike anything else being played at the time. This was a time of experimentation for him: while playing everyone else's music, he was internalizing bits and parts he liked most for himself. "I was open, I was learning," he said at the time. "I went with them because everybody's music is an experience. I like Indian music as much as Charlie Parker, and Beethoven quartets, especially 9 and 12."

Mingus's first major break as an innovator came during the end of the war, when there was a musician's strike. As an artist who wasn't a member of the union, he was offered the chance to record under his own name, The Charles Mingus Sextet. He combined jazz with blues, plus his own eclectic mix of influences, and recorded a dozen tunes. The record didn't sell very well, but he was beginning to find his own voice as a musician instead of just playing other people's music.

Creation and Procreation

Mingus fell in love constantly, repeatedly, and with complete abandon, just the way he played the bass. He fancied himself a ladies' man and did indeed attract his share of groupies. In his autobiography, he claimed to be a pimp with his own stable of whores at his beck and call (another of his exaggerations). What is true is that he did have a certain magnetism that attracted women of all ages and races.

Jeanne Gross lived in the Minguses' old Los Angeles neighborhood but on a lot big enough to hold a chicken farm. The Grosses were a successful family around town, with Jeanne's father an educated man whose house was filled with books. Jeanne thought it was scandalous to take up with a musician, even someone raised by the exacting standards of Sergeant Mingus, but both families approved of the union— mostly because Jeanne was pregnant. Charles agreed that the only right thing he could do was to marry her.

From the first days of their marriage right after the new year of 1944, the couple fought and argued because Jeanne wanted her husband to get a regular job, perhaps working for the postal service like his father. With a new baby, and a shortage of money, it didn't seem like he could possibly support a family making a few dollars a day playing gigs. But Mingus was determined to stick with the commitment to music, whatever the cost, and if Jeanne didn't like it, that was too bad for her. Jeanne got so mad, she smashed him in the face with a telephone and chipped his tooth. During the best of times, Mingus never smiled much, but after this incident he would almost always be seen scowling in public to hide his fractured tooth.

Once their son was born, things got even worse. Mingus was inclined to hide in the closet to practice his bass. He said he couldn't stand the sound of the baby crying and screaming all the time, nor could he tolerate the smell of soiled diapers.

By 1946, Mingus's career was enjoying some limited, if temporary, success. Dimitri Tiomkin, who scored films for Hollywood but had limited imagination, hired Mingus, and others like him, to infuse the scores with something other than the usual soundtracks. During this year, Mingus recorded some of his own compositions while he enjoyed steady work for the first time. It was not to last any longer than his marriage.

Mingus was experimenting with a sound that was built upon the work of Duke Ellington and others, and yet it was so completely original that there was no way to quite describe it. One music critic tried describing what Mingus was trying to do:

> There was a pedal point—*a bass note extended over measures and chord changes. There was polytonality—more than one key signature to a piece. There was striking counterpoint that wound two songs against each other, often ironically. And there was extended form, where measures were added and subtracted.*

One need not be a music theorist to appreciate that during a time of experimentation and innovation in American jazz, Mingus was creating a whole new domain of musical expression. By the age of twenty-four, he was already one of the most radical composers operating anywhere in the world.

If Mingus was coming into his own as a composer, he was making even more of a mark as a musician, both on the piano and the bass. "I began playing and didn't stop for a long time," he told one interviewer. "It was suddenly *me;* it wasn't the bass any more. Now I'm not conscious of the instrument as an instrument when I play." The bass had now become an extension of Mingus's own volatile, passionate, unstable personality.

A Time of Madness

The lives of Charles Mingus and Charlie "Bird" Parker would continue to intersect throughout the 1940s, as each struggled to maintain some sort of stability in the face of increasing internal pressures. Their paths would cross again and again, and during that time Mingus would alternate between feeling absolute reverence for Bird's brilliance and feeling disdain for his weakness in giving in to the temptations of drugs and the insanity that came with them.

During the summer of 1946, Parker was back in L.A. under less than optimal circumstances. He was strung out on heroin and fell apart during one of his recording sessions, which ended up having him shipped out to a rehabilitation center for six months. The shock therapy and drugs he received didn't seem to put a dent in his madness, other than to scare him into pretending he was more normal, at least until he could get out of the treatment facility.

Parker, as well as many of his followers, believed that the drugs and madness were an integral part of his creative productivity. They were what made it possible for him to move beyond *swing* and the prevailing conventions of the time. During Bird's stable times, when coherent and in control, Mingus greatly enjoyed their time together. He saw Bird as the best possible teacher on the planet for him, if only he could minimize the undercurrents of bad craziness that had them both enslaved.

"I studied Bird's creative vein," Mingus said, "with the same passion and understanding with which I'd studied the scores of my favorite classical composers, because I found purity in his music that until then I had only found in classical music." To Mingus, Charlie Parker was on a par with Stravinksy or Schoenberg: an absolute genius.

Meanwhile Mingus and Jeanne continued to grow apart, their battles now more and more frequent. After three years together, Jeanne moved out in September 1946, and Mingus went into a deep funk. His ability to get work as a musician took a nose dive. As a result, he was not only dealing with the breakup of his family, but he was forced to do the one thing in life he had vowed never to do: work for the postal service to make ends meet. A second vow he made was also broken when he began using heroin like his mentor, Bird; this only made him more paranoid and erratic than usual.

Even during the depth of his depression, Mingus managed to remain creative, writing his first piece to win widespread popularity: "Mingus Fingers." He wouldn't earn a cent from its recording because the band leader, Lionel Hampton, claimed the royalties, but it established Mingus as a composer on the rise.

The association with the Hampton band would last less than a year, before Mingus began feuding with the other musicians. During one show, he became so enraged that he knocked the drummer, Curley

Hamner, off the stage, sending him flying into the audience. This was his way of saying he quit.

About the only good news in his life was that he met Celia Gemanis, who would soon become his second wife. For a man who felt so ambivalent about his own racial composition, who purported to hate white people much of the time, it must have been even more confusing to fall in love with a white woman. Remember, this was the fifties in America, when interracial relationships could easily spark violent reactions in some quarters. It is hard enough to make a new marriage work between two passionate individuals, but Charles and Celia had their work cut out for them when the Mingus family all but disowned him, and they found it difficult to find a place that would allow them to live together, even as man and wife. It is more than a little interesting that the composer who sought to integrate disparate forms of music—classical, bebop, gospel, swing—also did the same thing in his personal life.

Charles and Celia were married in April 1951 and then headed East to make a new life for themselves. Mingus was hopeful that it would be easier to find work in New York, which had emerged as the cultural center of the world for music and the arts, supplanting Paris during the days of Hemingway. During the next decade, they would hang out within a culture that not only accepted a degree of madness in artists but even seemed to encourage it. Mingus played in clubs and hung out at social gatherings frequented by the most creative—and deranged—artists alive. There was Jack Kerouac, Allen Ginsberg, William Burroughs, the other beat poets, some of whom would collaborate with Mingus on dual performances. There was radical comedian Lenny Bruce, entertainer Judy Garland, actor Marlon Brando, writer Norman Mailer, artists Jackson Pollock and Mark Rothko, all of whom would run into one another at jazz clubs. They were all known not only for their creative brilliance but also for their rather eccentric behavior. There was a zeitgeist of those times that made it possible for musicians like Mingus and Parker to operate in their craft while engaging in behavior that was both self-destructive and dangerous to others.

Hellview of Bellevue

Once Charles and Celia joined forces, they were inspired to do something together that was relatively unprecedented in the music scene: to create their own label—Debut Records. Mingus, Parker, Gillespie, Powell, were all frustrated by being held hostage by the large record companies that would pay them nominal fees for distributing their work. The Minguses came up with the idea of starting their own company, which could produce and distribute the recordings of their group of friends. Celia would become the business manager, and Charles would lean on his friends to join them in the venture.

Debut started small and remained that way for a long time. It was the first black-owned, and one of the first artist-owned, record companies, a radical step in those days. The company limped along, producing four, then eight records a year, barely breaking even. But it wasn't the financial success of the company that mattered as much as the idea that black musicians did not need to be victims of corporate suits who continually exploited them; they could take their fate into their own hands. This idea inspired others—Thelonious Monk, Miles Davis, Hank Mobley—to try the same thing (with mixed results). Although Debut only lasted a few years before it folded, producing recordings by Dizzy Gillespie, Max Roach, and The Mingus Workshop, it signaled Mingus's commitment to break new ground in as many areas of music as he could.

If Mingus was enjoying some success, or at least satisfaction, from his music enterprises, he was dismayed at the number of his compatriots who were succumbing to drugs and madness. In 1955, the year that Parker died, Bud Powell was committed to a psychiatric ward, and Miles Davis was sent to jail for failing to pay child support.

But in spite of the apprehension related to watching his friends spin out of control, Mingus was finding his stride in creative composition. He had long been frustrated with the process of trying to write out his compositions and then giving the scores to the musicians. Most of the jazz players couldn't read them anyway, and those who could were used to going their own way. Mingus valued improvisation but not to the point that the musicians strayed from the central theme of the piece. He needed a way to instill a certain discipline on the band and yet still give them creative freedom to build on one another's efforts.

"Creativity is more than just being different," he said in perhaps his most famous quote. "Anybody can play weird; that's easy. What's hard is to be as simple as Bach. Making the simple, awesomely simple, that's creativity."

What became known as the Jazz Workshop was a structure invented by Mingus that was half group therapy and half group improvisation. Once he had an arrangement clearly in his head, a compilation of all the musical hallucinations he collected and assembled, he would then carefully instruct, cue, and drill each of the musicians in their part.

During rehearsals, he would hum a particular musical phrase and then demand that the player play it back perfectly, before going on to the next one, and the one after that. It was exhausting and challenging for the band, but the result provided both a level of control by the composer, and room for creative inspirations that would emerge during the performance or recording.

The work was taking a lot out of Mingus, both physically and emotionally. He started taking speed, the way most of his friends did, to boost his energy, then downers and tranquilizers to help him calm down afterward. In an eerie replay of Judy Garland's drug-induced madness, Mingus began to experience chronic insomnia and increased paranoia. He and Celia also began fighting, just as Jeanne, his first wife, and he had done. As the marriage began to fall apart, so too did the viability of Debut Records.

Mingus began to lose touch with reality, relying on drugs more and more to moderate his mood swings and control his depression. In desperation, he checked himself into Bellevue, the same psychiatric unit that had housed so many of his friends. He knew that he was out of control, even by his own standards. He had lost a lot of weight, which for him, was a sign of illness and distress.

Like many distraught black men of his day who showed up at a hospital complaining of emotional problems, Mingus was diagnosed by the doctors as a *paranoid schizophrenic*. He was certainly depressed, but that particular label was then and is now bestowed far more often on minorities and the poor than it is on those who are privileged and more likely to be considered "eccentric" or "emotionally exhausted." Mingus was indeed depleted and depressed but hardly psychotic. He tried to explain this to his therapist, Dr. Pollock:

"I've been reading about you in a magazine," Pollock said to him. "You didn't tell me you were such a famous musician."

"That don't mean shit," Mingus answered. "That's a system those that own us use. They make us famous and give us names—the King of this, the Count of that, the Duke of *what!* We die broke anyhow—and sometimes I think I dig death more than I dig facing this white world."

Now one can see how this might sound a bit paranoid to doctors on a mental ward examining a patient, but this was a black man in the sixties. And it ain't paranoid if it's true.

Mingus demanded that he be released from the facility, claiming that he changed his mind and wasn't crazy after all. "We're here to help you," one of the psychiatrists tried to reassure him. "But you sit down and write out the reasons you think your own doctor would be better."

Mingus did exactly that, writing out a long list complaining about the toilets, insects, and lowlifes on the ward. Two of the items on his list included:

> *Dr. Bonk keeps saying I'm a failure. I did not come here to discuss my career or I would have brought my press agent.*
>
> *Dr. Bonk talks to me two minutes at a time and hurries me off. What does he expect me to say in two minutes? When I ask for more time he complains he is overworked and the wards are overcrowded. My doctor is not overworked and his office is not overcrowded and he does not do all the talking.*

Always enjoying the possibility of stirring up a little trouble, not to mention fighting for the downtrodden, Mingus began to organize the patients on the ward into group activities and talk sessions. The doctors at Bellevue favored strong drugs and electroconvulsive shock therapy, so they didn't exactly appreciate their patient's effort. When Mingus requested that the staff supply them with art materials, one psychiatrist responded to him, "May I comment that compulsive organization is one of the prime traits of paranoia?"

If Mingus had not been in a rage before this type of interaction, he was furious afterward, although he did his best to hide his anger so he could get the hell out of there. By the time he was released, Mingus was so indignant at his treatment there that he composed a song in honor of the experience: "Hellview of Bellevue."

Fame and Prosperity

> *You, my audience, are all a bunch of motherfuckers. A bunch of tumbling weeds, tumbling 'round, running from your subconscious . . . minds. Minds? Minds that won't let you stop to listen to a word of artistic or meaningful truth. . . . You don't want to see your ugly selves, the untruths, the lies you give to life.*
>
> *So you come to me, you sit in the front row, as noisy as can be. I listen to your millions of conversations, sometimes pulling them all up and putting them together and writing a symphony. But you never hear that symphony . . .*

Woe to any member of the audience, especially sitting up front, who had the audacity to talk while his band was playing. With a certain amount of menace, Mingus would announce before beginning a show that he didn't want to hear any talking (or even whispering), nor did he want to hear any cash registers ringing or glasses clinking. If people wanted a sip of their drinks, they should do it before the show started. And, oh yeah, he wasn't interested in hearing any applause, at least until the end of the set, when it wouldn't make any difference anyway.

If Mingus could be called eccentric, even irascible, he would go off on an endless rant against a perceived offender, especially a white guy, who showed him the slightest disrespect. Whatever ambivalence he felt toward men of the dominant culture, he continued to feel attracted to women who were white, developing huge crushes on a few coeds who swooned in the presence of the jazz master.

The new love of his life, and soon to become his third wife, was Judy Starkey, a tall blonde who was beginning her career as a nurse. This was in 1959, about the time comedian Lenny Bruce was stirring up audiences with his own brand of craziness in another part of town. The couple got married a few months later in the beginning of the new year. It was the first time Mingus married a woman who wasn't pregnant with his child.

The sixties were to become a time of prosperity for Mingus. By that time, he was famous and in demand. He'd appeared regularly at the Newport Jazz Festival. He was rolling in dough, spending it as fast as he could pull it in—buying clothes, going on shopping sprees, and acquiring Cadillacs (limousines!). Even the politics had changed for the better with the Kennedys in power and the civil rights movement in full blossom.

It had even become part of Mingus's act to become crazy! Audiences began to expect it. They were disappointed if he didn't throw a tantrum or throw someone off stage or humiliate someone in the audience. Charles Mingus, and Lenny Bruce, with whom he would sometimes share the stage, were the bad boys of the entertainment industry, but their acts seemed to be selling to sold-out crowds. By that time, Mingus was featured at the major jazz festivals and concert halls, as well as at universities and the usual clubs.

Mingus's fluency and productivity as a composer were increasing significantly now that he was in his prime. He hired trombonist Jimmy Knepper to work full time just to transpose music scores for the players. When Knepper couldn't keep up with the workload on his own, there were more arrangers added to the staff, all trying to keep up with the flow of music and get it ready for performances. The pressure on

Knepper, in particular, was getting out of hand, and he was doing the best he could to keep up with his boss's perfectionistic demands. At one point, Mingus became so irate at what he perceived as Knepper's loafing that he started calling Knepper names and accusing him of betrayal, crazy stuff that Knepper couldn't begin to fathom. Mingus worked himself into a frenzy, and then, without warning, he punched the astonished musician in the mouth, knocking out a front tooth. For a trombonist who had made a living blowing a horn, this was akin to destroying his career. In fact, after dental repair work, Jimmy lost a substantial amount of his range and dexterity. He would never be quite the same again. He initiated legal action against his former employer to recover damages.

There was a performance at Town Hall, and things were appearing ominous. The musicians were not prepared to perform to Mingus's exacting standards, to a large extent because he kept making last-minute changes in the program. The show was an absolute mess, with the band not playing together and losing track of the score. The producer had no choice but to give all the people in the audience their money back. Mingus lost complete control of himself after the performance, alternating between violent bellows of rage and uncontrollable sobs and tears. They called for his therapist, Dr. Pollock, to help Mingus pull himself together.

Mingus needed to get his head screwed back on straight, and the only way he could think to do that was to head back to Farwell Taylor, his longtime mentor, in California. Taylor took him in with open, loving arms, nourished and nurtured him, controlled his diet, and reintroduced him to Hindu philosophy. This seemed to do the job—or at least to patch the broken man back together enough to return to New York.

Mingus had by then been discovered by the popular press. He was a major celebrity, one of the reigning kings of jazz. There were feature articles about him in *Newsweek* and *Time,* proclaiming him the heir to Duke Ellington, as well as accounts of his exploits in the tabloids and papers. He was great press, not only because of his music but also because of his crazy antics.

Losing His Mind

By 1965, just as he was at the height of his popularity, Mingus became even more impossibly violent and unpredictable, attacking one of the members of his band, Jaki Byard, with an ax. Byard fended Mingus off with a fire extinguisher. The behavior was perhaps fueled by an assortment of drugs, because Mingus had been seen backstage with Thelonious Monk swallowing handfuls of pills that neither one of them could identify.

His troubles were getting even worse. His third wife, Judy, caught him in bed with his soon-to-be fourth wife, Susan Graham. They married in 1966 but may not have bothered to divorce their previous spouses. Mingus needed a woman to take care of him, to keep him grounded, in the same way that Hemingway went from one successive wife to another, lining up the next candidate before he dumped the previous one.

More disturbing, Mingus was beginning to lose any semblance of self-control. He had become a bully just like the father he so feared. He picked on the weakest member of his band, at this time the placid Hobart Dotson. Mingus would constantly threaten and intimidate the musician, who was completely cowed. One time, Mingus showed up to a gig wearing a kimono and carrying a bullwhip, which he proceeded to slash all over the place in a crazy frenzy. Another time, he drove his Corvette through the front window of the car dealership because they wouldn't fix it right.

Mingus was soon evicted from the loft where he was living for destroying the place. He was abandoned by his ex-wife, Judy. And his new wife, Sue, was keeping as much distance as she could from him; she was scared. The musicians in the Mingus Workshop got tired of his tirades and abandoned ship. He was reduced to living in hotels, drinking wine, flat broke until he finally settled alone into a tiny apartment in a bad part of town. "For about three years," Mingus admitted, "I thought I was finished. Sometimes I couldn't even get out of bed. I wasn't asleep; I just lay there."

There were weeks he couldn't leave home. He doodled on his piano and bass but couldn't write or compose music; he couldn't even play a song to completion most of the time. Yet there was something about the mixed, working-class neighborhood that revived him. Nobody knew who the hell he was, nor did they care. All they saw was a man who was floundering, dying, so the Ukrainians, Puerto Ricans, and blacks adopted him as one of their own.

"We all look out for each other," he said. "Not just against muggers and robbers. There was a time when I had no money left at all, but the tailor on the block made sure I had enough to eat. I don't know if I could have come out of the graveyard had it not been for them."

Ashes in the River

By the time Mingus reemerged from this working-class neighborhood, he had some of his sanity back, but not much else. He was still a celebrity in some circles, invited to join the merry band of Allen Ginsberg, Andy Warhol, Timothy Leary, and others during some of their experimental forays into drugs, filmmaking, and debauchery. He was drinking a lot, still popping downers and Demerol, but strangely proud that he could resist both heroin and LSD. He had to draw the line somewhere. Then he started taking Thorazine to control psychotic symptoms that started appearing, and which were frightening even to him.

Amidst the personal struggles and depression, Mingus managed to sign record contracts, first with BMI, and then with Columbia, which gave him some spending money. He was given another chance to save himself, another opportunity to revive his career, but it still didn't change his behavior. His weight ballooned out of control, which he attempted to moderate by going to weight loss spas in upstate New York. After one visit, a friend asked him how he had managed to spend a week at a fat farm and not lose a single pound. It was easy, Mingus explained. He paid a taxi driver each night to sneak him out and drive him to a cooking school nearby, where he ate himself sick. After all the gluttony and drugs, "His body was like an extended chemistry experiment," writes Gene Santoro. "Agents and reagents and catalysts swirling in a dense, cumulative mix."

Mingus's domestic life was no less chaotic in his fifties, a time when most men settle down and enjoy the fruits of their creative labors. He had made up with Sue, his fourth wife, and they were doing reasonably well, considering their volatile relationship. He had fathered four sons and two daughters from his various marriages but had minimal contact with any of them. Occasionally, he would see Charles III, Eric, or Eugene, three of the boys now grown, but the connections were tenuous at best. The one saving grace for which he was proud was that he never raised his hand to children, regardless of the situation. In this way, at least, he had escaped his father's legacy.

In the middle of the 1970s, Mingus enjoyed a resurgence once again. He was awarded a Guggenheim Fellowship to support his collaboration with choreographer Alvin Ailey to create a special composition for the Joffrey Ballet. It was to be called "The Mingus Dances." He was earning a sizable income from his various music copyrights, plus the concerts

and tours he had resumed. He lost some of the speed with his finger-
ing on the bass, and by then he used amplification on the instrument
to save his strength, but he was still holding his own. The one thing that
had changed since he had been on the antipsychotic drug was that he
seemed like he was in a fog most of the time. His ferocious spirit
seemed tamed.

In 1977, Mingus was so heavy that he could barely walk. He was
having problems with his legs, which seemed unable to support his
bulk. When he checked into a hospital for tests, it was discovered that
he had amyotrophic lateral sclerosis, better known as ALS or Lou
Gehrig's disease. It was degenerative, progressive, and invariably fatal.
At best, he was given a year left to live, and most of that would be in
excruciating pain.

Sue refused to allow her husband the indignity of dying in the hospital, so she conspired with a friend to help him escape the doctors'
care so that he could continue his life as normally as possible, even if
confined to a wheelchair. Nurses and doctors treated him with the best
that science had to offer, but with no cure, all that the injections could
do was postpone the inevitable. They also increased his hallucinations.
The only bright spot was that he stopped taking the antipsychotic
drugs (what was the use?); he regained some of his previous passion
and seemed to come out of his psychological fog.

Mingus refused to surrender to his illness, and with Sue's support,
he launched himself back into music composition with a fervor. He
had some ideas that he still wanted to make come alive and some musical hallucinations that he wanted to make real. His last collaborator,
folk singer Joni Mitchell, expected the worst in her relationship with
the madman who was rumored to be an ogre, but she actually found
him "sweet" and "sensitive." Mingus called her a hillbilly, affection-
ately, and she doted on him like a devoted daughter. Together they
produced a collaborative work, setting the poetry of T. S. Eliot to music,
with Mitchell's angelic voice to sing the melodies.

Mingus had other plans as well. He contacted Leonard Bernstein
about collaborating on a symphony together. He wrote a string quar-
tet. Even his old friend Jimmy Knepper, whom he had bashed in the
mouth and compromised his career, returned to help his friend transpose and arrange his music. Mingus knew his days were literally numbered, but he was absolutely driven to write as much as his failing
body and mind would allow.

The disease not only produced constant agony for Mingus but also crippled him to the point that he could no longer use his hands. Unbowed, he began to sing melodies into a tape recorder and asked Knepper and other friends to write the scores, which he would later check, still with a volatile temper. He was calming down considerably from aging, the disease, and medications, but not *that* much.

Mingus was also becoming more contemplative, as you'd expect from someone facing imminent death. "Most people are forced to do things they don't want to most of the time," Mingus said in one of his last interviews, "and so they get to the point where they feel they no longer have any choice about anything important, including who they are. We create our own slavery."

Mingus was determined that he was going to die the way he wanted, but before that day came, he still had work to do.

He and Sue traveled down to Mexico, where the doctors were rumored to have some experimental treatments for ALS. Even if this was not the case, he decided this would be a good place to die, near to the spot where he had been born fifty-seven years earlier. Mingus made it clear that he didn't want a fuss made over his funeral, nor did he want to be exploited the way his friend and mentor, Bird Parker, had been years earlier. He remembered that it had been a circus at Parker's memorials, with everyone trying to steal a piece of him by association.

On January 5, 1979, Charles Mingus died in the arms of his son Eugene, who had been transferring his father to his wheelchair when Mingus took his last breath. Following his last wish, his wife, Sue, carried Mingus's ashes to India, where she scattered them into the current of the Ganges River. His remains finally found peace in a place of Hindu serenity, a state he could never seem to find while he was alive.

CHAPTER EIGHT

Vaslav Nijinsky

A Method to His Madness

I n what was to be the centerpiece of his career, Vaslav Nijinsky was laboring to compose a ballet set to Igor Stravinsky's *Le Sacre du Printemps*, "The Rite of Spring." To the composer and dancer, the return of spring, after a long, harsh Russian winter, was indeed an event to be celebrated. This particular piece of music was intended to explore the most ancient, primitive core of springtime fertility. Its chords were dissonant, its rhythms and melodies seemingly as explosive and chaotic as the rebirth of Spring itself. This piece of music by Stravinsky, now regarded as his greatest work, was heard as radical, heretical, and even blasphemous to audiences when it first debuted as a symphonic piece in 1912.

Stravinsky and Diaghilev, the director of the Paris-based Ballet Russe, had wanted to work with Vaslav Nijinsky in the role of master choreographer because, at the ripe old age of twenty-three, he was already considered the greatest dancer alive, perhaps the greatest male dancer who ever lived. He was described as "the god of dance" because of his remarkable athletic abilities and passion as a performer. Nobody could elevate as high and stay aloft, so beautifully, for so long. Yet it was not only his virtually perfect technique that distinguished him;

he was also among the most passionate and erotic performers who has ever taken a stage. It was this passion that the composer and producer were hoping could be translated into the performances of all the dancers, not just the famed high leaper.

The way Nijinksy conceived the ballet, the dancers would display power and elegance but also the eroticism and sensuality of the process. There was to be a virgin who sacrificed herself by dancing to death. The other dancers would honor the surface chaos of the music; all traditional symmetry and familiarity were to be abandoned, and the choreography was rearranged to staging and movements that went beyond anything that anyone had ever seen—or imagined—before.

Nijinsky was working under incredible pressure. He had to deal with Stravinsky, as well as additional composers, like Debussy, who were contributing other works to the program. The dancers rebelled against Nijinsky's direction that they take on positions and arrangements that more resembled bestial animals than human dancers. What he asked of them seemed beyond what anyone could possibly do. Some of the dancers themselves said that they felt "misshapen," "maimed," and "struck by paralysis." Nijinsky was asking them to abandon a lifetime of classical training in order to reposition their arms, postures, and gestures in what could only have seemed like the orders of a madman. What nobody understood at the time was that he was patterning the movements after patients with neurological disease.

Adding to his company's image of Nijinsky as an *enfant terrible* was his appearance when he arrived to rehearse them, still wearing his costume for *L'après-midi d'un faune* ("The Afternoon of a Faun"). He would show up for rehearsals still dressed as a monster with horns: like the wild beasts he was trying to turn them into.

Nijinsky was not only young and inexperienced in his new role as choreographer but also relatively inarticulate. Whether in his native language, Russian, or in French or German, he found it hard to make himself understood. Then there were the problems with his moods and violent temper tantrums.

The dancer who had been cast in the role of the virgin was none other than Nijinsky's sister, Bronislava. It happened that she disclosed her pregnancy just at the point that rehearsals were in full swing. Nijinsky went nuts, ranting and raving that there was nobody else who could play the demanding role.

"You are deliberately trying to destroy my work, just like all the others," he screamed at her, demonstrating both the increasing paranoia and narcissism that would haunt him throughout his life.

When Bronislava's husband entered the scene and attempted to calm things down, Nijinsky tried to strangle his brother-in-law because the man had the audacity to impregnate his lead dancer. It took several other dancers to calm Nijinsky down and restore order. For some time afterward, he seriously considered playing the role of the virgin himself—the idea of dancing himself to death held great appeal.

On May 29, 1913, the ballet *Le Sacre du Printemps* premiered at the *Théâtre des Champs-Élysées.* Located in a ritzy part of Paris, the palace-like facility had just opened a few months earlier. The performance was sold out, largely as a result of advance publicity that warned of "semi-savagery" and "frenetic human clusters wrenched incessantly by the most astonishing polyrhythm ever to come from the mind of a musician." This certainly played a part in stirring up passions.

From the first opening notes of music, the audience came immediately to life in ways that were quite unexpected. By the second minute of the score, people started whistling and calling out their protests. The well-heeled theatergoers felt violated and offended by the music, and then, as the dancers began, by the choreography that was to them beyond modern; it was an abomination.

The audience began to riot. Men stood up on their chairs and demanded that the performance be called to a halt. Younger members of the audience took offense at the disruption and called for the others to behave themselves. Fistfights broke out between the two groups. Men challenged one another to duels. Women were screaming hysterically. Meanwhile the orchestra continued to play and the dancers continued to act out the primitive rite of Spring.

It was not until the house lights were turned on that Nijinsky and Stravinsky could see the nature of the riot that was now in full swing. The choreographer had tried to keep some semblance of control, screaming to be heard over the bedlam of the crowd, urging the dancers to keep going and the orchestra to keep playing. In spite of the tumult going on all around them, the performers continued to press onward. By the time it was Nijinsky's turn to dance, things had actually quieted down. Those who had been most irate or most injured had already been removed from the theater, and the rest must have grown exhausted from their efforts.

Both Diaghilev and Stravinsky were secretly thrilled by the scandal, realizing that *any* publicity was favorable for promoting future shows. It may have been a testimony to the influence of the three collaborators that by the second show, one week later, the audience was both prepared and responsive to the performance. The audiences of

Paris were dragged kicking and screaming into the twentieth century by the radical music of Stravinsky and the progressive choreography of Nijinsky. That first performance of *Le Sacre* is now regarded as one of the seminal events in the history of dance.

Just four years after this memorable evening, Nijinsky's career, crippled by mental illness, would be over. He would spend the following thirty years looking for peace of mind, seeking treatment from the most accomplished experts in the world. And throughout this odyssey, beginning in 1919 just before entering an asylum, Nijinsky would keep detailed notes about his experiences. He would leave behind not only a legacy as perhaps the most creative dancer and choreographer who ever graced the stage but also as a running commentary on his inner journey of madness.

Child Prodigy

In the year 1889 (or perhaps 1890, the exact birth date is unknown) Eleonora and Thomas Nijinsky, professional ballet dancers from Poland, gave birth to a second son. One year later, they would have a daughter. The three young children, Stanislav, Vaslav, and Bronislava, were given Russian names as befitting their new home in St. Petersburg, the capital city. Not surprisingly, given their lineage and home environment, all three children showed early talent as dancers; so they began their professional preparation at the same time they learned to walk.

The Nijinsky home, although an excellent training ground for dance, was not a happy place to grow up. Eleonora was often depressed, as had been both of her parents. In fact, she had blackmailed Thomas to marry her in the first place by threatening to kill herself unless he would make a commitment. When Thomas began an affair with another dancer and moved out several years later, Eleonora was required to keep her family together, struggling with poverty and her own sense of despair.

Among the children, Vaslav, and his sister, Bronislava, showed extraordinary talent, even as young children. So close in age, they developed a close bond based on their total devotion to ballet. They practiced together, drilled each other, and became constant companions—almost extensions of the other. Their older brother, Stanislav, had also shown early promise as a dancer but had been critically injured while falling (possibly jumping) out of a fourth-floor window. The boy was never the same after that and was eventually confined to an asylum because of his raving behavior.

Vaslav seemed to share his older brother's inclination toward reck-lessness, a predicament that would drive his mother half crazy with worry. Already one of her sons was permanently disabled; she didn't want to lose another. But Vaslav could not be restrained: he was al-ways restless—jumping, leaping, running, dancing, climbing—any-thing to stay in motion. His mother needn't have worried: the boy's sense of balance and athletic skills were uncanny. He also seemed to have inherited the ability to leap from his father, who was known for his high jumps on stage.

Whatever talent Vaslav exhibited in the domain of dancing, he was handicapped in others areas, like many brilliant young people. Pablo Picasso, for example, was a dismal academic student, barely able to master basic lessons. Albert Einstein is well-known to have been a poor student as a child. In Vaslav's case, he was inarticulate, almost mute, in speech. The only way he seemed to be able to express his thoughts and feelings was through dance.

By the time Vaslav was admitted to the Imperial School of Ballet, the primary training facility for Russian dancers, he was already con-sidered a prodigy. He was eight years old, able to demonstrate a vari-ety of complex dance maneuvers, but was severely challenged in academic matters, especially anything that involved speaking.

The other boys were jealous of Vaslav because he could jump higher than anyone else in the school and seem to stay aloft for im-possible lengths of time. It was this ability that some boys decided to test one day. They challenged Vaslav to see if he could jump over a bar-rier, but unbeknownst to him, they had spread soap all over the floor and when he launched himself toward the wooden beam, they raised it still higher. Vaslav crashed and fell, suffering severe internal injuries that kept him in a coma for almost a week. He spent the next year con-fined in a hospital, and although he would recover physically from the injury, he would always remain fearful of death.

Rising Star

During adolescence, Nijinsky enjoyed the benefit of several talented teachers who helped him to refine his raw abilities into perfect con-trol. Emotionally, however, he was both volatile and unpredictable. He discovered early, as did Charles Mingus and the controversial come-dian Lenny Bruce, that the more crazy and eccentrically he behaved, the more he was declared to have a distinguished stage presence. It's unclear whether his temper tantrums were the lingering result of his physical trauma or the very beginnings of a far more disturbing mental disorder.

During his first public performances before even graduating from school, Nijinksy immediately captured the attention of critics and the audience alike. He was a slight youth with a body that seemed to have been created from the parts of both men and women. He was quite short, just five feet four inches tall, but he had powerful legs that seemed to have been sculpted for a much taller man. The top half of his body appeared almost feminine, with a small chest, waist, and delicate arms. The combination of the parts seemed to make him a creature especially built for flying. People would often ask to examine and touch his body, especially his feet, to see if they could figure out how it was possible that he could soar so high and so far. What few realized was how hard he had worked to develop this talent—strengthening the muscles in his calves and thighs, strengthening his Achilles tendons, learning to control his breathing and even the way he turned his body in flight so as to give the impression of weightlessness.

By the age of seventeen, Nijinsky was already well-known throughout the dance world in his country. He was sought out by other dancers, directors, choreographers, potential students, who wanted to work with him, even though he had established a reputation for being "difficult." He could make his body do almost anything, but he found it challenging to communicate with anyone except his sister.

It was during the year 1907 that Nijinsky made a journey to visit his father, whom he had not seen in many years. Thomas initiated the contact, having heard about his son as a rising star. The meeting did not go well and the two of them had a heated argument. Although Vaslav had intended to stay for a week, he left after a single day. His father was so furious about their conversation that he refused to send child support to his ex-wife thereafter. For his part, Vaslav returned so depressed that he could barely function for weeks afterward.

"I was no longer cheerful because I felt death," he confessed to his sister. "I was afraid of people and used to lock myself in the room. My room was narrow with a high ceiling. I liked looking at the walls and at the ceiling because all this spoke to me of death."

Even the public acclaim that Nijinsky was experiencing failed to lift his spirits. As flamboyant as he could be on stage, as narcissistic and self-centered as he could be in his daily interactions, he was strangely humbled and restrained when he received applause, almost embarrassed by the attention. Part of this modesty came from his belief that the audience was applauding the wrong parts of his performance—

they were blown away by his great leaps but seemed not to notice the more subtle aspects of his craft.

At age seventeen, Nijinsky was a true sensation, a dancer quite unlike any other that the world had ever seen. Yet as accomplished as he was as a performer, he seemed almost retarded in his social skills. Celebrities, royalty, and fans would flock to his side at parties or receptions only to find him mute. Both women and men would attempt to seduce him but he remained unresponsive. He had actually stopped masturbating at the age of thirteen because he believed that spilling his seed would compromise his artistic energies and ability. His ambivalence about masturbation and orgasms would remain a lifelong obsession and source of guilt.

Nijinsky had very few friends and had yet to have a lover. When the Russian Prince Pavel Lvov lavished him with gifts and began a determined effort to seduce him, Nijinsky accepted the advances out of gratitude for the attention. The prince was twice Nijinsky's age and was very well connected within the aristocracy, as well as the world of dance. It is unknown whether Nijinsky entered into a relationship with the older man because he so desperately wanted to be loved by someone or if he wanted to take advantage of the career opportunities made possible by the prince. During the next year that they lived together, Lvov mentored the boy in all ways that were necessary in the upper echelons of Russian society. Nijinsky learned how to dress and how to handle himself at social functions. He developed a level of poise and confidence that began to manifest not only in his social behavior but also in his dancing. Perhaps the most important consequence of all for Nijinsky was that the prince introduced him to the person who would become his next lover and his most important mentor: Sergei Pavlovitch Diaghilev.

Diaghilev was twenty years older than Nijinsky's eighteen years. He was an important figure in the world of Russian ballet, perhaps the single most important dance producer and promoter on the scene. A deal had been struck with the prince in which the impressionable young man would be "transferred" to the control of Diaghilev. It was exactly like the kind of Machiavellian maneuvers that would take place between Judy Garland's mother and Louis B. Mayer, in which Judy too had been passed around like a commodity, used not only for her artistry but also for her body.

There has been ongoing debate regarding Nijinsky's sexual orientation. Throughout his life, he would have relationships with both women and men, but perhaps the clearest clue as to his preferences are revealed in his masturbation fantasies, which he wrote about frankly in his notebooks: "I liked lying in bed thinking about women, but I came afterward and decided that I should make myself my own object of lust. I looked at my own erect penis and lusted." This disclosure reveals a level of narcissistic disturbance—being most sexually aroused by the image of his own body—that would only heighten the severity of his other problems. It also demonstrates, quite clearly, that he entered into the relationship with his next lover, Diaghilev, not because of sexual attraction but because of what he viewed as another solid career move.

Nijinsky wrote about their first encounter in his diary: "Diaghilev asked me to come to the Hotel Europe where he lived. I disliked him for his too self-assured voice, but went to seek my luck. I found my luck. At once I allowed him to make love to me. I trembled like a leaf. I hated him, but pretended, because I knew that my mother and I would die of hunger otherwise."

It turned out that Diaghilev was the best possible mentor for Nijinsky, at least as far as for opening doors. The patron of the arts started his own independent ballet company, separate from the official Imperial Ballet, and wanted Nijinsky as his featured dancer. This would be a convenient arrangement for both of them: for the next few years, from 1908 to 1912, they would live together as lovers and work well as producer and star performer.

Shaping a Dance

Nijinsky's master and lover would waste little time making the most of the opportunities that opened before them. Diaghilev assembled a cast of the best dancers available, including Nijinsky's sister, Bronislava, who had just graduated from the Imperial Ballet School. He hired up-and-coming composers like Igor Stravinsky and Claude Debussy to write music for the ballets. Then he took the show to Paris and other European capitals, where Nijinsky was featured as the principal dancer.

It was during a performance of *Le Pavillion d'Armida* in Paris on May 18, 1909, that Nijinksy established his reputation as the "god of dance," demonstrating for the first time his signature exit. It was considered normal for a soloist to walk calmly off stage after a performance, perhaps with a slight bow. In this production, however, Nijinsky was playing the role of a slave, a part that involved a simulated *ménage à trois*, a sexual threesome with his sister and the other female lead.

This was provocative enough, but when the number came to an end, rather than making a modest departure, Nijinsky quite literally soared off stage, flying into the wings, where he landed on a mattress to break his fall. The audience went absolutely wild, stopping the orchestra until the noise could subside. Nobody had ever seen—or heard of— a dancer like this before.

Nijinsky may have been enjoying the career benefits of his association with Diaghilev, but he did not at all enjoy the forced sex or domestic life. It was a situation that had to be endured for the sake of his career. In one sense, he truly loved his mentor. Nijinsky appreciated the older man's devotion and caring, even as he despised what he had to do to stay in his mentor's good graces. For his part, Diaghilev seemed to believe that he had a responsibility to nurture a national treasure, the greatest creative genius his country had produced since Dostoyevsky or Tolstoy.

During the years 1910 and 1911, Nijinsky and Diaghilev collaborated on a number of successful productions. By this time, Nijinsky was taking a far more active role in the set designs, the costumes, and the choreography. Because of his close relationship with the producer, he had access and opportunities that allowed him to exert far more influence than his age and experience would normally allow. It was assumed that because he was the greatest dancing talent the world had ever seen, naturally he could infuse this passion into the work of the whole troupe. Indeed, Nijinsky did have ideas for staging and dance arrangements that went far beyond anything that anyone had ever imagined before. This is how he managed to find himself in the position of collaborating with Stravinsky on the century's most notorious artistic event.

Nijinsky's behavior, however, became more and more outrageous both on stage and off. He seemed to delight in provoking people, dressing in costumes that consisted mostly of tights and a jock strap (stuffed with padding). He claimed that the less he wore, the higher he could fly. He added routines to his dances that became even more daring, at one point leaping out of a window (a reenactment of the way his older brother had fallen). During a performance of *L'après-midi,* in which he played a faun who is seduced by seven nubile women (including his sister), he simulated masturbation with the fallen scarf from one of the maidens. Off stage, his long periods of silence, mood swings, continuing difficulty in expressing himself, and petulance could only be described as eccentric and were indulged only because of his creative genius.

While in London, Nijinsky had captured the interest of the Blooms-bury Circle, the group of writers including Virginia Woolf and her cousin Lytton Strachey (Freud's translator). They were drawn not only because of his artistic accomplishments but also because he was con-sidered a prominent gay figure who had come out of the closet. Stra-chey, in particular, had fallen in love with him, sending him flowers and gifts, hoping for a brief liaison. It was not to be, because Diaghilev kept such tight control over his protégé, a situation that was becom-ing increasingly conflicted.

There were some who would say that Nijinsky was an even greater choreographer than he was a dancer. In terms of the level and depth of this creativity, this may certainly be true. The problem was that he was required not only to envision a particular scenario but also to de-scribe it to others and then teach them the movements. He could do this with his sister, not through speech, but by shaping her body into desired positions.

"I am like a piece of clay that he is molding," Bronislava explained, "shaping into each pose and change of movement . . . we are com-pletely absorbed in our work . . . but sometimes emotions run high and we lose our tempers with each other." This method was not an option with the rest of the cast.

The year 1912 was a particularly tough one for Nijinsky. First, he "lost" his sister when she married. Second, his attempts at choreogra-phy were deemed financial, if not artistic, failures (at least by the crit-ics of his time). Third, his relationship with Diaghilev was unraveling, and he could no longer pretend to enjoy the sex between them. Fourth, his father, whom he had not spoken to since their breach, had died. Finally, Nijinsky had never been in good health for very long since his time in the hospital after his "accident" at school. And he was now complaining of a number of physical problems that sometimes prevented him from showing up at work. His employer suspected that this was malingering; Diaghilev was considerably less sympathetic now that Nijinsky was locking his door to him.

Breakdown

The ballet touring company headed to South America during the sum-mer of 1913, and it was on the cruise that Nijinsky was stalked by an attractive Hungarian woman with the aristocratic name of Romola Lu-dovika Polyxena Flavia Pulszky. She was a little younger than Nijinsky, quite beautiful and exotic, a member of European high society, and totally obsessed by the dancer. Ever since she had first seen him dance, she had been so enthralled by his beauty and grace that she announced to a friend sitting with her that she would someday marry him.

By the time they met on the cruise months later, Romola had been following Nijinsky whenever she could, gathering information about his whereabouts and personal habits. Romola believed that she could convince the dancer to marry her if only she could get him alone. Once she heard rumors about Nijinsky's break with his mentor and discovered he was traveling abroad, she managed to find a space on board the ship.

Nijinsky and Romola enjoyed a whirlwind courtship lasting all of one month. Nijinsky was flattered by the attentions of a suitor in the same way he had been with Diaghilev. But this time, he had connected with someone the same age as his sister. In addition, Romola was a woman of striking beauty and a member of the highest level of European society. For her part, Romola was determined to save Nijinsky from what she considered his depraved homosexuality. (He was, in fact, attracted to both men and women throughout his life.) They were married in 1913 and would remain so for the next thirty-five years, even though they would not live together during much of that time.

Four days into the marriage, Nijinsky believed that he had made a terrible mistake. More worrisome to him than their sexual incompatibility (he liked to troll the streets for whores) was that his wife showed little interest in learning about dance. As Nijinsky didn't like to talk much anyway (even if he wanted to, he spoke no Hungarian and poor French), their time together in these first years must have been excruciatingly difficult. Nevertheless they did manage to have sex, because Romola became pregnant.

The one good part of the marriage, as far as he was concerned, was that the announcement of Romola's pregnancy would finally get Diaghilev off his back (literally). What he failed to anticipate was that his rejected lover would no longer remain committed to furthering his career. A few months after his marriage to Romola, Nijinsky was fired.

In 1914, there were only a few ballet groups that could possibly hire a dancer and choreographer of Nijinsky's caliber. He couldn't return to Russia, even if he wanted to, or he would have been drafted into the army for the coming world war. He saw that his only choice was to create his own ballet company, which he attempted to do by recruiting his sister, her husband, and a dozen other relatively inexperienced dancers. They would open in London as *Saison Nijinsky,* and even though the performance was regarded as excellent, it was not seen as up to his godlike prowess. In part, this may have been because of the relatively modest budget of the production, but it was also because of the stress Nijinsky was under. His leaps were just as high but didn't seem nearly as magical as they once had been. He was distracted by the upcoming birth of his child, the responsibilities of running the company, and he seemed even more moody than usual.

Nijinsky managed to complete the scheduled performances but not without a high degree of turmoil. He picked fights with stagehands, even striking one man who he imagined was lusting after his sister. He screamed and humiliated one of his female leads, reducing her to tears. His behavior deteriorated to the point that even his sister no longer wanted to deal with him. The final blow came when the Palace Theatre canceled the rest of the shows because they were tired of Nijinsky's rants.

Nijinsky, along with his very pregnant wife, retreated to a health spa in the Austrian mountains to recover from the successive disappointments. He was still being offered invitations to perform at private functions, by the king and queen of Spain, for instance, and had even begun negotiating with other ballet companies, but Nijinsky was finding it difficult to remain focused for long. He was clearly depressed, with all of the most pervasive symptoms, including lethargy, insomnia, skittishness, and irrational fears, especially about his health.

The Language of Dance

Kyra Nijinsky was born in June 1914 to an indifferent mother and a father who, even though initially apprehensive, soon made her the center of his life, at least for the first few years of it, until he lost his ability to relate to anyone. She would resemble her father not only in physical appearance but also in her ability to dance. Nijinsky was so taken by the little girl that from her earliest infancy he threw her in the air as if teaching her to fly.

Nijinsky was by no means a well man. The year 1915, when Nijinsky was twenty-five, was a time when he struggled to control his excitable condition. Without any warning, he was prone to wild displays of movement, resembling dance, but also of a frenzied animal. About the only thing that seemed to calm him, besides playing with Kyra, was a new project that he had undertaken to develop a notation system for recording ballets in the same way that music was scored. He was attempting to develop a language of dance that would make it possible to recreate productions by following the notational scripts. It was a fabulous idea, composed of musical notes, drawings, words in several languages, geometric shapes—the only problem is that nobody else could decipher their meaning.

At the time, the Nijinskys had moved to Budapest and were living at the home of Romola's mother. World War I had begun, and as a Russian, Nijinsky was considered a prisoner of war. He was required to check in with the police every week to report his activities. When word leaked out that the strange foreigner was engaged in private scribblings in a notebook, authorities were called in to investigate. They were convinced that he was a spy who had developed a secret code that was being used to transmit military intelligence to the enemy. Unable to decipher the writings, the police called in mathematics and music experts, who eventually helped them to understand that the notations were nothing more than a new attempt to describe the essence of dance.

Back in the West, Diaghilev decided that he needed Nijinsky to revive his struggling ballet company. The war had decimated the ranks of his dancers, and he was desperate to regain his star attraction. Based on his considerable influence (as well as the intervention of the king of Spain), Diaghilev managed to get his former protégé exchanged for a comparable prisoner of war, and Nijinsky was able to leave Budapest. Nijinsky, who had by then fully recovered from his earlier depression, launched into the midst of a manic phase in which he was bubbling over with new ideas. He was hallucinating dances in his head in the same way that Virginia Woolf had done with her stories, Sylvia Plath with her poetry, and Charles Mingus with his music.

In the revived collaboration with his former lover, Nijinsky was promised exorbitant fees for his services—the staggering sum of $1,000 for each performance, which would be on par with any rock star today. Plus he was promised almost total creative control, even appointed as the director of the company on their planned tour of the United States to be partially subsidized by the Metropolitan Opera in New York. The frightening thing about this trip, however, was that he would have to function at the highest possible level without the support of either his sister or his former mentor. The Metropolitan Opera refused to work with Diaghilev directly, because they found him to be unprofessional. Because Diaghilev was relieved to keep as much distance as possible from his increasingly difficult and strange star performer, he was (unwisely) content to let Nijinsky handle the tour on his own. Perhaps Diaghilev thought this would teach his wayward protégé a lesson and bring him back into the fold.

Nijinsky's reputation as potentially violent and unpredictable made it difficult for him to attract all the personnel he would have liked for the American tour. He was forced to hire a stage designer, Robert Jones, after arriving in America, because none of the usual Russians would make themselves available. Describing the first impression of his new boss, Jones was struck immediately by the great dancer's charisma and energy.

> *He seems tired, bored, excited, all at once. I observe that he has a disturbing habit of picking at the flesh on the sides of his thumbs until they bleed. Through all my memories of this great artist runs the recurring image of those raw red thumbs. He broods and dreams, goes far away into reverie, returns again. At intervals his face lights up with a brief, dazzling smile. His manner is simple, ingratiating, so direct as to be almost humble.*

If that was Jones's first impression, his second was much less laudatory: "The maestro is waiting for me in a flame of rage. Torrents of Russian imprecations pour from his lips. . . . He lashes out at me with an insensate blind hate. It is a nightmare set in a blast furnace."

If his designer was bewildered and frustrated, the Russian dancers were even more confused. They already knew, by reputation if not from personal experience, that Nijinsky was the most innovative and eccentric choreographer in the world. Still, many were totally unprepared for the level of incoherent instructions that they would receive from their director. Because Nijinsky found it almost impossible to explain himself with words, all he could do was show what he wanted, even though so few others could precisely duplicate his movements. Eventually, the dancers went on strike, demanding better treatment. Then the conductor quit, complaining of ill treatment. The stress got to be so much that Nijinsky accidentally injured his ankle and was confined to his bed.

When Romola could not console him, another of the Russian dancers, Dmitri Kostrovsky, went to visit him, and they soon struck up a close friendship that some suspected developed into a sexual affair. Regardless of the particular kind of relationship, the companionship proved reassuring, but not sufficient to get Nijinsky out of bed. The American premiere at the Metropolitan Opera seemed in jeopardy with the lead dancer and director out of commission, but the management refused to cancel the performance; they had already invested too much money.

Without Nijinsky available to offer direction, the dancers were mystified as to how to complete their final rehearsals. At this point, they still had not been instructed about how the ballet was to end—they were left to their own devices to make up their own choreography on the eve of opening night. All Nijinsky could do was show up with a pronounced limp and no idea about what he would do during his own dance performances. When the music began, he improvised totally, dancing with abandon to a routine that was being made up as he went along. Nevertheless the audience loved the entire performance, having no idea that what they had seen was created from thin air.

Nijinsky introduced ballet to the masses in America and did so with performances that amazed the crowds in over fifty cities in four months. Charlie Chaplin saw one of his performances and was so moved that he called every one of the dancer's movements an act of poetry and every leap "a flight into strange fancy." Yet Chaplin was also struck by Nijinsky's essential sadness. He found that he couldn't stand to be around Nijinsky for very long or he would lose his own comical ability.

Tug of War

Upon returning from America and settling in Switzerland, Nijinsky was exhausted and depleted. He had realized while he was away that as much as he enjoyed the attention and adulation in America, he yearned desperately for his homeland. His wife, Romola, was from the privileged class, but he was a peasant at heart. He wanted badly to return to Russia, to live a simple life. It was a last attempt to save himself, to disconnect from the pressures of creativity and performance that were driving him crazy. Unfortunately, Romola would have no part of this. She enjoyed her luxuries and pleasures and absolutely insisted that her husband continue dancing, whatever the cost. It was not the creating of new ballets that Nijinsky found distasteful—he lived for that—but he was puzzled why furs and jewelry and clothes were so important to her; they meant absolutely nothing to him.

While Romola was pressuring her husband to go after the most lucrative possible jobs, he was getting pressure from another, familiar source as well—from Diaghilev, who wanted Nijinsky to rejoin his company. The two antagonists—wife and creative partner—began a battle of will, vying not only to influence Nijinsky but also to negotiate terms of a contract that would be favorable to one or the other. They were playing a tug-of-war over his future, yet Nijinsky seemed unconcerned about the outcome; he just didn't like the conflict between these two giants in his life. At one point, Romola threatened to leave him unless he would do her bidding and excise all the Russians from his life. To cement the deal, this highly manipulative woman actually arranged for a friend, the Duchess of Durcal, to have an affair with her husband, in order to keep him more malleable.

Nijinsky became more than a little suspicious and paranoid, perhaps with good reason. He no longer knew whom he could trust. When he accidentally stepped on a nail, he believed it was part of a conspiracy by Diaghilev to harm him. He believed further that there were attempts to assassinate him. It is no wonder, then, that he walked around so terrified and depressed. His personality was disintegrating, but he was still forced to dance.

An Amateur's Analysis

Nijinsky not only became dysfunctional in his personal life, but he could no longer perform on stage. During his final professional tour, scheduled for South America as World War I was winding down, he began to exhibit clear signs that he was losing complete control over himself. During rehearsals, he would sometimes refuse to allow himself to be lowered on a platform, convinced that there was a conspiracy to injure him as had happened to him as a child. During one performance toward the end of 1917, he actually froze, like a deer caught in the headlights, when the curtain was raised, and then he ran into the wings. The stage manager had to threaten him repeatedly to force him back on stage and begin his dance.

Finally, when she had no other choice, Romola had to admit that her husband was far too sick to continue. She arranged for them to move to St. Moritz in Switzerland, so he would have time to recover and she could acquaint herself with ski society.

Once resettled in the Alps, Romola socialized with the "beautiful people," while Nijinsky contented himself to hang out with the servants and children. He was still a simple man at heart, uncomfortable being around those he found pretentious.

There was one acquaintance of his wife whom Nijinsky found particularly sinister—a doctor by the name of Hans Frenkel, who was the house physician at one of the ski resorts. Romola was most likely having an affair with the surgeon, a situation that Nijinsky immediately suspected.

For reasons that Nijinsky could not fathom, Frenkel had a deep interest in him and decided that he would take the dancer on as a project, to cure him. For his part, Nijinsky distrusted the doctor's motives, this time his paranoia having some basis in reality.

It is probable that Nijinsky would provide endless interest and entertainment for any physician, psychiatrically trained or not, given the variety, intensity, and sheer weirdness of his symptoms. He was inclined to respond violently to the slightest imagined threat or provocation. To keep himself occupied while his wife was out skiing or carrying on with the doctor, Nijinsky began planning a new ballet—one in which the main character was a lunatic. As the dancer cast to play the lead, Nijinsky was now empowered to act as crazy as he wanted and consider it all part of the performance. There was now a method to his madness.

If there was one role that Nijinsky knew how to play instinctually—and dance with abandon—it was a madman. His main problem, however, was that he could not seem to shrug off the lunatic role once he removed his costume. He wandered around the town mumbling to himself, calling out to imagined companions, carrying a large cross and claiming that he was God (after all, he had been called the god of dance his whole adult life), yelling at those who looked at him for too long. He had become an embarrassment to his wife, who called for Frenkel to sedate her husband, which the doctor proceeded to do with a strong dose of chloral hydrate. Being drugged by his wife's lover did not quiet Nijinsky down as much as they had hoped. The only thing that seemed to calm him was working on the new ballet that he intended to perform for the villagers.

The idea for this dance performance, the very first one he would give since his return from tours in North and South America, was based on the most personal of motives. This was to be an enactment of a madman during the birth of creation. It would show the agony and the internal conflict of the artist at work. Nijinsky would "pretend" to be a lunatic expressing his most terrifying inner turmoil.

The well-heeled St. Moritz crowd of several hundred gathered together for the performance that was to be held in the ballroom of the elegant Suvretta Hotel overlooking a lake. It was a Sunday evening, January 19, 1919, with not much else to do in town. Besides, it wasn't every day that the world's most accomplished dancer would offer a private recital.

When a pianist began playing a piece by Schumann, Nijinsky walked out onto the impromptu stage wearing a loose-fitting white silk outfit that resembled pajamas. He carried with him a chair, which he proceeded to place in the center of the stage, arranged carefully, and then seated himself facing the audience. There were a few nervous coughs in the crowd, some whispers of anticipation, but otherwise people waited breathlessly to see what the brilliant but strange artist would do next.

Nijinsky sat perfectly still in the chair, staring out into the crowd, but seeming to look inward. He appeared to be comfortably arranged, feet planted on the floor, arms resting on his lap, yet he also appeared like a statue. Meanwhile the music played on, the Schumann filling some of the silence but not nearly enough without the accompaniment of the dancer.

One minute, two, five minutes, turned into ten, and Nijinsky just sat there, not moving a muscle, not even tapping a toe to the music. He just continued to stare forward as if in a fugue state, as if catatonic, as if he were truly a lunatic who was incapable of doing anything but taking a breath.

The crowd began to become restless, then a little agitated. They started whispering, then crying out in outrage about what was going on. Nijinsky failed to respond or even acknowledge that he heard them. He remained frozen.

Romola was so embarrassed that she started to walk onto the stage to end the debacle. She felt totally humiliated with all her friends in the audience. She kept looking nervously toward Dr. Frenkel, though whether she was looking for support from her lover, or assistance from her husband's analyst, was unclear. Before she could decide what to do, the pianist changed the music from Schumann to Chopin, which seemed to elicit a reaction in Nijinsky, the very first sign that he was even alive.

Still sitting in the chair, staring out into space, Nijinsky began to move one hand in time to the music, then the other. He stretched out his arms over his head, to the sides, then let them drop. Once again, he returned to an immobile state. He was doing an excellent job, he said to himself (later noted in his journal). He was trying to transmit to the audience a state of intense nervousness so that they might understand what it felt like to be crazy. The message seemed to go over their heads because people began leaving, muttering that Nijinsky was a fraud and an idiot for wasting their time.

Suddenly, the dancer jumped from the seat as if levitating and proceeded to whirl around the stage in some semblance of a dance but appeared as much like a chaos of movement. Yet compared with the sitting, those who were still in attendance appreciated the action. It would not last long.

Nijinsky stopped the dance as abruptly as it had begun and walked to the front of the audience, facing them directly. He then began to give a disjointed sermon, in halting French, about the horrors of war that were raging in Europe and that had kept him a prisoner in Hungary for so long. He next announced that he would do a dance of war and began leaping and twirling around the stage with such wild abandon that the audience was both amazed and horrified: it looked as if he might actually hurt himself (or someone else) by the reckless way he was soaring across the room. Then he collapsed on the floor.

Unsure whether to applaud or call a doctor, the audience filed out of the hotel convinced that what they had seen was the strangest, yet most interesting, dance that had ever been performed. They were never quite sure whether they had seen a madman in action or merely someone pretending to be one.

Frenkel decided that he would get to the bottom of things, once and for all, and make the determination whether Nijinsky was truly crazy or merely an excellent actor who enjoyed playing with other people's minds. Frenkel had read a bit of Sigmund Freud and Carl Jung, enough so that he got the general idea that he should help probe his patient's past in order to provide some insight into his current maladies. The main thing that Frenkel failed to understand (besides the impropriety of treating his lover's husband) was that such a therapeutic relationship must be built on trust, and Nijinsky clearly recognized the doctor as a dilettante who only had his own selfish interests in mind.

Treatment by the Masters

After two months of Frenkel's futile attempt at analyzing Nijinsky, Romola had no choice but to consider other options. Nijinsky, at this time, was so depressed that he could barely function at all, managing to write in his notebook:

I want to weep but I cannot because my soul hurts so much that I fear for myself. I feel pain. I am sick in my soul but not in my brain. The doctor

*[Frenkel] does not understand my sickness. I know what I need in order
to be well. My sickness is too great for me to be cured soon. I am not incurable. I am sick in my soul. I am poor. I am a beggar. I am unhappy.
I'm hideous. . . . I suffer. I suffer.*

There was certainly no way that anyone could mistake the degree
and depth of Nijinsky's suffering. He needed help desperately, and for
the next decade he would receive treatment from the most famous
psychiatrists and psychoanalysts in the world.

At only twenty-eight years of age, Nijinsky was so disturbed, depressed, and disoriented that he could no longer function. His daughter was being looked after by a nanny, because Romola showed so little
interest in the child and Nijinsky was now incapable of caring for her.
He was frightening to be around, volatile in his moods, as likely to lash
out at others as to hurt himself. Romola was beside herself and so
began research to find the best doctors available to restore her husband
to his previous "working order," so he could continue to dance and earn
money; that is, continue to be the goose who laid the golden egg.

Nijinsky's doctors during the 1920s represented a "who's who" in
the annals of psychiatry. He had the privilege of consulting the world's
most famous experts on mental illness, none of whom could do him
much good. First in the lineup was Professor Eugen Bleuler, the
world's authority on *schizophrenia,* who had invented that term to describe the phenomenon of "split mind." Upon examination of the patient, Bleuler concluded that indeed such a diagnosis was warranted:
Nijinsky was most certainly insane, perhaps incurably.

After consulting the world's most distinguished diagnostician,
Nijinsky was next carted off to the most exclusive psychiatric facility
in Europe, the Kuranstalt Bellevue, directed by none other than Dr.
Ludwig Binswanger, a psychoanalyst who was known far and wide for
his psychoanalytic expertise, his friendship with Freud, and his spe-
cialty of working with creative but unstable individuals. He would also
become one of the authors of a new movement in therapy, called *existential analysis,* which examined emotional problems in the larger
context of their personal meaning.

Binswanger tried an assortment of methods with his famous patient, including individual psychotherapy and analysis. One can only
imagine how challenging this must have been, considering that he
spoke German and French, and Nijinsky spoke Russian and Polish—
when he spoke at all.

Still, as a practitioner, the doctor was remarkably sympathetic, innovative, and pragmatic. He even organized a special ballet recital for Nijinsky, who performed a rather bizarre spectacle, pounding on the piano (he couldn't actually play the instrument) before beginning what was described as a "suicide-madness" dance, before he collapsed. Soon afterward, he lapsed into a catatonic stupor. So much for existential analysis.

Nijinsky remained at the Bellevue Sanatorium with Binswanger for over a year, receiving the best possible care from an assortment of doctors and attendants. There were times when he would appear charming and cooperative and other times when he would become violent or mute. The case notes by staff describe a man who met every imaginable definition of psychotic:

Sits in the same spot for 1½ hours. . . . I try to put him to bed. He jumps on the floor and moves around on his hands and feet like an animal, an ape, and eats like one too, until he goes back to the corner.

During the next decade, from 1919 to 1930, Nijinsky would be sent off to see dozens of other distinguished doctors and psychiatric experts. He would consult with Manfred Sakel, the inventor of insulin shock therapy, and receive hundreds of injections designed to produce seizures not unlike electroshock therapy. Binswanger and others thought it was a stretch to call it "therapy," rather than a primitive form of torture with no proven scientific rationale other than the observation that sometimes it seemed to shake a screw loose—or rather shake it back into place.

Romola finally consulted about her husband's condition with the greatest master of all, Sigmund Freud, but he didn't believe that psychoanalysis would be of much use to a patient like Nijinsky, who was in such an advanced state of deterioration. About that, he was assuredly correct.

Doctors tried an assortment of medications to suppress the most bothersome psychotic symptoms—neuroleptics, morphine, opium, scopolamine, bromides, barbiturates, insulin—none of them proved particularly useful. Nijinsky's psychosis seemed so severe—and so intractable—that his case appeared hopeless. Still, Romola would not give up, although her persistence again seemed based less on devotion to her husband and more on reviving their income and replenishing their dwindling savings. They had accumulated sizable wealth during

Nijinsky's best earning years, so she was used to indulging herself as if she were royalty.

Romola would occasionally visit her husband during the next years, checking on his condition (and hoping for a miracle cure), but she began a new life for herself, traveling around the capitals of Europe before eventually settling in America. She was, after all, the wife of the most famous dancer in the world and as such in great demand at social functions.

Last Resort

By 1930, Nijinsky was in his forties and had gained considerable weight over the years. Neither Romola, nor his daughter, had seen him in over three years because he was considered too dangerous to be around. (There is some possibility that he abused Kyra physically, if not sexually.) Romola had given birth to another child, Tamara, in 1920, at the recommendation of one of the doctors, who thought this might lead to a cure, but the actual paternity of the child was never determined.

When Binswanger followed up on Nijinsky's case in 1930 out of concern for his welfare (Binswanger had always been suspicious of Romola, whom he described as psychopathic), he found Nijinsky locked in a small apartment, raving and incoherent, smearing his own feces all over the walls, while at the same time Romola was staying at the elegant Savoy Hotel in London. Binswanger brought Nijinsky back to Bellevue to help him regain some semblance of functionality but Nijinsky's health was by then severely compromised; he exhibited both heart and digestive problems. Most disturbing of all, he began to cease moving and speaking, entering periodic catatonic states, occasionally awaking from them long enough to launch into frenzied (but artistic) dances before falling back into a stupor. It was as if the memory in his dancer's nervous system would spontaneously ignite.

In October 1934, after an absence of four years, Romola suddenly appeared at Bellevue accompanied by her lesbian lover and a distinguished expert from Vienna, Alfred Adler. Adler was one of the most famous disciples of Freud and the creator of what has become known as *individual psychology,* an approach to therapy that still enjoys considerable popularity because of its emphasis on family dynamics, early recollections and their impact on current behavior, and *social interest*—that is, the need for everyone to make altruistic contributions. Adler also invented the concepts of *inferiority* and *superiority complexes.* Unlike Freud, who had a rather pessimistic view of humankind—ruled by instincts and genetics—Adler favored a far more optimistic framework that instilled hope in his patients and their families. It is no wonder that Romola convinced him with all her persuasive powers to consult on the case. It must have seemed like a last resort.

Because Adler could not get much of a history from a patient who refused to respond much of the time, he was dependent on Romola to fill him in on Nijinsky's early history and life experiences. After Adler heard about the legacy of Nijinsky's dysfunctional family, his lack of a traditional education, his difficulties communicating in the best of times, and his predicament of coming from the lower-middle classes and being forced to operate with the upper class, it did not take him long to pronounce that his patient had an inferiority complex. As for a prognosis, he could not make that determination without assessing the likelihood of establishing some sort of alliance with the man. Adler was also one of the first theorists to advocate an equal, collaborative relationship between patient and therapist.

Romola disagreed in the strongest possible terms with Adler's diagnosis, insisting that her husband needed not greater understanding, but better medicines. After firing Adler, she contacted Freud's other great disciple, the mystic Carl Jung. Perhaps it was indeed some sort of mystical premonition that led Jung to have the good sense to avoid meddling in a case with so many complex extraneous factors that would make sound treatment almost impossible.

Nijinsky's heart problems continued to worsen as he approached fifty. He was now morbidly obese and totally weird. He would laugh inappropriately in a disturbing cackle. Even more upsetting for others was his tendency to masturbate publicly whenever the impulse struck him. He might be sitting in the dining hall, or the activity room, and all of a sudden whip out his penis and start stroking himself with sensuous enjoyment. Rather than feeling any shame, he appeared to enjoy the attention for his autoeroticism. In many ways, this is what it felt like for him to dance before an audience.

The Cure of His Comrades

War was coming to Europe again, and Romola was frustrated with the lack of progress at the expensive sanatorium, which had done her husband no good. She was running out of money, especially with her lavish purchases, and so she retrieved Nijinsky from Bellevue and decided to bring him back to Hungary with her.

Romola never appreciated just how much of a handful Nijinsky would be without doctors and attendants around to keep things under control. The change of scenery, the conflicts in the home, combined with the sounds of war, seemed to agitate him more. He would attack people without provocation; he once tried to kill Romola with a knife and only missed his opportunity because his coordination was so impaired. This was the last straw, and so she had him confined to a hospital in Budapest.

In March of 1945, as the war was coming to a close, the Russians began to invade German-occupied Hungary. When the bombing came dangerously close to the facility where Nijinsky was interned, he escaped with one of his attendants, who was concerned for their safety. It was while walking the streets that the strangest thing happened: as soon as Nijinsky saw the Russian soldiers and heard his own language, he came alive in a way that he had not for decades. The soldiers immediately recognized their famous countryman (even with a disheveled appearance)—Nijinsky was a living legend, one of the greatest Russians of the century—and so they embraced him as an old comrade.

Speaking his own language, being with his own people, revived him in ways that two decades of psychotherapy, two hundred injections of insulin, and dozens of other medications could not. So many years ago, he had told Romola, begged her even, that all he needed to be truly happy was to live as a peasant back in Russia. All he ever wanted was just to dance and to live in his homeland.

Nijinsky made a remarkable recovery of sorts during the next days he spent with his comrades. He joined them for meals, sat around their fire, sang Russian folk songs, and at one point, began to dance in a way that he had not been able to for many years. He danced Cossack dances with a passion that brought the crowd to their feet, clapping their hands and stamping their feet. At fifty-six, he was like a man reborn, a man who had finally found himself once again. During the hours that he danced for the soldiers, he was no longer psychotic or out of control. He appeared relaxed, composed, sociable, and yes, happy.

The Curtain Falls

Soon after the war ended, Romola insisted that they move to England, where Nijinsky could find better medical care than in Russia. He spent the last few years of his life seeking treatment for heart disease and kidney problems, although he stopped looking for psychiatric care because many of his symptoms had abated. He still continued to experience sleeplessness, moodiness, and irritability, but he could at times appear both coherent and charming.

Vaslav Nijinsky died of renal failure at the age of sixty on April 5, 1950. He remains today one of the most influential ballet dancers and choreographers who ever appeared on stage, virtually inventing the prominent role of male dancing to highlight his trademark leaps and artistic expressiveness, a role model for Nureyev, Baryshnikov, and many others. With his unique creativity, Nijinsky revolutionized the art of dance in a period of just eight intense years, before mental illness exerted its final grip.

Romola lived another thirty years after her husband's death, during which time she traveled the world, enjoyed lesbian affairs, and fell deeply in love with a transvestite actor who held an eerie resemblance to Nijinsky. She also became the protector of his reputation, writing two books about his life, and selectively editing his diaries for publication.

During all the years that Romola, the doctors, and the greatest mental health experts of the day tried to understand Vaslav Nijinsky and the source of his madness, all they really needed to do was read his own words in his diary. "People will say that Nijinsky has gone mad," he wrote, eternally frustrated that he was so misunderstood. "I am an ordinary man," he said quite simply. "I am a dancer. You will understand me when you see me dance."

CHAPTER NINE

Marilyn Monroe
Killed by Kindness

In May 1933, during the depths of the Depression, Tilford Hogan became another casualty of hopelessness. In poor health, as was his wife, unable to support his family, Tilford hanged himself in the barn at the age of seventy-five.

When Gladys Baker Mortensen heard about her grandfather's suicide, she became inconsolably depressed. She had already lost both of her parents to mysterious illnesses that had been rumored to be forms of insanity, so although she didn't know her grandfather, the very idea that he too might have been struck down by madness filled her with despair. She believed, with all her heart, that her turn was next. During the following weeks, Gladys became increasingly unstable. She stopped eating and sleeping, pacing the house all hours of the night while repeating prayers from the Bible. Then she started drinking to calm her nerves.

Gladys's daughter, Norma Jeane, was only seven, but she already had responsibilities well beyond her age. Norma Jeane could never be certain who her real father was because Gladys had been involved with several different men at the time she became pregnant. In the best of circumstances, Gladys was not exactly right in the head and was usually unable to care for her daughter. Norma Jeane could tell already that this latest stint at motherhood, less than a year long, was not going to last.

During the brief times she spent with her mother, Norma Jeane was always uncomfortable, perhaps in large part because Gladys had no idea how to respond to a child. She was a nervous, agitated woman, who could become upset by almost anything the little girl would do. When Norma Jeane would sit quietly reading a book, she had to be particularly cautious about turning the pages without making a single sound because her mother complained that the noise was too loud. Gladys complained constantly about the burdens of parenthood, how that alone was driving her crazy. There is some indication that at one point, she may have tried to kill her daughter during a loss of control.

Norma Jeane was plain in those days, with dirty blonde hair, green eyes, a slight build, but a bewitching smile. She was terrified about the changes her mother was undergoing but felt utterly helpless to do anything about it, except to keep out of the way. She had already lived in as many foster homes as years she had been alive. She could see that she would soon be on her way to another one.

When Gladys failed to improve, she was taken to a hospital for psychiatric care, with a poor prognosis. She didn't respond to medications prescribed and became only more withdrawn over time. Norma Jeane was an orphan again and would spend her childhood being shuttled from one home to the next, exchanged from one mother figure to another.

No Need for an Introduction

It hardly seems necessary to identify young Norma Jeane as the child who would grow up to be Marilyn Monroe. There have been over six hundred books written about her, plus a critical biography of the *other* biographies and an encyclopedia that lists everything you could ever want to know. Yet in the volumes written about Marilyn Monroe, there is almost always a focus on her mysterious death, her lurid affairs, her marriages to famous personalities, and her reputation as a blonde bombshell and sex goddess. What is much less understood is not only how emotionally tortured she was but also how that fundamental inner loss and vulnerability made her so powerful as an actress and performer.

Marilyn Monroe's work in films has not always been taken seriously. It has been said that she was only a pinup girl, a dumb blonde, who happened to capitalize on her sexuality to entrap powerful men—

the Kennedys, Joe DiMaggio, playwright Arthur Miller, and Frank Sinatra—to mention a few. It was as if only luck, or pure sexual magnetism, opened all those doors to make her known as perhaps the most famous celebrity of all time. There is nobody whose image is more recognizable and few who have attained such lofty popularity upon a tragic death.

Yet even feminists like Gloria Steinem became a convert to Monroe's power as an entertainer, as well as her victimization as a sex symbol. In the films *Some Like It Hot, The Seven Year Itch,* and *Gentlemen Prefer Blondes,* Marilyn Monroe established herself as a whole new category of comedic charisma. It was more than her acting ability but also her pure energy, her passion, and her sense of humor that captured and delighted audiences. She was not a creative genius in the same sense as some others in this book, but she distinguished herself as an artist who essentially created herself, who transformed plain little Norma Jeane into the luminous, irresistible, sensual icon—Marilyn Monroe! And in this role, she shared Judy Garland's ability to move audiences like nobody else even imagined was possible.

Some would say that Marilyn Monroe was not so much a great singer, or actor, but rather a brilliant *presence.* It was said that the camera "loved her." She worked very hard during the early years of her career to create an image, a way of using her eyes, her body, her hair and voice, to transcend ordinary beauty and sexual attractiveness to reach a higher, almost spiritual level of human connection with her audience. She was able to reveal simultaneously an innocence, sadness, and vulnerability, as well as a strong, unerring moral intelligence. Her still photographs continue to be both alluring and captivating. Unfortunately, as much as anyone profiled in this book, Marilyn Monroe's psychological instability was at the core of her creative performances.

The Good Girl

Norma Jeane had first been placed as a foster child with Wayne and Ida Bolender when she was an infant. Gladys had just been too busy, too preoccupied with her work as a film splicer in the movie industry, and too involved in her social life to take care of a baby. She figured the kid would be better off in a good home.

The Bolenders were paid $20 per month by the state of California to take in foster children, a significant contribution to their household income, supplementing Wayne's salary as a mailman. These were religious people, strict in their ways, harsh in their discipline; yet they were essentially caring toward the abandoned child. This devotion to foster parenting, however, was in no way compromised by their insistence on strict adherence to rules and their complete intolerance for disobedience. There would be no dancing, no card playing, no bad manners or back talk. Most of all, the Bolenders considered Hollywood, located just a few miles down the road, as a place of devil worship, where they made those horrid movies. Ida made it clear that going to movie theaters was a mortal sin that would surely condemn Norma Jeane to burn in hell.

In spite of their good intentions, the Bolenders were inclined to punish transgressions of their laws with brutal force. More than once, Norma Jeane was seen beaten by a razor strap, beginning in infancy when she wouldn't stop crying. Her mother would rescue her for a period of time, but she just couldn't sustain any lasting interest in parenting.

Within the pious and rigid atmosphere of her foster home, Norma Jeane tried to fit in as best she could. She was frightened that any lapse on her part could very well land her out in the street. She overheard "Aunt Ida" say on more than a few occasions that she wanted to get rid of that strange little girl who made her nervous. So Norma Jeane did what she was told, as much as possible, and tried not to call too much attention to herself.

Such was the situation when one day in late 1933, when Norma Jeane was almost eight, one of the borders staying in the house yelled her name: "Come here, Norma," Mr. Kimmel called out to her from his room. He could hear her soft footsteps tiptoeing down the hallway.

Norma Jeane approached the room diffidently, assuming that he had some sort of errand for her to run. Perhaps he'd allow her to keep the change, enough to buy an ice cream.

"Yes, Mr. Kimmel?" Norma Jeane said, sticking her head in the door. She could see the man sitting on the bed with a funny smile on his face.

"Come on in," he repeated again, gesturing with his hand. Norma Jeane was a little afraid of Mr. Kimmel, who could be mean at times. She couldn't recall even hearing whether he had a first name or not. He was always Mr. Kimmel, even to the Bolenders.

As soon as Norma Jeane stepped fully into the room, Kimmel quickly walked to the door, shut it slowly, and turned the key in the lock. "Now you can't get out," he said with a smile that was less than reassuring. He was pretending this was some sort of game, but Norma Jeane already knew enough about men to recognize that was not at all a good situation to find herself in.

"I stood staring at him," she recalled years after the incident. "I was frightened, but I didn't dare yell. I knew if I yelled, I would be sent back to the orphanage in disgrace again. Mr. Kimmel knew this too."

Kimmel reached out to grab Norma Jeane, and she stood there powerless to resist him. As soon as he put his arms around her and started to hug and kiss her, she started to fight back, to punch and kick, trying not to make any noise that would get her in trouble. There was something terribly wrong about this, but she just knew that she would be the one blamed for the trouble.

"He was stronger than I was," she remembered, "and wouldn't let me go. He kept whispering to me to be a good girl."

A good girl seemed to mean that she would take off all her clothes and let him put his thing inside of her. He was so big, and she was so small, there was nothing she could do. He kept telling her, over and over again, to be a good girl, and all she could think of was that if she didn't do what he said, she'd be out of the house before nightfall.

When Kimmel finally unlocked the door and let Norma Jeane out, she immediately ran down to Ida, her foster mother, to tell her what happened. But before she could get even a few words out, before she could even say, "Mr. Kimmel did something . . . ," Ida shushed her and told her to keep her mouth shut. It was as if Ida knew exactly what had happened but didn't want to risk losing her boarder by any sort of embarrassing scandal. She looked at Norma Jeane with the sort of accusing stare that seemed to imply that whatever trouble she found herself in was all her own darned fault.

Although Norma Jeane did not exactly lead a life out of Dickens, in which she was cruelly beaten, neglected, and abused in orphanages, she did experience more challenges than any child should ever have to face. Apart from the rape incident, which is more than enough to spoil any childhood memories and sense of trust, she was treated reasonably well in the Bolender household. It's not known whether Kimmel ever tried to assault her again or even how much longer he remained in the house, but Norma Jeane spent the rest of her childhood living in an oppressive atmosphere that left her with permanent wounds and a lasting sense of abandonment, painful separation, and a yearning for attachment and security that could never be filled.

A Mantra to Become a Star

It was soon after the incident with Mr. Kimmel that Gladys reappeared in her daughter's life, whisking her away from the foster home and taking her to live in a small bungalow that she had purchased in the Venice Beach area of Los Angeles, a short commute to where Gladys then worked, cutting film at Consolidated Film Industries during the editing process. Gladys never would have attempted to care for this eight-year-old girl on her own, if not for her friend and supervisor, Grace McKee, with whom she shared an active social life. The two were inseparable and Grace, more so than Gladys, took a keen interest in this child who showed so much sparkle.

This was all very confusing for Norma Jeane, who had always called her foster mother Aunt Ida, and now she was largely under the care of this strange red-headed woman, Gladys, who sometimes flitted in and out of her life. She was supposed to call this woman mother, but it was actually Grace who seemed to take more responsibility for Norma Jeane's care. It was even more confusing for the little girl that whereas she had always been told that going to films would corrupt her soul, her mother and Grace were now dropping her off at movie theaters every chance they got. They used the movies of Claudette Colbert, Jean Harlow, or Mae West to baby-sit the little girl while they went carousing about town.

As the head of an important department in the film industry, Grace, who was now at Columbia Pictures, was exposed daily to the inner world of filmmaking. She was obsessed with Hollywood stars, and without a family of her own, she was determined to launch the acting career of her surrogate daughter. When Gladys was committed to a psychiatric hospital for an indefinite period of time, Grace became the major guardian in Norma Jeane's life.

For her part, Norma Jeane had always been shy, malleable, and eager to please—qualities that were critical for her survival when she was living in other people's homes. She was not permitted to rebel openly or to be defiant in any way. But that did not stop her from engaging in a rich fantasy life. One of her favorites foreshadowed the major obsession of her life:

I dreamed that I was standing up in church without any clothes on, and all the people there were lying at my feet on the floor of the church, and I walked naked, with a sense of freedom, over their prostrate forms, being careful not to step on anyone.

The screen divas with whom Norma Jeane now shared her week-ends only fueled her fantasies further. She dreamed of a time that she, too, might feel some sense of power and control over her life, just like Harlow or West, or make people laugh, just like Charlie Chaplin. Grace repeated to the impressionable girl, over and over like a mantra, "You're going to be a star. You're going to be big, bigger than all the rest of them." In time, even Norma Jeane believed it could be so.

Center of Attention

During the mid-1930s, from age eight to twelve, Norma Jeane would be shifted back and forth between a half dozen foster homes and or-phanages. Grace had promised to take care of her and was now her legal guardian, but a new romance had shifted Grace's priorities in an-other direction; and she couldn't always make time for the full time responsibilities of a parent. She would dutifully visit Norma Jeane in the orphanages and foster homes, however, taking her on outings to see movies. As a special treat, they would visit Grauman's Chinese Theatre, where Norma Jeane would place her small hands inside the impressions of the stars she was destined to follow. Among them, Jean Harlow, the erotic, platinum blonde and comedienne, would be the model they would follow. "There's no reason you can't grow up to be just like her," Grace would tell Norma Jeane again and again. Even when Norma Jeane was only eight years old, Grace was already taking her to beauty parlors to fix her hair and makeup.

The trauma of her sexual molestation in the Bolenders' foster home was repeated again once Norma Jeane finally moved in with Grace and her new husband, Doc Goddard. One night, Doc got drunk and forced himself on the eleven-year-old girl, fondling and kissing her until she pushed him off and ran away sobbing and crying. Grace could see more trouble brewing unless she took some action, so Norma Jeane was sent off again, this time to live with members of her mother's fam-ily. Her already traumatic childhood would only grow worse.

While she was living with an aunt and cousins, one of the boys, two years older than Norma Jeane, attempted to rape her. She was by that time twelve years old and already the veteran of several sexual assaults in various foster homes. These events would make an indelible im-pression on her, affecting her sense of trust in relationships, her sex-uality, and the image of sexual pleasure that she would use ultimately to enthrall generations of men.

Norma Jeane was next sent to live with Grace's aunt, Ana, the first truly stable, consistent, and genuinely caring adult in her life. Yet as hard as Ana tried to get through to the shell-shocked adolescent, Norma Jeane was beyond the point where she could ever trust another mother figure. Much of her time was spent in a fantasy world, reliving scenes from her favorite movies, picturing herself as the sultry Jean Harlow playing opposite Clark Gable.

At the time that Norma Jeane began junior high school in 1939 while living with Aunt Ana, she was in the most secure living situation of her life. The biggest change in her life, however, occurred as if her fondest wish had come true. She desperately wanted to fill the shoes of the stars at Grauman's Theatre, as well as Grace's expectations: now the fantasy began to become real. By the age of thirteen, Norma Jeane had begun turning into a voluptuous beauty, developing physical assets that she was never shy about displaying in the most provocative way possible. She rarely wore a bra beneath her tight-fitting sweaters and was sometimes sent home from school for wearing skirts that were either too tight or too short. For the first time in her life, she was enjoying being the center of attention.

Norma Jeane spent hours in front of the mirror staring at herself, as if amazed at the person who looked back. She was frequently discovered in the girls' bathroom primping and preening, freshening her makeup, brushing her hair. It was as if every day she was preparing to go on stage, which in a sense was very much how her life felt. This was a girl who, no matter how hard she tried to stay out of the way, had been repeatedly rejected by women and assaulted by men. Now, finally, she was enjoying a degree of acceptance from peers, and more than that, the discovery of her power over men—based purely on the way she looked.

"At thirteen everyone said I looked eighteen," Norma Jeane recalled later, "and the boys in their twenties were trying to date me. I may have been a baby on the inside, but on the outside I had the body of a woman."

One such older man, Jim Dougherty, took an interest in Norma Jeane about the time she turned fifteen. Although Dougherty was reluctant to pursue his attraction because Norma Jeane was so young, Grace actually encouraged the relationship, thinking it would help the girl mirror Jean Harlow, who had also married so young and experienced chronic abuse. Norma Jeane was essentially given a choice: either marry Jim or go back to the orphanage.

Norma Jeane gave the matter some thought. She liked Jim and appreciated the way he treated her like a proper woman instead of a girl. He was handsome and had a nice car. With nowhere else to go, and adamant about not returning to the orphanage, she told Grace that she had just one question.

"What's that, dear?" Grace said with a gentle smile. She was glad that Norma Jeane was at least considering the proposal. She felt terribly guilty about abandoning the girl again.

"I was wondering," Norma Jeane said shyly.

"Yes, go ahead."

"Well, I was wondering if I could marry Jim, but we wouldn't have sex."

"Don't worry," Grace tried to reassure her. "You'll learn."

It is difficult to imagine just how terrified Norma Jeane must have been. She was still a child in so many ways, still so innocent and sheltered. But she was also a girl without many choices. She married Jim two days after she turned sixteen. He was twenty-one. At least now, she would finally have her own home, from which nobody could ever send her away.

Screen Test

Norma Jeane called Jim "Daddy" and responded to him that way, out of deep need for him to take care of her. When he enlisted in the Merchant Marines in 1943 and then was sent to the Pacific, Norma Jeane went to work at Burbank Airport, where she folded parachutes for the war effort. It was there that army photographers first discovered her, and it was there that the world finally discovered just how alluring and photographic this young woman really was.

One photographer, David Conover, took a special interest in her, producing a portfolio of publicity shots that were used in army propaganda recruiting, and he later helped her to begin a modeling career. In her file at the modeling agency, it was noted that she had a perfect figure, 36-24-34 and she had perfect teeth, but they recommended that she bleach her hair.

Norma Jeane learned quickly and was able to work with photographers to produce studio and outdoor work that had an enormous appeal. She soon became more in demand, with many sessions and new appearances in print. In 1946, by the time Norma Jeane was twenty, she had appeared on over thirty magazine covers, including

Parade and *Glamorous Models.* She was noted for her easy, playful laugh, but few realized that its source was not amusement but often contempt for how phony the business was. "They thought that was great, they had a great smile from you, and they just snapped away, thinking that, well, I was having a good time."

While Jim was still overseas, Norma Jeane's modeling career really started to flourish when she joined the biggest and most prestigious agency: Miss Snively. With financial independence, she realized that she didn't need to be married anymore in order to survive. She wrote to Jim and told him that the marriage was over. Then she made the transition to bathing suits and started bleaching her hair, because she was told that gentlemen prefer blondes.

It was no less than Howard Hughes who first considered Norma Jeane as a film actress, having seen her photograph on a magazine cover. Once Fox Studios heard about Hughes's interest, they made contact with the new sensation and signed her right away. She had been asked to make a screen test, one that was so successful that the producer, Leon Shamroy, was totally blown away.

"You've got it, baby," he pronounced after seeing the film. When Darryl F. Zanuck, head of 20th Century Fox, reviewed the test, he immediately signed her to a contract, after changing her name to Marilyn Monroe.

For Fox to invest in a young, unknown talent, one without any experience in the industry, was a certain risk, which was motivated primarily by trumping Howard Hughes. But once she signed, the studio demanded that their new employee take acting and singing lessons, at her own expense. This meant starving on her meager salary of $75 per week, as well as trying to keep her self-respect, a prospect that became increasingly difficult as money ran short. When the studio did not renew her contract after the first term, Marilyn was forced to trade sexual favors on the street in order to survive. She drew the line at accepting money but gratefully accepted a meal from a customer cruising Santa Monica Boulevard.

Marilyn was by then devoting herself to the serious study of acting. She began attending The Actors Lab, a group of stage actors who met on a regular basis to read plays and critique one another's performances. Marilyn appeared in several amateur productions, but her low self-esteem, combined with a tendency to stutter uncontrollably when she was nervous, made her the subject of ridicule. Nevertheless she was admired for her persistence, her ambition, her sheer drive to succeed. Few had any doubt that someday she would indeed become a star.

Mentors

While attending a party in February 1948, one of the most powerful Hollywood producers, Joseph Schenck of Fox, became totally entranced with Marilyn Monroe. This was not a young man with a mild infatuation; Schenck was actually sixty-nine and had been around the most beautiful women in the world all his life. But there was something about this woman that was so radiant, so captivating, that he could not think about anything else.

Schenck and Monroe would become lovers of sorts, striking a deal that he would help her with her career if she would become his occasional companion. As Schenck was an old man in poor health, it took all of Marilyn's considerable charms and skill to bring him to satisfaction. During those rare times when he could manage an erection, Marilyn was immediately called to take the situation in hand. If she arrived too late, they would both giggle and spend the evening having a leisurely dinner instead.

Schenck would be the first of several such powerful mentors who would aid Marilyn's career in exchange for sexual favors, a kind of reciprocal exploitation. He got her a new contract at Columbia Studios that helped in the short run, but far more significantly, he signed her up to study acting under the tutelage of Natasha Lytess, one of the most renowned coaches in Hollywood. Natasha became even more infatuated with Marilyn than Schenck had been and spent the next six years during their often tumultuous relationship mooning over her and hoping to consummate her love. Just as Marilyn had leveraged her position with other mentors in order to gain some advantage, so too was she able to do so with Natasha, but without having to deliver anything more than mild flirtations.

One might say that part of Marilyn's creative genius was her ability to persuade both men and women to act as her advocate by casting herself in the most persuasive role. For Schenck, it was a naive vixen; for Natasha, it was the ingénue devoted to her mistress. Natasha was later to admit, "I wish I had one-tenth of Marilyn's cleverness. The truth is, my life and my feelings were very much in her hands. I was the older woman, the teacher, but she knew the depth of my attachment to her." She would not be the last to confess such an obsession.

Another mentor who helped Marilyn significantly during this period was Johnny Hyde, an executive at the William Morris Agency and one of the most important agents in the film industry at that time. When he met Marilyn at a New Year's Eve party, he fell so hard for her that she was to become the complete focus of his life. Although he was twice her age, she appreciated the way he took care of her and decided to let him manage her career. In a sense, he shaped her into the perfect embodiment of our culture's fantasy of beauty. In addition to her elocution lessons with Natasha, Hyde put the finishing touches on her appearance, paying for orthodontics to correct a slight overbite and plastic surgery to remove a small bump on her nose. He also schooled her in how to behave in the highest echelons of Hollywood culture. Although she never made it past tenth grade, Marilyn started devouring books by Marcel Proust, Thomas Wolfe, Sigmund Freud, and Dostoyevsky. She took a literature class at UCLA. She became one of the first women devotees of weightlifting and jogging to hone her body and increase her physical stamina. In addition, Hyde taught her to use all of her physical attributes to become the perfect lover.

Hyde made it the major priority of his life to help his girlfriend launch her movie career. Her first appearance in a major film, described in the opening credits as "Introducing Marilyn Monroe," was in the Marx Brothers' *Love Happy*. During Marilyn's cameo, Groucho opens the door to find this goddess in a slinky dress.

"What can I do for you?" he asked with a leer and the distinctive raising of a thick eyebrow. Then he looks directly at the camera and says, "What a ridiculous question."

Based on his many contacts and obsessive persistence, Hyde eventually succeeded in landing Marilyn breakthrough parts with two of the best directors in the business—Joe Mankiewicz for *All About Eve* and John Huston for *The Asphalt Jungle,* both major dramatic films released in 1950 to wide acclaim. Hyde never lived to see his efforts come to fruition: he died the same year at the age of fifty-four. His last words were asking about Marilyn.

Another parting gift from Johnny Hyde to his protégé and lover was a newly negotiated contract with 20th Century Fox on far different terms than what had been offered just a few years earlier. Rather than making $75 per week, Marilyn would get a salary starting at $500, which would double every year thereafter. To her credit, Marilyn cared little about the money, as long as she had enough to eat.

"I just want to be wonderful," she declared, more out of relief that she would be working rather than from any joy over the level of compensation.

Puffy Eyes

Marilyn may not have been "in love" with Johnny Hyde, but she was certainly strongly attached to him and grateful for all his help. After he died, she felt abandoned and alone again. She was by then living with her acting coach, Natasha, but Natasha's attentions paled in comparison to that of her lover, Johnny Hyde, who had sacrificed his family, his reputation, and much of his career, in order to help her. Although warned to stay away from his funeral so that she didn't embarrass Hyde's widow and children, Marilyn nevertheless attended, becoming hysterical at the sight of his coffin.

A few days later, Natasha returned home to her apartment to find Marilyn's bedroom door shut and a note on her own pillow that read, "I leave my car and fur stole to Natasha." When she rushed to Marilyn's room, she found another note on the door that warned Natasha's daughter not to enter under any conditions. With a sense of complete dread, Natasha entered the room to find Marilyn unconscious, having taken an overdose of sleeping pills. Not knowing what else to do, Natasha reached inside Marilyn's mouth to find a glob of melted pills that had regurgitated. At age twenty-five, Marilyn confessed that this had actually been her third attempt at suicide, having tried twice previously after her divorce from Jim Dougherty.

One of the recurring patterns of Marilyn's life, beginning since early childhood, was fear of abandonment. She had never known her father, told by her mother that he had left them and later died in a car accident. (This was not true, but Gladys was never sure who the real father was.) Then her mother abandoned her, not once, but over and over again, as she pawned Marilyn off to foster homes and orphanages. Marilyn would spend her whole life looking for older men to take care of her, yet she could never commit to deep intimacy with any of them, fearing she would be left alone all over again.

It could be theorized that this most recent suicide attempt—even *all* the later such efforts, including the final one, were never actually intended to be serious. Equally likely is that although Marilyn felt sufficient despair to end her life on several occasions, there was a counterbalanced will to survive that in the end overrode her self-destructive urges.

Whether this latest pill-swallowing binge represented serious suicidal intent or not, it was clear that her reaction to loss and her feelings of abandonment led her to operate on the edge.

During this same period, Marilyn was playing the part of a seductive secretary in the movie *As Young as You Feel* and was already showing early signs of the emotional fragility that would frustrate directors to no end. The director, Harmon Jones, tried everything to calm her down, but she could not seem to stop crying at the most inopportune moments. The worst part, as far as he was concerned, is that his actress would develop puffy eyes, which could not be concealed with makeup alone. Until she could regain control of herself, he would have to work around her scenes.

This time, her liaison with a previous lover would be replaced by two candidates, both friends, who were introduced to her at the same time. Elia Kazan, a noted actor and director, would become her lover for a few months in 1952, and his companion, playwright Arthur Miller, would someday become her husband. It is interesting that both were towering intellectuals who had established their reputations on the New York stage. Miller had already written one of the most important plays of the century, *Death of a Salesman,* which had been awarded a Pulitzer Prize. He would go on to write other plays that established him as one of the most memorable writers for stage, and eventually for the screen, writing *The Misfits* for Marilyn.

During this same time, in 1953, a story broke connecting the new Fox star to a nude calendar based on photographs that were taken of her four years earlier. One of those photos of Marilyn was purchased by Hugh Hefner and appeared in the inaugural issue of *Playboy* magazine. If Marilyn Monroe had not been known based on her brief film career, the scandal and thrill associated with her nude photographs catapulted her to fame. Contemporary politicians could take a lesson from the way she handled the affair. Rather than denying the accusations, she humbly and apologetically acknowledged that during a time when she was dirt poor, she tried to earn extra money so she had enough to eat. She then observed wryly that the photos did not reveal her at her best angle.

Marilyn Monroe was now officially the heir to Jean Harlow, a genuine sex goddess, and also the biggest star at Fox Studio since Shirley Temple and Betty Grable. She received over two thousand letters per week from fans, more than any other star. She was the champion pinup girl among soldiers stationed in Korea. There were feature articles written about her in dozens of major magazines. She had yet to star in a major motion picture, and yet she was already a sensation, America's naughty sweetheart.

A Storybook Romance with an Unhappy Ending

Marilyn continued to work on improving herself, not only under the guidance of Natasha, who was retained on a salary higher than that of the star, but also with Michael Chekhov, another acting coach and cousin to the immortal Russian playwright. Between her two teachers, she was pushing herself to new levels of acting so that she could hold her own with the established professionals on the set. Indeed the training seemed to pay off, as costars like Joseph Cotton (*Niagara*), Betty Grable (*How to Marry a Millionaire*), Cary Grant (*Monkey Business*), Anne Bancroft (*Don't Bother to Knock*), and Robert Mitchum (*River of No Return*) expressed nothing but admiration for her performances.

During 1952, the same year she became friendly with Kazan and Miller, she met another superstar of American culture, perhaps the only man alive who could approach her level of fame: Joe DiMaggio. One of the greatest baseball players of all time had just retired when he saw a picture of Marilyn in the newspaper. He contrived to set up a meeting with her, but, by her account, "he struck out." Even though he called her every day for two weeks, she refused to go out with him again, that is, until she began to learn more about him. They began a slow courtship, lasting over a year, during which time DiMaggio described their chemistry as "a good double-play combination."

In retrospect, it is easy to see how their relationship could not possibly have lasted. Two of the most famous people in the world weren't used to sharing center stage. To add to the challenges, Marilyn Monroe was the most desired woman alive, and DiMaggio was a very jealous man, not to mention being the most dour of fellows. They had absolutely nothing in common except their fame and an intense sexual attraction. Their marriage was doomed almost from the start.

It was while traveling to Japan with DiMaggio on one of his baseball appearances that Marilyn agreed to entertain the combat troops then stationed in Korea. She had never performed before a live audience in her life but immediately agreed (without her husband's consent) to do a one-woman show in six different locations. Even though it was the dead of winter, she appeared in a tight, formfitting, low-cut dress, and sang her heart out, including her signature "Do It to Me" and "Diamonds Are a Girl's Best Friend." The audiences almost started a riot, and for Marilyn, it was the absolute highlight of her life. Like

Judy Garland, she only felt truly accepted and loved when she was in front of ten thousand adoring fans.

The more famous Marilyn became, the more possessive DiMaggio became. She had been careful to omit the word *obey* from their marriage vows because she had no intention of giving up her career or deferring all important decisions to her husband. As proud as Marilyn was of her appearances in Korea, DiMaggio started to sulk, because she was getting far more attention. The last straw seems to have been the now-classic photograph taken of Marilyn on Lexington Avenue in New York during the filming of *The Seven Year Itch* with Tom Ewell. She is captured on film standing over a grate on the sidewalk with her dress blown in the air, showing her in a pair of scanty underwear. The next day, she appeared with bruises on her shoulder, only one of several instances in which DiMaggio beat her when she wouldn't do his bidding. Marilyn filed for divorce two weeks later.

Until his death, DiMaggio would never speak about his relationship with Marilyn, not in any interview, nor to any reporter, nor in any autobiography. He remained devoted to her throughout his life, never remarrying. He would be the one to make her funeral arrangements, the one who would break down at the side of her casket, and the one who would have fresh roses delivered to her grave in perpetuity.

Studying in New York

One thing that DiMaggio had given to Marilyn was the confidence and the resources to stand up to 20th Century Fox, which had been taking advantage of their star in the same way that MGM had done with Judy Garland. Marilyn was still being paid only a fraction of her worth and had no control whatsoever over her roles. She was tired of being the sexy blonde and longed to stretch herself creatively.

Marilyn not only cut ties with her husband, but she also was trying to extricate herself from the complex relationship with Natasha, the coach who insisted on being present at every one of her protégé's takes on the set. Natasha was driving the directors crazy, and according to most who were present at the time, she was not helping Marilyn much as an actress. Natasha was so obsessed with correct pronunciation that it was hampering Marilyn's ability to become a more natural actress. Although Natasha would be kept on the studio payroll for a number of years, by the beginning of 1954 she was kept off the sets as much as possible and was not allowed access to her former pupil.

Another final ending in Marilyn's life was far more tragic: Grace, her surrogate mother and mentor, was found dead after years of alcohol and drug abuse. Like so many of the important people in Marilyn's life, another woman killed her pain through suicide. At this time, Gladys was still in and out of mental institutions, all but dead to Marilyn as well.

Marilyn went to New York, as much to reinvent herself as to escape Hollywood. She longed to be a serious actress, someone respected for her artistry rather than her sex appeal. For this transformation, she sought the counsel of Lee Strasberg, chief acting coach at the legendary Actors Studio. Lee Strasberg and his wife, Paula, were advocates of the Russian Stanislavky's *method acting* and had worked with Marlon Brando, James Dean, Paul Newman, Rod Steiger, Steve McQueen, and Shelley Winters, teaching these and other famous actors how to draw on their own past and inner life to achieve total psychological immersion into a role.

Strasberg found Marilyn Monroe to be the most nervous, self-conscious actor he had ever seen, but he saw this as a sign of strength in her sensitivity. "It was almost as if she had been waiting for a button to be pushed and when it was pushed a door opened and you saw a treasure of gold and jewels." In the coming years, he would become her rabbi, therapist, teacher, and friend. He would also be quoted as saying that the two greatest actors he had ever worked with were Marlon Brando—and Marilyn Monroe.

Marilyn was privileged to receive three months of private lessons from Strasberg before she was considered ready to join his famed Actors Studio, an experimental laboratory and encounter group where actors were given the opportunity to extend the limits of their abilities. The effects of his influence could hardly be underestimated with his prize pupil. In the next two years, from 1954 to 1956, Marilyn Monroe went from making vapid recreational movies to *Bus Stop,* her finest performance (some would say one of the best of all time). With Strasberg's guidance, she had chosen her own material, director, and cinematographer, designed her own costumes and makeup, and finally discovered her creative potential.

Unconscious Excavations and Their Consequences

During their work together, Strasberg could hardly ignore the deep emotional fragility of the actress, far more challenging than he could handle. He referred her to Dr. Margaret Hohenberg, a psychiatrist and psychoanalyst, whose assignment was to mine Marilyn's unconscious, to unleash even more of her creative potential. Unfortunately, nobody seemed to explain to Marilyn the concept of *informed consent,* that there were serious risks to such an undertaking, because once traumas from the past are stirred up, they can regain momentum and take on a life of their own.

Almost immediately after beginning therapy, Marilyn developed severe insomnia and anxiety attacks, for which she was sedated with barbiturates and sedatives prescribed by other doctors (without consulting her psychiatrist). This business of stirring up the past was very disturbing to her, especially with therapy sessions four days a week, and twice weekly meetings with Strasberg that could be even more emotionally evocative. She may have been discovering her deeper creative potential, but it was coming at the expense of her mental health.

"But I do want to be wonderful, you know?" Marilyn explained. "I know some people may laugh about that, but it's true. . . . I'm trying to become an artist, and to be true, and I sometimes feel I'm on the verge of craziness."

Both her therapist and acting coach urged her to keep a journal of the thoughts and feelings that came up during her psychological work. From reviewing these notes, it can be seen that she was exploring her lifelong depression and its origins in her childhood and especially how she used her sexuality to hide from feelings that she had buried long ago. As interesting as these insights might have been, the effects on her behavior were far from helpful. She appeared to grow far worse from the therapy, a not unusual occurrence during the early stages, but a circumstance that was hardly practical for an actress who was only going to be available for a few months' worth of treatment.

Beauty and the Brain

Marilyn's second order of business in returning to New York was to rekindle the attraction to Arthur Miller. Many years earlier, in 1950 when she was shooting *As Young as You Feel,* she met the famous writer in the studio cafeteria and reported it was love at first sight. She vowed she would someday marry him. Miller, as well, had remained obsessed with the actress from the time of their first meeting, feeling shivers when he first shook her hand. Their relationship ignited during Marilyn's period in New York at the Actors Studio. Although there was a strong physical magnetism between them, as well as the attraction of opposites, there were also warning signs about their basic incompatibility. Marilyn, in particular, loved the *idea* of being with the great Arthur Miller but felt intimidated by his intellect. Miller didn't make this any easier by sometimes ridiculing his fiancée as only an uneducated actress.

They were called the Beauty and the Brain, the odd couple composed of America's most glamorous film star and one of the country's most famous playwrights. The media went crazy, calling the union as strange a mismatch as could be imagined.

Nevertheless, at least for a while, Marilyn and Miller were madly in love. Miller continued to experience physical tremors at the very thought of being with his new love. Marilyn admired Miller's work more and more, not only *Death of a Salesman* but also *All My Sons,* for which he had won the New York Drama Critics Award, *The Crucible,* and *View from the Bridge.* Just the fact that someone so brilliant was interested in her seemed to bolster Marilyn's confidence and her growing belief that she wasn't just a dumb blonde. Between her new beau, her famous acting coach, and her therapist, she was beginning to believe that she could do truly great things.

Things of a far more sinister nature were also taking place, however, events that would later give conspiracy theorists reason to speculate on the eventual cause of her death. Because of Marilyn's involvement with Miller and Strasberg, both liberal, politically active figures (and later with the Kennedys), the FBI and CIA began to take a major interest in her life. This was during the McCarthy Era, when anyone who showed the slightest sympathy toward the downtrodden might be labeled a traitor and a Communist. Declassified records now show that a huge file had been compiled on Marilyn, carefully documenting her associations with any "suspicious" figures. The House Un-American Activities Committee called her "the darling of the left-wing intelligentsia" and a "Red sympathizer."

When Miller was called before the committee in 1956 to give testimony as a possible traitor, he became one of the most articulate voices of reason against censorship and repression of freedom. And unlike his former friend Elia Kazan, when asked to name names as part of the committee's witch-hunt to blacklist writers, actors, and artists, Arthur Miller refused to do so.

By the year 1955, Marilyn Monroe had started her own production company in partnership with friend and photographer, Milton Greene.

This would allow her to have greater control over the roles she played and the supporting talent involved. It also gave her leverage in negotiation with Fox to insist on more creative input into her films. As she was now the biggest box office draw in the world, the studio had no choice but to make some gradual accommodations, hiking her salary up to $100,000 per film. *Time* magazine called her a very shrewd businesswoman.

With the release of *The Seven Year Itch* in 1955, and then *Bus Stop* in 1956, Marilyn was now established as the most bankable and versatile actress in films. Even more influential, her personal strike against Fox Studios, refusing to work until they renegotiated their contract on her terms, broke the back of their monopoly over actors. She has been credited with launching the demise of the Hollywood star system, giving actors far more creative freedom and artistic control over their work.

At the same time as she was asserting such independence and personal initiative in her career and business affairs, every facet of her personal life was being controlled by her psychoanalyst, Dr. Hohenberg. As was the case with so many of the celebrities described in this book, when treating Marilyn's mental illness, the doctor sometimes compromised her professional judgment in favor of the personal benefits of being associated with the rich and famous star. The usual boundaries between doctor and patient collapsed. In Marilyn's case, first with Hohenberg, and then with others, her doctors took on the role of business adviser and friend rather than maintaining the necessary ethical boundaries as her psychotherapist. So many of these therapists were trained in psychoanalysis, so they certainly were well aware of Freud's admonishment about the dangers of countertransference and about personal feelings having the potential to sabotage the therapeutic relationship. They also should have known better than to reinforce dependency in patients who were already struggling with lack of confidence and poor self-esteem.

Hohenberg gave official permission (in writing!) for Marilyn to marry Arthur Miller, even though Marilyn herself was feeling ambivalent about going through with the ceremony. She had just recently survived the disastrous marriage with DiMaggio, another man with whom she had little in common except their sexual attraction. The same pattern seemed to be repeating itself: a foster child who never graduated high school and was now the world's sex symbol was marrying America's foremost intellectual, who happened to be both Jewish and a spokesperson for the oppressed. They say opposites attract, but a lasting relationship can usually be sustained only when there is a core of shared values and life experiences.

Marilyn seemed to know that she was making a mistake, just as she had with DiMaggio, but she felt helpless to alter her fate. She was being pressured by Miller in a number of ways to fit in with his ideal of a mate and to please his family, who were already upset that he had left his wife and children. Marilyn converted to Judaism in a brief cere- mony just prior to the wedding. She was going to be the perfect house- wife, who would take care of the author's home and produce children who would be a perfect blending of her beauty and his brain.

Before they could fully settle into domestic life, however, Marilyn had other things weighing on her mind, such as an upcoming trip to England, where she was to work with Laurence Olivier, who was con- sidered to be the greatest actor in the world. She would coproduce and star in the movie *The Prince and the Showgirl.* Olivier would direct and also appear as her costar and romantic lead. It was a collabora- tion fraught with conflict in their personal and professional styles, but each ended up with grudging respect for the other.

The honeymoon period between the Beauty and the Brain was not to last long, even though they would remain married for almost five years, the longest relationship of Marilyn's life. From 1957 onward, she would begin a slow decline in her emotional functioning, become increasingly dependent on drugs and alcohol, and exhibit progres- sively more erratic and self-destructive behavior.

From Bad Therapy to Worse

Marilyn was coping with the stresses of her success, her challenging love life, and new creative demands the same way that Judy Garland had—with the aid of chemicals. She medicated herself with barbitu- rates to take the edge off her continual self-doubt and anxiety, but this only plummeted her deeper into depressions. She stopped making films altogether in 1957 to try out for the role of Jewish American housewife for Arthur Miller. There had never been a part that was more difficult for her to play, and for which she was more unsuited.

In addition to trying to cook matzo ball soup and keep Miller's house, Marilyn resumed her acting lessons with Strasberg and decided to re- sume therapy. She contacted Anna Freud in London for help and was referred to Freud's friend, Dr. Marianne Kris, an analyst who had been friends with the Freuds for years. Marilyn would remain in therapy with Kris for the next four years, becoming highly dependent on her and leaving a sizable portion of her estate to the doctor in her will. This is just another example of the ways that codependency was fostered by experts who were supposed to be encouraging greater self-sufficiency.

Kris was primarily a child therapist, who accepted Marilyn Monroe as a patient largely because of her fame and notoriety. As part of her theoretical orientation, she believed (like most analysts) that in order to work on current problems, one must first come to terms with unresolved issues of childhood. The problem seemed to be that her patient had spent the first twenty years of her life burying the past in a way that made it possible for her to function reasonably well. Nevertheless Kris continually challenged her patient to go back into the past, even when there was survival-based resistance to doing so. If Marilyn felt like she was a lousy actress pretending to attain only a rudimentary level of competence, she saw herself as an even worse patient in therapy. No matter how hard Kris would press her to deal with issues related to her father (whom she never knew), her mother (who was still deranged), and her abandonment (which was still too painful to explore), Marilyn felt blocked and was unable to fully comply with the directives.

One would hope that contemporary therapists might treat Marilyn Monroe, Judy Garland, Charles Mingus, Sylvia Plath, and Virginia Woolf quite differently than what occurred thirty, forty, fifty, or sixty years ago. In reality, there is some evidence in Marilyn's case that therapy may have made things worse for her rather than better. Certainly, she needed all the support she could get, as well as help improving her sense of personal effectiveness, but what she needed most was a sense of personal empowerment—encouragement to make her own responsible decisions and to stand on her own two feet instead of constantly depending on surrogate parents.

Both Marilyn and Arthur Miller were confronted with legal problems that increased their levels of stress. Miller was held in contempt of Congress for failing to respond to more interrogations by the House Un-American Activities Committee. Marilyn Monroe Productions began to experience financial and management problems as Arthur Miller came in direct conflict with Milton Greene, the managing partner and other major shareholder. Increasingly, Miller was taking over control of Marilyn's life (along with Strasberg and Kris), and there was no room for old friends and associates like Greene.

Marilyn felt it was time to get back to work. She had been away from Hollywood for over two years, which was like a lifetime for a film star. If imitation is the most sincere form of flattery, then a whole new herd of Marilyns were on the scene, trying to fill her tight sweaters. Although she was not exactly forgotten, she feared that Fox would do their best to replace her.

But then she got lucky. Billy Wilder presented Marilyn with the first good script she had seen in years, a comedy called *Some Like It Hot,* costarring Jack Lemmon, Tony Curtis, and George Raft. Yet even with all her experience and formidable reputation, Marilyn was still a bundle of nerves once filming had begun. She was almost impossible for the cast to work with, showing up late and constantly keeping the crew waiting. She insisted on redoing her lines over and over again, at one point requiring sixty-five takes for one three-word line. Tony Curtis, in particular, found her to be the most selfish, arrogant, and unprofessional actor he'd ever worked with.

Director Wilder recalled, "I used to worry: What character is she going to be today? Will she be cooperative or obstructive? Will she explode, and we won't get one single shot? I can cope with anything, but I need to know what is in store. I never knew with Marilyn." Even with all the challenges, Wilder grudgingly admitted that she was a comic genius and that the final product was worth it. It's generally agreed that *Some Like It Hot* is a wonderful film, with stellar performances by Jack Lemmon, Tony Curtis, and Joe E. Brown, and it also had Marilyn in her most brilliant comedic role, a lovely combination of innocence, sensuality, and self-parody.

After having spent almost two years living in relative leisure, both of their creative forces dimmed by domestic life, Miller and Marilyn began to collaborate on turning one of Miller's short stories, *The Misfits,* into a screenplay. The film would eventually star Marilyn with her all-time fantasy leading men, Clark Gable, Montgomery Clift, and Eli Wallach, directed by John Huston. One could hardly imagine a more impressive ensemble of talent, with the greatest director, writer, and leading men working in concert.

Clark Gable was paid a fortune for his participation, close to a million dollars, but that wasn't enough to compensate for all the aggravation associated with the film. Arthur Miller kept rewriting scenes at the last minute, never satisfied with the dialogue. A screen actors' strike stopped production, even though Miller continued to labor on the script. This, more than anything else in their marriage, destroyed any respect that Marilyn had for her husband. Here he was supposed to be the champion of the working class, and yet he was breaking the strike for his own benefit. For that, Marilyn could never forgive him.

The production had been plagued with other problems from the very beginning. The movie was filmed in the desert—in *summer*—with temperatures soaring over 110 degrees. There was a clash of egos between the stars and power struggles between Miller and Huston, with Marilyn often stuck in the middle. Perhaps not surprisingly, Marilyn was the one who most reflected the stress of the whole ensemble. She showed up late at the sets, if at all. She was wigged-out on drugs and sometimes so shaky she could barely remember her lines.

The one bright spot for Marilyn was her relationship with Clark Gable, her hero since the time she'd kept a picture of him on her wall as a child. Gable was sick with heart problems at the time but took a fatherly interest in his costar, sensing her fragility and wanting to do everything in his power to support her. He was solicitous and unfailingly polite. No matter how many times she botched her lines while fogged with drugs, Gable was patient and understanding, and this mutual affection showed in what was otherwise a somewhat disappointing film. Clark Gable suffered a massive heart attack the day after filming was completed. He died a week later.

Marilyn was trying so hard to reach beyond her own caricature. She was tired of playing herself and had hoped that her close association with one of America's greatest writers might help her break free.

"When I married him," she said, referring to Miller, "one of the fantasies in my mind was that I could get away from Marilyn Monroe through him, and here I find myself back doing the same thing, and I just couldn't take it, I had to get out of there."

She was trying to escape a failing marriage, a film that was falling apart, and most of all, she was trying to escape from herself, a task that was becoming increasingly difficult, with continued therapeutic "assaults" on her fragile defense system. Marilyn had been awarded a best actress Golden Globe for *Some Like It Hot,* but this still did nothing to bolster her confidence. A note of her scribblings was discovered by a reporter while waiting on the set. It read, "What am I afraid of? Do I think I can't act? I know I can act but I am afraid. I am afraid and I should not be and I must not be."

Such self-affirmations could not put a dent in her disintegrating composure. She asked Kris for a referral in Los Angeles and was given the name of a founder of the Los Angeles Psychoanalytic Society and a professor of psychiatry at UCLA. Dr. Ralph Greenson was a therapist who specialized in treating celebrities. He was a controversial figure, described by colleagues as both a lightweight and a charismatic practitioner.

If we give him the benefit of the doubt, it seems as if he really did have his patient's best interests in mind (at first anyway) when he devoted himself so completely to her care. Greenson diagnosed his patient as suffering from severe depression accompanied by paranoia and showing signs of schizophrenia. He scheduled her in therapy for sessions six days a week, at one point increased to seven days, including meetings twice per day. In today's climate, where it is a luxury to see a patient for even once a week for several months, this can only be seen as excessive if not bizarre. To add to the picture, for reasons that are not entirely clear, nor rational, Greenson insisted that the sessions be held in his home rather than his office. He gave the reason that this would ensure his famous patient's privacy, but given that his house was on a busy street, this didn't make much sense. Later he would justify this unusual arrangement as part of a plan to provide Marilyn with all the warmth, affection, and love for which she had been deprived in her childhood. A more cynical explanation would be that he wanted his wife and children to have the opportunity to interact with the most famous woman in the world.

If this ethical breach was the only one that occurred, the effects of his misguided treatment might not have been so detrimental to his patient. Not unlike his colleague on the East Coast, Greenson reveled in self-importance that he was the therapist chosen by Marilyn Monroe to be her savior. It was up to him to complete what others had failed before him. In a letter to Dr. Kris, he said, "I had become the most important person in her life, but I also felt guilty that I put a burden on my own family." This so-called burden was assigning his wife as Marilyn's companion and his children to do errands for her and pick up and deliver her drug prescriptions. There is no evidence that Greenson ever attempted to betray Monroe's trust or behave seductively in any way. He was a compassionate man, and no one would doubt his devotion to any of his patients. His greatest professional lapse was to repeat the same mistakes of his predecessors, to cast himself in the role of a Svengali, who would rescue the distressed maiden.

It's strange and perplexing how traditionally trained orthodox psychoanalysts like Kris and Greenson, who not only had practiced for many years but had supervised other analysts, could have breached one of the most important tenets of therapy: let the patient do the work. Instead Greenson encouraged Marilyn to completely rely on him, to follow his directions to the letter, to take the pills he offered, and to treat him as a benevolent father who would take care of her and would even take her into his own family. He provided her with any medications she requested to help her sleep and relax, and then he continued the work of Kris to unearth as much repressed trauma as he could find. The combination would prove lethal.

Nut House

Marilyn Monroe and her publicist chose the end of January 1961 to announce her divorce from Arthur Miller. This was the same week that John F. Kennedy was inaugurated as president, so Marilyn and her publicist hoped their own news item would get buried. Kennedy had long been a fan of the star, having hung a poster of her over his bed when recuperating from one of his back injuries.

There are many conflicting accounts of her relationship with John Kennedy and his brother Robert. Some reports alleged that Kennedy and Marilyn had been having an ongoing affair since the time he was a senator. Others say their liaison began during the presidential campaign. Whatever happened (and whenever it began), there can be little doubt that to Kennedy, at least, their time together was for sexual recreation rather than anything resembling love. It was as if Marilyn were a call girl again, but this time she was servicing the highest officer in the land.

What is known for sure is that Marilyn spent time with Kennedy, both alone and in the company of others. They most likely had sexual trysts on at least two occasions, and probably one other time, all in 1962 (but probably not before). It is unlikely that Kennedy (or few others) could have tolerated prolonged periods of time with Marilyn during her period of greatest emotional instability. Another rumor that can be put to rest is that Marilyn had an affair with Bobby Kennedy. It is highly improbable that they had anything more than a friendship. In spite of rumors that they had indulged in a long and passionate affair—and even that he was the last person to see her alive—more solid evidence and detailed investigations revealed that he was not even in the same city as Marilyn during the times that they had supposedly been together. The controversy about this relationship, as well as Marilyn's liaison with the president, still rages to this day.

Soon after the announcement of her divorce from Arthur Miller, Marilyn experienced severe depression and a major breakdown. It was another in a series of traumatic losses, one from which she would never recover. Even when she was to initiate the breaks in her romantic relationships or with her mentors, often for her own good, she would remain wracked with remorse and panic at the fear of abandonment. She would forget the abuse and humiliation she had suffered and concentrate only on her own failings and inadequacies as a woman.

Following her divorce, Marilyn had been spending a lot of time alone, locked in her room, refusing to eat, listening to music in the dark, and trying to regulate her moods with pills prescribed by her doctors and laxatives to control her weight. Throughout the latter part of her life, she had also been using enemas as a means to reduce bloating, so she could pour herself into tight dresses. Between the neglect and chronic stress, she was in poor health and not thinking clearly.

As she was on the East Coast at the time, Dr. Kris, her East Coast therapist, arranged for Marilyn's admission into a psychiatric facility for rest and treatment. When Marilyn realized that she was confined to a locked and padded room, she had immediate flashbacks to her family history: she had now become like her mother, who had spent the majority of her life in such facilities. It is difficult to determine which was cause and which effect—whether being involuntarily committed made her crazy or whether it was her madness that necessitated such drastic steps—but Marilyn was beginning to act quite psychotic. She began screaming and yelling, alternated by periods of uncontrolled sobbing. She banged on the door until her fists bled. It seemed to her that she was a prisoner, being held against her will, for a crime she did not commit. She was not far wrong.

Marilyn convinced a sympathetic nurse's aide to smuggle a note out of the hospital, addressed to the Strasbergs, pleading to help her escape. "Dr. Kris has put me in the hospital under the care of two idiot doctors," the note began quite simply (and accurately). "They both should not be my doctors. I'm locked up with these poor nutty people. I'm sure to end up a nut too if I stay in this nightmare. Please help me."

Try as they might, the Strasbergs could not secure her release. They appealed to Kris on behalf of their friend, but the doctor only rebuffed them, saying that she was not permitted to talk about her patient.

It was Joe DiMaggio who would come to the rescue.

Even though he had not seen his former wife in over six years, when he heard about Marilyn's plight, he immediately rushed to New York to see what he could do. He demanded her release, and when the doctors did not immediately comply, he threatened to take the place apart, brick by brick.

Kris later admitted that she had made a horrible error in clinical judgment by committing her patient without Marilyn's consent or co-operation. It was one of many such decisions made by doctors (and others) on her behalf: treating Marilyn as if she were a child incapable of making her own choices. The one good outcome of the crisis was that now the great Joe DiMaggio was back at her side, fighting the good fight. First of all, they agreed to fire Kris, a decision that was made far too late, given the damage she'd already done. Second, DiMaggio found another, more appropriate hospital where Marilyn could recuperate. She was in absolutely horrid shape, both physically and mentally. DiMaggio would remain by her side, visiting her daily, obviously grateful to be back in her life on any terms.

Marilyn would have other affairs in the few years that were left her—with Frank Sinatra for instance—but it would always be Joe DiMaggio who wanted nothing else from her but to be in her company.

Her therapy with Greenson resumed in 1961, when she returned to Los Angeles. Marilyn's friends became increasingly concerned about the relationship because it seemed so unconventional, and the doctor seemed to exert so much control over her. Some of their sessions involved drinking champagne with his wife or Marilyn staying for dinner. It was his continuing strategy (or fantasy) to help Marilyn feel like a part of a family, thinking that this would help heal her. If it was his goal to promote more dependence on him and her new family, then he succeeded in spades—Marilyn would call at all hours of the day and night, visit the house several times each day, and not consider making the most rudimentary decision without first consulting Greenson. He even dismissed some of her staff, like her favorite driver, because he didn't want her attached to anyone other than him. Instead he installed a handpicked spy to live in her midst, Eunice Murray, a woman who was universally regarded as downright weird.

On top of everything else she was dealing with, Marilyn now encountered contractual problems with Fox. She had not made a movie for them in over a year, and they wanted her to star in *Something's Got to Give,* with Dean Martin, Phil Silvers, Cyd Charisse, and Wally Cox. This was more of the same kind of drivel she had done earlier in her career so she resisted. Fox then decided to hire Dr. Greenson as a consultant; it was to be his job to convince his patient to do something that she didn't want to do. That this was a grievous conflict of interest was only the latest in a series of such professional lapses. Nevertheless, after her therapist's continued harping (for which he was paid), Marilyn agreed to make the film.

If Marilyn had managed to extricate herself from one dependent relationship, with her former acting coach Natasha, she had quickly found another—Lee Strasberg's wife, Paula Strasberg, a formidable acting coach steeped in the *method,* who had been working with Marilyn during the past several films. Marilyn's strings were already being pulled by Greenson during most of her waking hours, and while on the set she was totally controlled by Paula, who remained glued to her side. Whenever directors like John Huston, Billy Wilder, Josh Logan, or George Cukor tried to give some guidance, Paula would interrupt and offer her own often contradictory advice. Laurence Olivier actually had her banned from the set because he found her presence so disruptive.

No matter what she accomplished, how much acclaim she received, Marilyn remained painfully insecure throughout her life. She depended increasingly on advisers, doctors, and coaches to tell her what to do and reassure her that she was doing well. After each take, she would look immediately to Natasha, and later Paula, for feedback that what she had done was acceptable. More often than not, they would shake their heads in the negative, no matter what the opinion of the greatest living directors. She had thus been trained perfectly to become the obedient student of whichever coach, or therapist, controlled her life. It is mind-boggling to consider how much better she could have been—and how much more she could have done—if Marilyn had ever been allowed to follow her own inner spirit.

The Doctor Assumes Full Control

Just as there had been rumors that Marilyn was involved with President Kennedy, so too, as we have seen previously, were there reports that she had been "passed along" to Attorney General Robert Kennedy. This was absolutely not the case, and there is fairly compelling evidence that even though they were social friends, there was no sexual relationship.

Marilyn was also friends with Peter Lawford, a brother-in-law of the Kennedys. When a celebration at New York's Madison Square Garden was planned to honor the president's upcoming birthday in which

Marilyn (and others) would be asked to perform, there were two concerns that immediately arose. First, the studio refused to release her from the production schedule of *Something's Got to Give,* as it had already been delayed because she was so often sick or late. And second, she was quite weak and disoriented, most likely the result of chronic overmedication for her depression and anxiety.

The variety of prescription drugs given to Marilyn by various doctors was becoming a major problem. Greenson had referred her to another one of his cronies, an internist by the name of Hyman Engleberg, to manage the various medications. The good doctor created a concoction he called "vitamin shots" for his patient, a combination of Nembutal, Seconal, and Phenobarbital, plus chloral hydrate to help her sleep. She would wake up in the mornings so hung over from the drugs that she could barely function until noon. This put the production schedule behind, and the studio was in no mood to compromise any longer.

Marilyn was now living with Greenson and his family while another home he picked out for her a few blocks away was being refurbished. The doctor restricted all access to Marilyn, keeping away all visitors except those that he personally approved. Again it was Joe DiMaggio who came to the rescue, forcibly removing Marilyn from Greenson's clutches, where she was virtually held captive, and installing her in her new house. Unfortunately, Eunice the spy was already living in the residence, where she could continue to exert the doctor's control.

Just prior to her scheduled appearance at President Kennedy's birthday celebration at Madison Square Garden, progress on the new film had been slow and erratic due to a combination of factors. For example, Marilyn could only work a few hours each day because Greenson still required her to have two sessions per day with him. Nevertheless things limped along until the most extraordinary decision of all was made: the doctor who had worked so hard to make his patient completely dependent on him decided to go on a vacation for five weeks in Europe, leaving his acutely dependent and unstable patient to fend for herself. His solution to this absence was to prescribe an additional quick-acting antidepressant combined with a sedative. Incredibly, recognizing the significance of his abandonment, he explained himself in this way:

I can condense the situation by saying that, at the time of my vacation, I felt that she would be unable to bear the depressive anxieties of being alone. The administering of the pill was an attempt to give her something of me to swallow, to take in, so that she could overcome the sense of ter-rible emptiness that would depress and infuriate her.

It is difficult to avoid a sense of the doctor's own narcissism, self-importance, and negligence, not to mention the sexual metaphor in his conceived role to fill her up, to give her something of himself to swallow. He may have found it surprising that once he did leave, Marilyn initially demonstrated a streak of independence, firing his stooge, Eunice, and then demonstrating greater self-control without him around. Unfortunately, Eunice, under orders from the doctor, refused to leave the house and instead decided to lie low for awhile, returning when Marilyn left town.

The Late Marilyn Monroe

In spite of Fox's insistence that she could not attend the president's birthday party, Marilyn took off to New York to be featured at the festivities at Madison Square Garden. She had been giving considerable thought not only to how she wanted to appear but also to the way she wanted to sing the song—sultry, seductive, but with a touch of innocence.

A number of performers appeared on stage before Marilyn was scheduled to appear—Ella Fitzgerald, Jack Benny, Harry Belafonte, and Peggy Lee. Marilyn was constantly late, and this was no exception. She had prepared a special gown to wear, one that was essentially a sheer body stocking with sequins in a few strategic places. There was no underwear, nothing to break up the flow of the tight dress along the molds of her body. Because the only way she could get the dress on was to be literally sewed in, Marilyn was even later than usual, requiring the other performers to stall.

When Marilyn finally tiptoed on stage, breathlessly (it was hard to walk and breathe at the same time while wearing the dress), the master of ceremonies, Peter Lawford, turned as she appeared and quipped, "And here she is, ladies and gentlemen, . . . the late Marilyn Monroe." In less than two months, this unintended prediction would come true.

At the time, however, Marilyn believed that this night was the most important of her life. Singing the simple song "Happy Birthday" in her inimitable and highly effective style, she had created a sensation that struck President Kennedy deep in the heart. His wife, Jackie, was said to have become furious at the display, but for the millions who watched, it became one of the most enduring moments of the decade.

Marilyn's earliest fantasy from childhood had been to stand up in church without any clothes on, with all the people lying at her feet, and she would walk naked among them, "with a sense of freedom, over their prostrate forms." Now she had made that fantasy come true, appearing virtually naked before the whole world, singing memorably to the most powerful man in the world.

Nudity had long been a prevalent theme in Marilyn's life, far beyond the erotic photographs she had created for men's magazines and calendars. She was observed walking around naked on a regular basis by house staff, friends, hairdressers, wardrobe personnel, completely unconcerned. Natasha Lytess observed, "Being naked seems to soothe her—almost hypnotize her. If she caught sight of herself in a full-length mirror, she'd sit down—or just stand there—with her lips hanging slack and eyes droopily half shut like a cat being tickled, absorbed in the mirror's reflection of herself." It was as if she were always looking for her *self,* her identity that had been so carefully disguised and manufactured by experts.

Marilyn herself once said:

> My work is the only ground I've ever had to stand on. I seem to have a whole superstructure without a foundation—but I'm working on the foundation. . . . I'm beginning to look at things—really look. To find the real inside center of me—and then to look out at the world in a new way. First I'm trying to prove to myself that I'm a person. Then maybe I'll convince myself that I'm an actress.

After President Kennedy's birthday party, Marilyn returned from her appearance stripped naked before the world, and her defenses seemed to lose control. It was as if once she was pried out of that sequin dress that was holding her together, she began to unravel. She struggled to keep filming but each day it became more and more impossible. She continued to self-medicate profusely, mixing every combination of drugs she had with large quantities of alcohol. The search to find her center became distracted, and once again she was operating in a primitive survival mode.

In the beginning of August 1962, the last week of her life, nobody noticed anything particularly different about her, at least based on phone calls, which was now the primary way she communicated. She had conversations with Gene Kelly about doing a movie together. She talked to Frank Sinatra and composer Jule Styne about plans to do a musical as well. She spoke at length to Marlon Brando, who seemed to lift her spirits. She called other old friends, just to chat. Later it was apparent she was saying her good-byes.

A few days earlier, Marilyn had been able to weasel additional supplies of Nembutal and chloral hydrate from her internist, Dr. Engleberg, and her gynecologist, Dr. Siegel. They were only trying to be helpful, trying to pacify their patient's hysterical rants for relief from insomnia and anxiety. Neither one of them thought to communicate with each other, nor with Greenson.

On Saturday, August 4, the last day of her life, Marilyn awoke in a foul mood, sleep deprived and envious of her publicity assistant, Pat Newcomb, who had spent the night and slept like a log. Marilyn wondered how it was possible that anyone could enjoy a full night's rest without the aid of chemicals.

Greenson visited and stayed with her for a two-hour session. He may or may not have known about the drug deliveries from the other doctors, but it should not have been difficult for a trained psychiatrist (or anyone else) to notice that she was heavily medicated with tranquilizers. Joe DiMaggio called Marilyn twice that day to see how she was doing, but Eunice, prickly and controlling as ever, told him she wasn't at home. Peter Lawford also called to invite her to a barbecue but was turned away. Several other friends called that late afternoon as well, but this time Greenson answered, abruptly notified them that Marilyn wasn't available, and hung up. Later he was to claim that they had been involved in an all-day marathon therapy session. If so, it has to go down as the most ineffective therapeutic session in history, considering that after more than eight hours of treatment, the patient decided to kill herself.

Both Lawford and DiMaggio persisted in trying to reach Marilyn, finally getting through to her in the early evening and finding her voice slurred and her thinking disoriented. When Peter Lawford continued to press her about whether she was truly OK, to please reassure him that she was fine to be alone, Marilyn hesitated and said what might have been her final words: "Say good-bye to Pat [Lawford's wife], say goodbye to the president, and say good-bye to yourself, because you're a nice guy."

Lawford was so distressed by the phone call that he made efforts to raise some help for his friend, who was obviously in trouble. Eunice, who was staying in the guest cottage on the property, was eventually reached and said she would check on her employer. She returned to the phone a minute or two later and reported in a bored voice that everything was fine. There is some question whether she ever bothered to look.

For reasons that are still unclear (and perhaps contribute to the conspiracy theories surrounding her death), Marilyn's dead body was not discovered until three in the morning, at least five hours after Lawford first raised the alarm that something was amiss. Greenson and Eunice told conflicting stories about what had happened, who found the body, and what time all of this occurred. Details of their stories would change again over the coming weeks. Because an autopsy revealed that Marilyn had actually died from drugs administered through an enema suppository likely administered by someone else, suspicion fell on either Eunice or Greenson as the culprit, whether acting in the role of a healer or a murderer.

Even if nothing sinister occurred, Greenson's neglect, self-aggrandizement, ethical breaches, and incompetence certainly contributed to Marilyn Monroe's death. At best, he can be seen as a well-intended, essentially compassionate man, who lost his objectivity—and also his patient. At worst, he committed murder, if not by his own hand then as an accomplice to a wounded, disoriented woman who was crying out for help.

Although there can be no doubt that Marilyn took lethal doses of medications in her possession, enough to kill anyone several times, there is some speculation that she never intended to die. At least a half dozen other times in her life, she had attempted suicide but was careful each time to notify others who might intervene. Given that she called just about everyone she could think of the night of her final attempt, crying out for help as well as leaving messages, and that she actually died with the phone gripped tightly in her hand, she may very well have been expecting a last-minute rescue. The problem is that help arrived a few hours too late.

A Luminous Paradox

The final tragedy of Marilyn Monroe's life is that she was never awarded during her lifetime the recognition she deserved as a dramatic and comedic actress of unparalleled skill.

"She had a luminous quality," Lee Strasberg said in her eulogy, "a combination of wistfulness, radiance, yearning—to set her apart and yet make everyone wish to be part of it."

It was this luminosity that not only distinguished her as an actress but also as a model. One of her photographers, Eve Arnold, commented that Marilyn's brilliance cannot be attributed solely to her spectacular appearance but also to her unique ability to project her persona, however that was constructed in the moment, to the camera lens.

One of the aspects of her life that made her such a fine actress—and yet contributed to her psychological troubles—was that she was systematically stripped of any core identity that once belonged to her. She was never sure what her real name was nor who fathered her. She never developed the usual attachments, nurturance, and bonding that are so critical in early childhood, making later healthy relationships possible. She was raised by a dozen different parents, all of whom attempted to mold her into their own image, and each of whom—she felt—abandoned her. She was literally refashioned by Hollywood experts who changed her hair color and her name. She was fed drugs to control her behavior and was subjected to psychotherapy that more resembled a form of brainwashing. She was cast (with her active participation) into the ultimate symbol of men's fantasies, and women's ideal. She was not entitled to a moment of privacy nor even permitted to lead anything close to a normal life without her every movement being reported in the papers. It is no wonder that she was confused and disoriented at times. The true miracle was that she managed to accomplish as much as she did without being permitted to enjoy even the most basic sense of trust in relationships.

If ever anyone could be called a "legend," someone who embodies a fantasy far bigger than life, surely Marilyn Monroe would qualify. She has been portrayed as the paradoxical image of the innocent victim and the promiscuous harlot, the virgin and the whore, the postwar ideal of the all-American girl and the aggressive sexual predator. She has been vilified as a betrayer of women's rights and yet lauded by many feminists as an icon and role model for women's rights. She has been called a victim and a perpetrator, brilliant and dim-witted, cheap and complex, punished and powerful, pathetic and heroic, superficial and deep, manufactured and genuine, helpless and resourceful, unaware and calculating, a talentless sex symbol and a creative genius. She's a visionary or she's insane. Of course, she was all of these. And so much more.

CHAPTER TEN

Lenny Bruce
Sick and Dirty Comic

"We are living in a degenerate, debauched society," the comedian announced to begin his show. He paused for a moment, waiting impatiently for a guy in a front table to stop talking to his girlfriend. He could tolerate the clinking glasses, but it was the wandering attention that really boiled in his gut. It was 1963 now, and he was finding it more and more difficult to concentrate on one thing at a time. "And I am one of the huge cornerstones in the second tower of Babel that we of Satan's growing army are building."

There were a few nervous laughs, but they seemed to be less in response to the comedian's words than to the visible police presence standing in the back of the room. The men dressed in blue stood at attention, slapping empty notebooks in the palms of their hands, where they were to write down any alleged transgressions of decency. They were under orders to arrest Lenny Bruce immediately if he used any of those "dirty" words. Just in case there was any doubt about how that was defined, the prosecutor gave them a list, including several in Yiddish.

"Sixty thousand dollars, that's the amount I'll earn next year as a nightclub comedian. Amazing, isn't it?" Lenny Bruce said, shaking his head, as if even he couldn't believe it. That was indeed a lot of money for those days.

Bruce was a remarkably handsome man in miniature scale, less than five feet two inches and weighing 120 pounds with his shoes on. He was wearing his trademark skinny black tie, white shirt, and dark suit, fitted so tightly to his body because he had a tailor resew every seam.

"A United States senator earns about a third of that. A school-teacher, less than $7,000," Bruce continued, his voice rising in volume, trembling with passion.

"Hey, you should hear what *I* make . . ." someone in the audience called out, but Bruce cut him off with a look that froze him cold. He was boiling over with rage and wanted to go out in the audience and strangle the guy. But the police were watching his every move. They were always watching. The only place he felt truly safe was sitting on the toilet.

"You might assume that I am an extremely moral individual, suffering pangs of conscience in an unjust society," Bruce continued. "But I'm not. I am just a hustler like everyone else. And I continue taking your money as long as this mass madness continues. At least I know what I'm doing is wrong, even if I continue doing it." Bruce looked meaningfully at the cops standing in the back of the room. He knew most of them already from previous arrests, even liked a few of them, but they were still following orders without questioning the absurdity in this war of censorship.

"I just want to say that I am not the sick, bad-taste comic they accuse me of being." He looked again toward the back of the room, as if challenging the police to come and get him. They were concentrating hard, trying to remember the list of words they'd been given by the district attorney that were supposed to signal an immediate arrest.

"And even if I were, it amazes me that these pillars of society would take time to give me space in their columns when there are so many truly bad-taste areas in show business that warrant inspection." Bruce shook his head in disgust. He was pacing back and forth on stage, working himself up, obviously in a battle with himself about how far to take things on this particular night. He was just so tired. He felt so depressed that he often thought about just giving up. All he could think of was how much he wanted to get back to his hotel room where he'd stashed the methedrine and a syringe. If the cops searched the room, they'd never find it. And this thought made him giggle, but it also made him want to hurry this up and get the hell out of there. The depression was closing in on him again, and the only thing that could take care of that was the meth.

"Why go after me when there's the critic who peers over the bed board of the uneasy marriage of convenience between the advertising department and the editorial room? Now that's sick.

"Then there's the unhealthy liaison between the advertising department and the bread-and-butter showbiz columnist resulting in an ill-conceived pregnancy that cries out for an abortion."

That got a laugh. Some people came to the show hoping for the spectacle of an arrest, something to tell their kids: that they saw the great Lenny Bruce hauled off to jail for obscenity. Some had heard that the guy was stone crazy, liable to do most anything, and they wanted to see him freak out. Some probably came hoping that the rebellious criminal would get what he deserved. But there were genuine fans in the audience as well, who loved his edge and his anger. As he scanned the crowd, Bruce recognized two dark-skinned men, one comically tall and the other short, surrounded by a gaggle of white models. Bruce nodded in the direction of Wilt Chamberlain and Sammy Davis, who saluted back.

"Without taking you to Tijuana, I, Dr. Bruce, will attempt to perform this abortion."

The applause was wild and enthusiastic. Whistles. Catcalls. Stomping on the floor. Even the policemen in the back of the room smiled a little, leaned against the back walls to relax their postures. They seemed to recognize that in spite of their assigned jobs, they were in the presence of a true phenomenon. They didn't like this dirty-mouthed smart-ass one bit, but they had to admit he was funny.

Forty minutes later, Lenny Bruce was in a cab heading back to his hotel. He'd stuffed an extra five dollars in the driver's hand, telling him to hurry. His foot was tapping nervously on the floor, but his head was tilted back. It was as if one part of him was jumping out of his skin, and the other was about to crash. He hadn't slept in over thirty hours, and he didn't plan to sleep any time soon. When he closed his eyes, he might see people coming after him. He would remember that his ex-wife, the only person who had ever truly loved him, was gone and out of reach.

Once in the room, he tried to remember where he'd hidden his stash. His hands were too unsteady to manage the screws in the light plate where he thought he'd put the meth, but maybe that was in another hotel in another city. Besides, he couldn't wait that long: he needed a fix *now*.

Under the mattress. Now he remembered. It was a stupid place, the first one the cops would check if they raided him. But then he grinned, recalling that he had a letter from that young doctor, Norman Rotenberg, the orthopedic surgeon in Los Angeles who had given him a get-out-of-jail-free card. The fool had been so happy just to be in the presence of the great Lenny Bruce that he'd agreed to write him a letter, one that Bruce carried with him at all times, which read in part:

> Methedrine, in ampoules of 20mg, together with disposable syringes, has been prescribed for intravenous use as needed.
>
>   Mr. Bruce has asked that I write this letter in order that any peace officer observing fresh needle marks on Mr. Bruce's arm may be assured that they are the result of Methedrine injections for therapeutic reasons.

Therapeutic indeed.

Bruce was cackling to himself, dancing a little jig, as he reached under the mattress and pulled out his works and supply. He was talking to himself more and more now, as if answering the voices inside his head. Sometimes he couldn't tell what was real and what was part of his imagination. Most of the time he didn't care.

One bottle of Dilaudid, two hundred pills, prescribed for pain, usually in terminal cancer patients or gunshot wounds. Check. He sure had some pain.

One bottle of Tuinal, about forty tabs left. For sleeping. But he tossed those over to the side. He wouldn't be needing those in the near future.

Dozens of ampoules of methedrine, pharmaceutical speed, that glowed like jewels. That would perk him up some.

Ah, what's this? Tabs of mescaline for hallucinatory fun. Now *that* would be interesting. He counted out two, no, better three, tabs that he immediately popped into his mouth and chewed like baby aspirin while he began cooking the crystal meth in a spoon, before dissolving the Dilaudid.

The veins in his arms were so wasted that the only place he could find a decent injection point was the tiny blue vein behind the knuckle on his left hand. For this, he chose a number-thirty needle, which would only leave a tiny mark.

Bruce tied off his arm with an elastic belt, fumbling with the rituals that even after a dozen times each day he still couldn't get quite right. He lifted the plunger of the syringe, sucking in the brown goop that was bubbling in the spoon, and then carefully injected the chemical soup into his system.

One minute, two, then lift off.

An Outrageous Legacy

As much a social critic and provocateur as a comic, Lenny Bruce delighted in shocking people. He pushed the limits of what was considered acceptable, not just once, but over and over again, in as many ways as his creative mind could conceive. His use of four-letter words got all the attention, but the real crime for which he was punished was attacking the status quo and the privileged, regardless of their status or political affiliation.

Bruce's performances defied categorization. He had been a stand-up comic in clubs, but he also appeared on concert stages with Charles Mingus and the other jazz greats of the era. He performed a burlesque act for a while but then became transformed into passionate, angry social critic. He attacked the Pope and the president. He ridiculed organized religion, materialism, and capitalism. He talked about sex. A lot. And, yes, he used rather graphic language. A lot.

Lenny Bruce was so outrageous that he would do almost anything to garner attention for his messages. His favorite bit was to dress up in a prison uniform and walk around New York asking policemen for directions. One time at a show in Miami, he saw some of the retired residents of the hotel peering in through a window. He instructed the audience to start picking their noses—and one another's noses—in order to chase the spectators away.

Steve Allen introduced him on his national television show as "the most shocking comedian of our time." But he was so much more than just a comedian. During one of his several obscenity trials, he was described by defense witnesses like columnist Dorothy Kilgallen, cartoonist Jules Feiffer, and author Nat Hentoff as the most important social critic alive, on an exalted level with artists like Jonathan Swift and Rabelais. Comedians like Mort Sahl, George Carlin, and Richard Pryor followed in his footsteps and regarded him as a role model, a true visionary who made it possible for comics with an edge to talk about the most important problems of the day, to confront audiences with the subjects about which they felt most unsettled. One critic,

Kenneth Tyson, spoke for many when he described his reactions to Lenny:

I first saw Lenny Bruce in San Francisco and was puzzled. Then I saw him in Chicago and I was intrigued. I saw him in New York and was slightly scared by the nakedness with which this performer reveals himself. Then I began to laugh, to laugh at the wildness of one of the most bizarre imaginations that's ever been let loose on a nightclub audience. I've been laughing ever since.

Tyson was amazed at the sheer audacity of Lenny Bruce to take on the most heated issues of the day—Vietnam, racism, homophobia, censorship, oppression, fascism—and do so with unrelenting courage. "At his best he rises above mere evangelism and moral fervor into flights of fantasy, unscalable skyscrapers of sheer wit and baroque invention that, as far as I know, have never had any rival on the English-speaking stage."

In spite of his comic genius, or perhaps because of it, Lenny Bruce was a highly disturbed man. "All my humor," he once said, "is based on destruction and despair. If the whole world were tranquil, I'd be standing in the breadline, right in back of J. Edgar Hoover."

But the world was not a tranquil place, and Lenny Bruce was not like other people. Part of this had to do with the neglect he had suffered—pawned off on relatives and neighbors to take care of him, attending twenty-six different elementary schools. Part of his problem was that he was just born with a huge, dark, paranoid psychotic chip on his shoulder.

Bruce struggled constantly with depression, which he attempted to eradicate with drugs. He also claimed to suffer from chronic pain, for which he needed the medications, particularly favoring amphetamines to boost his energy, mescaline for producing hallucinations, and barbiturates to crash. The one drug he consistently stayed away from was marijuana, which he claimed made him think too much. As it was, his head held far too many ideas than he knew what to do with.

Bruce was most certainly hyperactive, even without the enhancement of amphetamines. He was clearly antisocial in his behavior, living by his own rules and resorting to manipulation, deceit, and distortion to indulge his fantasies and get his own way. And ultimately, the man who said he lived to confront hypocrisy appeared to end up believing his own lies.

Early Years

The Schneiders first arrived in America from England in 1905, when Mickey was an infant. They were pretty well off for Jewish immigrants, able to speak the language and earn a decent living in rural areas of New York State. They lived in several small farming towns that more resembled the Midwest than what you'd ever expect in a place that was just a few hours' train ride to the city on the Long Island Railway.

Mickey Schneider (Lenny's father) was trained as a physical therapist and podiatrist and later as a pharmacist. He was a serious man, strict in his ways, and perhaps inclined to a certain dour manner. When he married Sally Kitchenberg, there could not have been a more ill-suited match. Sally was everything that Mickey was not—outgoing, playful, irreverent, irresponsible, seductive, and from a lower-class family. Whereas the Schneiders liked to think of themselves as from the privileged class of English Jews, Sally's father was a rag peddler who could barely support his family, and her mother was certifiably insane.

On the day that Sally married Mickey in 1925, her mother was committed to a mental institution. She was more attracted to Mickey's relatively stable family than to her husband; she was eighteen and it was a way to begin a new life. In the same year that they married, they had a son, Leonard Alfred Schneider. They settled in the town of Bellmore, New York, a community of chicken farms.

Lenny was an absolutely miserable child, not only in his own company but in most other people's as well. He was described by relatives as a troublemaker and tough to be around. From Lenny's perspective, he found his father too rigid, strict, critical, conditional, and demanding—and the house too oppressive. Sally must have thought so as well, because in 1934, when Lenny was eight, she walked out, took off for Reno to get a divorce and seek a career in show business as an "exotic dancer."

Lenny, already an unhappy child, was even more devastated by this abandonment by his mother. He despised his father and tried everything in his rather persuasive powers to convince neighbors or other relatives to adopt him. "If you ever get divorced," he was later to comment, "let your wife keep the kid. Your kid is better off with a wife that sleeps with a different guy every week than with a family that doesn't want him."

Lenny grew up in a home in which he was neither wanted nor overtly loved. He would spend the rest of his life replicating exactly the pattern at home—desperately wanting people to understand and love him but doing everything he could think of to drive them away. And in a nutshell, that was also the essence of his stage performances.

During the rest of his childhood, Lenny would be shuttled back and forth between his parents, never feeling at home with either one of them. Mickey was absolutely stifling in his control, divvying out discipline but rarely displays of affection. Sally was a lot more fun to be around, but she was more concerned with her own needs than with taking care of a young boy. In later years, she would behave seductively around him, fixing him up with girlfriends, and relating to him more as a friend than a parent.

When Mickey remarried, the family settled into a house where Lenny would remain with his father, on and off, until he ran away to join the navy at sixteen, convincing his mother to sign for him. Until then, Lenny was provided with a comfortable life, including everything he might desire on a material level, despite his struggles with loneliness and alienation. Teachers described him as a disruptive influence in their classrooms: he was unruly, overly talkative, hyperactive, and mischievous. Still, they felt sorry for him as anyone could see how unhappy he was.

By the time he was thirteen, Lenny was spending as much time away from home (and all his parents' rules) as he possibly could. He began working at a neighbor's chicken farm and begged them to adopt him. They felt sorry for the boy, but not enough to make that kind of commitment. Like most people in the area, they thought Lenny was a bit strange, small for his age, almost too intense to be around. His father worried that he had inherited the insanity from his mother's side.

Weirdo of the Fleet

When Mickey did his patriotic duty and enlisted in the army in 1942, Lenny soon followed. He thought it romantic to sign up to fight the Nazis and was bursting with hope and optimism for the first time. It wouldn't last long.

For a young man who was already so tired of living under harsh discipline and strict rules, living on a warship was probably the worst possible environment. There were constantly horns blaring, sleep disrupted, orders being given, five-inch guns bombarding the coasts of North Africa and Italy. And there was no privacy.

Lenny's assigned task as a seaman first class on the cruiser *U.S.S. Brooklyn* was as a shell passer. It was his job to load the heavy shells into the breech of the gun and then step back as they continued pummeling the enemy positions. Hours later, they would see bodies floating toward them in the sea, drifting out toward the cruiser with the tide, bloody and bloated reminders of the damage Lenny and his crewmates had inflicted.

It was during a six-month refitting of the ship in New York harbor during 1945 that Lenny rekindled his relationship with Sally, his mother. She was trying to make it in show business at the time, singing and dancing in clubs, and living with a friend, Sandy Barton, who Lenny found to be wildly attractive. Sandy was married, seven years older, but she found the sailor kind of cute. Lenny's mother actually encouraged their relationship, perhaps thinking that her friend might teach her son a thing or two. She did.

Lenny was growing more and more dissatisfied with his days back on duty at the ship. He absolutely hated the navy, not only all its damn rules and regulations but just the tedium of doing the same things over and over. It probably didn't help that he had developed a reputation as a weirdo, not only because he was a Jew but because he was a strange one at that. He was subjected to anti-Semitism on board but also a more personal kind of harassment that he invited by his own behavior—Lenny was constantly clowning around. He loved to make the other guys laugh, but usually at his own expense.

It was while resting one evening in the arms of Sandy, his now full-time lover, that he devised a diabolical plan to escape the servitude of military life. It was to be the performance of his lifetime, and he would practice his role with complete dedication until he got every detail just right. His scheme was to begin to act so strangely that the authorities would have no choice but to release him from service.

Lenny began pretending that he was gay, walking with a swish and affecting a new accent. He started coming on to guys in the shower. When that failed to generate enough shock value, he started dressing in women's clothing. In doing so, he would later become the model for Klinger in the show *M*A*S*H*.

Enough was enough, the military soon agreed after this sailor's behavior became increasingly bizarre. He was granted his wish—an immediate discharge from the military. Lenny was now free to pursue his love full time, and that is exactly what he did, until Sandy's husband showed up, returning from the war that had ended two months after Lenny's antics.

Show Business

Cut loose from his father's rigid rules, all connections to the military, and a relationship that had taught him everything he thought he needed to know about women, Lenny decided to seek his fortune in the entertainment industry, following his mother's lead. He headed for Hollywood, where, after a brief acting course, he began appearing in amateur productions. After a year of training, he decided to return to New York and make his mark on the Broadway stage. In 1947, he changed his name to Lenny Bruce, deciding that Schneider was far too Jewish to make it in mainstream America. It was also another way to separate himself from his father

Lenny enjoyed some immediate success in the Broadway scene, winning awards and cash prizes in acting contests. His best act was doing a soliloquy of Shakespeare's *Hamlet,* pretending he was drunk. Even at the very beginning of his career, he showed a proclivity for satirizing the things that people hold most sacred.

Trying to earn a living appearing in these acting contests, Lenny made the circuit of all the clubs in the vicinity of New York City, Long Island, and New Jersey. He found himself competing with acts that included a guy who jumped off a chair and landed on his head and another fellow who performed patriotic songs using a sweet potato as an instrument. "The winner was selected by holding a hand over the contestant's head and asking for applause," Lenny recalled. "I never won. The sweet potato usually did."

After his initial success, Lenny may not have won many more contests, but he learned a lot from watching the other performers, as well as the crowd. He was amused by the ways that some of the other acts would play on patriotic themes or their experience as veterans in the war. "Since it struck me as funny that anyone who had been in the service would use that fact to gain rapport with the audience, I had a picture taken of all my campaign ribbons and medals, had it enlarged, and put it on." Then he had a band play martial music in the background as he appeared on stage with the blown-up photo of his medals pinned on his chest. This pissed off a lot of people in the club, which suited him just fine. He was so excited about the new ways he had discovered to get people riled up that he decided it was time to turn professional and make this his career.

Even before Lenny would ever start experimenting with drugs, people thought he was a pretty crazy guy. He seemed to operate without the usual inhibitions and limits to which most people subscribed. This is all the more remarkable when you consider the way he had been brought up by his father, with perfect manners and decorum. One reason for his rebelliousness, the image of himself as the Lone Ranger, the outcast who thrived on persecution, was a legacy of the cold, distanced relationship he maintained with his father. In adulthood, he would almost never mention the man's name.

Lenny confessed that he actually enjoyed stirring up hostility in others; it gave him a sense of power. It is also evidence of self-destructive behavior that would become increasingly florid as the years went on. He realized that because he presented a nonthreatening appearance, being small and quite handsome, he could get away with things that most people would never consider. In any career other than the one he chose, he could have been labeled a sociopath. It so happened that he managed to find an outlet for his creativity that allowed him to behave in the most outrageous ways, deliberately enrage people, and yet have it all be considered a part of his art.

Lenny was a con man and schemer before he made it as an entertainer. He enjoyed cheating people out of their money whenever he could, raising funds from naive fans by claiming that he was a film producer. He hustled one woman out of $7,000 by claiming that he was producing a television show. (He actually had to pretend to do the show when she became suspicious.) He would also go door to door with a friend who had his hand tied behind his back, pretending that the friend was a wounded veteran asking for donations. He even managed to get five bucks from poet Carl Sandburg during one of these forays.

When he wasn't devising new ways to separate fools from their money, Lenny began hanging out at comic "finishing school," better known as Hanson's Cafeteria in New York. This was, in 1948, the renaissance of Jewish comedy, when this half restaurant–half drugstore became the meeting spot for impressionists and comics, who tried out their routines on one another. Lenny would sit with comic veterans in the booths and spend the better part of an afternoon listening to their war stories about appearing on stage, as well as witnessing the development of new acts. Most of the participants in these impromptu rehearsals were up-and-comers like Lenny, but sometimes "graduates" like Milton Berle, Buddy Hackett, Joey Bishop, or Rodney Dangerfield would show up, more to check out the new talent than to share their material.

It was in this environment that Lenny was exposed to the best in the business. He had already tried his hand as an impressionist but found he wasn't very good at it. He was not much better in standard comedy because he lacked both confidence and polish in his delivery. Nevertheless he got his first big break when he won the talent contest on Arthur Godfrey's television show *Talent Scouts*. Although this could have been a turning point in his career, Lenny was a one-bit per-former: he had only one routine that he did well, an imagined con-versation, in German, between James Cagney, Humphrey Bogart, and Edward G. Robinson. Even this idea he had stolen from Red Buttons.

Perhaps because he never had the skills of a traditional comic, the sense of timing and delivery to tell conventional jokes, Lenny had am-bitions that far exceeded a mere performer. He admired jazz players like Charlie Parker and Charles Mingus and their ability to improvise within a structure that was carving a new niche in the world of music. Although he had not had much of an education, he also fancied him-self a philosopher and poet. And finally, he thought of himself as an actor. He wanted to use all of these disciplines to create a whole genre of performance, one that did more than merely entertain an audience.

Competing with Strippers

When Lenny met Honey Harlowe, a stripper from Baltimore, he fell in love with her "alabaster breasts." Once they were married a few months later, in 1951, he wanted to get her off the stage, feeling like he was her pimp. They devised a scam in which they would form a charity with a respectable-sounding name: The Brother Mathias Foun-dation. He managed to steal a priest's robe from a church, and while wearing it, he began collecting donations to support a leper colony in South America. He was so effective in his role that he managed to col-lect $8,000 panhandling in only three days. Overjoyed with his suc-cess—and feeling a little guilty—he sent a check for $2,500 to the leper colony, and he and Honey pocketed the rest for "administrative fees."

The Bruces were in Pittsburgh when their car was impounded. They used the last of their leper funds to get the car out of hock and were pulling out of the parking lot when they were hit by a truck. Both

Honey and Lenny were thrown from the vehicle, although Honey had the bad luck to land in a spot where she was run over, twice, left on the street bleeding profusely. Convinced she was dying, Lenny made a deal with God, promising to go straight if only He would spare his beloved.

Two months later, Honey did finally recover enough to leave the hospital. They got in a new Cadillac, which Lenny had bought with the insurance money, and decided to make their fortune on stage— Honey continuing her previous career as a stripper and Lenny trying out some new routines that he'd developed as a comic.

It was Honey who got the first break, an invitation to do some stripping in Las Vegas, and that was what drew them out West, eventually to Hollywood. Lenny and Honey managed to land gigs in the same strip clubs in the San Fernando Valley, blue-collar dives with names like Strip City and the Cobblestone Club. Lenny would be the master of ceremonies, whose job was to introduce the strippers, as well as perform his own evolving material. There could be no more sleazy, distracting, and depraved environment for an entertainer to develop his craft.

Lenny had to compete not only with the strippers but also with the drunk truck drivers and the pinball machines going off in the back of the room. He would sit back stage, watching his own wife doing the bump and grind, sometimes while getting oral sex from one of the other strippers. By the time it was his turn to go on, he would be so revved up, so crazy by the chaos going on all around him, that he tried things that nobody else would have ever dreamed of. He sank to the absolute depths of depravity in order to discover his own voice and his own creative genius. That he was destroying the relationship with the only person he would ever trust was an extra bonus for someone so hell-bent on self-destruction.

In one of his all-time most famous stunts, one night Lenny was frustrated and tired of trying to capture the attention of the mostly male audience, who were leering at the naked women and rubbing their own crotches. By this time, Lenny had already tried an assortment of crazy things—faking epileptic seizures, screaming incoherently in a psychotic rage, ridiculing the strippers, attacking members of the audience, even following some of the women into the bathroom with his microphone and describing what they were doing. Most of the time, he was still ignored.

Consequently, on this memorable evening, Lenny walked on stage completely naked to announce the next strip act. When the audience stared at him dumbfounded, he screamed at them, "What the hell are you looking at? Haven't you seen enough nudity on this stage?" More than anything else, this outrageous act signified his transformation into a whole other kind of performer, one who would resort to almost any means to shock the audience. But he wasn't doing this merely to get a rise out of people. He had a plan. Like a psychotherapist, he wanted to root out our greatest fears and inhibitions, all of the things that we avoid and repress and deny.

Rage on Stage

Hanging out in strip and jazz joints, Lenny began to embody the "hipster" culture, a period of hard drugs, fast talk, and good times. He thought of himself as an outlaw and acted the part. And what kind of self-respecting desperado would *not* be into the drug scene? It was one of Lenny's friends, Joe Maini, a jazz player, con man, and ex-convict, who first taught Lenny and Honey how to shoot up heroin, a skill that Lenny was never to master. Lenny was notorious for not being able to hit his own veins and usually needed someone else to aim the needle for him.

In between his stage appearances, Lenny continued to earn supplementary income as a hustler. He and Joe would compete with each other as to who could go into a drugstore or market and steal the most number of items. Whatever cash they could put together, they'd spend on drugs.

When Honey became pregnant, there had to be a period of reassessment. She had been warned that unless she stopped shooting up, their baby could end up with birth defects. Both of them tried to get their act together, to be more responsible and get clean, drug free.

In November 1955, their daughter, Kitty, was born, and this, more than anything else, changed Lenny's life. He was determined to be the best possible father and devoted himself to the task with the same passion that he had focused on being an entertainer. That doesn't mean that he and Honey stopped their partying, just that they did their best to make sure their baby was taken care of during those times when they were intoxicated or out of control.

Both Honey and Lenny were performing in 1956, ending their shows in the early morning and then staying up all night hanging out with musicians, strippers, and comics. It was in this uninhibited environment that the sex often got wild and crazy, partners switching as the mood suited them. This put tremendous strain on their relationship, even to the point of sabotaging their marriage.

Then Lenny was put out of commission after contracting a bad case of hepatitis. He spent weeks in a hospital, drying out, recovering his strength, and hovering in a depression. It was a period of deep reflection for him, most of it spent alone because Honey rarely came to visit. It was one thing for him to mess around with other women (he often bragged that he had slept with a different woman each night), but he couldn't stomach Honey doing the same thing. This double standard extended beyond their sex life to include the drugs as well—delusional and in denial, he didn't see that he had a drug problem but assumed that his wife did.

By the time he was fully recovered, he'd decided that he couldn't deal with Honey's drugging, stripping, and whoring any longer (if ever there was a projection of his own behavior!). Immediately after his release, he filed for divorce and went for full custody of Kitty, claiming that Honey was unsuitable as a mother. Ironically, he did just what he said had been done to him—being taken from his mother and forced to live with his father.

Lenny felt totally betrayed by Honey, and his wrath was something awful to behold. During a working trip to Hawaii, Honey had been arrested for possession of marijuana, released on bail, but kept under surveillance by the police. So Lenny deliberately gave her six more marijuana joints, then he called the police and tipped them off that she was in possession of drugs. Once she was arrested and jailed, Lenny took off with Kitty, leaving Honey to deal with the authorities.

If Lenny thought this desperate act would bring some peace to his family, he was wrong. He became depressed and acutely suicidal, begging Honey to come back to him. Even if she had wanted to, she was now out on bail and not permitted to leave Hawaii. She was eventually convicted and sentenced to two years in prison, thereby ending any possibility of their reconciliation in the near future. Lenny was awarded custody of Kitty based on his success (through private investigators) of getting more dirt on Honey than she could get on him. He portrayed her as an addicted whore, even though she had, by then, rehabilitated herself and had started a successful clothing business in Hawaii.

It is one of the interesting gender differences that men often convert their depression into anger, whereas women often do the opposite. In Lenny's case, his sense of despair turned into a rage so powerful and all-consuming that it completely changed him, not only as a person but as a performer. This was the turning point in his career, the critical incident in which his anger transformed him from a second-rate comic to a unique and original performance artist.

With the love of his life now out of his hair, and also bearing the responsibilities of sole parenthood, Lenny became even more obsessed with reaching the pinnacle of success. He started recording himself and refining his bits, methodically tweaking every nuance of his monologues just as Mingus might do with a jazz composition. More significantly, he now stopped holding his bitterness and anger in check—he used them with precision and without restraint, shaming and ridiculing people, attacking every sacred cow that crossed his vision. The audiences loved it, and his reputation around Los Angeles was building.

The more outrageous Lenny behaved, the more notoriety he earned. During his premiere at a new, exclusive club in town, he noticed that the audience was packed with comic celebrities—Don Rickles, Buddy Hackett, Georgie Jessel, the Three Stooges. Whatever initial excitement he might have felt was quickly gone when the crowd became unusually talkative. This was one thing that he could absolutely not tolerate, and he began to become increasingly frustrated. After asking the crowd to quiet down politely, then raising his voice to demand silence, he was still facing a raucous crowd that he felt was being disrespectful. Finally, in a fit of anger, he told the audience to go fuck themselves, gave them both middle fingers, and then stormed off the stage, creating a sensation. His main attraction was that nobody knew what to expect from him. He was becoming a cult figure no matter what he did, the crazier the better.

Skyrocketing to Fame

In 1959, Honey was doing her time in prison while Lenny was building his reputation as a madman who was quite capable of doing anything for a laugh, if not for pure shock value. By the end of the year, he had garnered some notoriety, earning a record contract and a gaggle of groupies. Whether he could be believed or not, he continued to boast that he had sex with a different woman every night, usually quickies or blow jobs back stage. His movie star looks, sleek suits, charisma, and literally smoldering eyes seemed to drive many of his female fans wild. He was called a rising star, a phenomenon, and a "sick and dirty comic." He was earning $2,000 per week, a great deal of money in those days. He had been discovered by no less than Hugh Hefner, who wanted to serialize Lenny's autobiography in *Playboy*.

Steve Allen, the host of the *Tonight Show* before Johnny Carson and Jay Leno, booked Lenny to appear before a live audience of millions in April 1959. Needless to say, this drove the producers and censors crazy with worry. How could they possibly trust that the most volatile, unpredictable, and filthy-mouthed guy in show business would possibly behave himself? Much to everyone's surprise, he did (mostly). Steve Allen introduced him to mainstream America with a warning that his satirical comments were likely to be disturbing—and perhaps offensive—but that was his job. "So ladies and gentlemen," Allen intoned, showing a bit of his own apprehension, "here is the very shocking comedian, the most shocking comedian of our time, a young man who is skyrocketing to fame, Lenny Bruce!"

Except for his very opening line, ad-libbed without telling the censors (ridiculing Elizabeth Taylor for her intermarriage to Mike Todd, who was a Jew), Lenny was a model of decorum, at least by his standards. Selecting his most tame material, Lenny was both cooperative and charming during the appearance. Steve Allen even invited him back a second time, but the network executives nixed that idea, figuring that they had just escaped a bullet and there was no way they would tempt fate again.

After his *Tonight* appearance, Lenny's fee was bumped to $3,000 per week, and he had money to burn, or at least enough to shoot as much heroin and methedrine as his veins could support. After his gigs in New York, Los Angeles, and everywhere in between, he'd party all night with his friends and with hangers-on, crashing about six in the morning. He'd sleep to about three in the afternoon, swallow a handful of uppers to get his heart going, and then continue the cycle all over again. He deluded himself into thinking that he did not have a drug problem like Honey because he could stop any time he wanted to—he just wasn't quite ready yet. He was still depressed and brooding over Honey, hoping they could reunite with their baby once she got out of prison. He acted as if the drugs were the only thing that kept him sane.

Lenny's behavior was becoming increasingly reckless. While in Las Vegas as the guest of the Tropicana Hotel, he fell into a rage watching a burlesque show, offended at what he considered exploitation. After making a scene, he then attended Shecky Greene's show, creating another disruption when he started heckling the comic to the point that he was asked to leave. Then the pièce de résistance occurred when he walked into another of the hotel's acts, by Pearl Bailey, an African American entertainer, who was in the middle of her routine. Lenny found her style to be "Uncle Tom" and told her so, getting up on the stage with her, pinching her ass, and then scolding her for promoting racial stereotypes. It looked like the bout of hysteria was about over, and everything was just about calmed down, as Lenny walked off— only to return with a fire extinguisher, which he proceeded to spray all over Bailey until she was a sheet of white. The audience howled with laughter, thinking this whole thing had been staged, the funniest thing they'd ever seen. An hour later, Lenny was sitting on the toilet (always his favorite spot), when three bouncers walked in, lifted him off the john, and threw him out of the hotel before he had time to even pull up his pants, much less pack his bags. He would never be invited to Vegas again.

Second Honeymoon

The one bright spot in Lenny's life during this period was that he had managed to convince Honey to set up house with him again and help raise Kitty. The problem seemed to be that Honey was now strung out on heroin all over again. This only made Lenny more determined to get her help, even if he couldn't get his own act together. The truth is that they never stopped loving each other, even if they were both too self-destructive to live together.

In August 1959, Lenny's worst nightmare came true: he was arrested as a drug user just outside the parking lot of the club where he was about to perform. The police scared the hell out of him and took him to the station to book him. Convinced this would ruin his reputation, if not his career, Lenny pleaded and begged for a break, or at least leniency.

The detectives, led by Sergeant Joel Lesnick, kept at him until their prisoner broke. Lenny agreed to become an informant. In fact, that very night he set a trap for his own dealer, who was arrested in time for Lenny to make his late show. Throughout the rest of his life, Lenny would become a partner with Sergeant Lesnick, calling in tips, informing on his dealers, providing evidence to convict other druggies. He even wrote a manual of advice for cops on the inner world of the hipster drug scene.

Like so many women in dysfunctional relationships, Honey became the "designated patient," the one who was labeled as sick and in need of professional help. Lenny would never in a million years see a therapist himself, but he spent considerable time finding help for his wife. After all, in his mind she was the one with the problem.

After purchasing a house together in Los Angeles, Honey and Lenny took off for Cuba in 1960 for a second honeymoon. They wanted to spend time together, away from the daily pressures, just to relax and restabilize their relationship, leaving Sally to take care of her granddaughter, Kitty, who was almost five. Lenny and Honey hung out in a luxury hotel in Havana, consumed a multitude of tropical drinks, and rested. On one occasion, feeling a bit tipsy, Lenny stood out on the balcony and did a hysterical impression of Fidel Castro, mocking the dictator's incoherent rants in swishy, fake Spanish. Honey collapsed in convulsive laughter, thinking it was the funniest think she'd ever seen.

Later, they ordered dinner from room service and enjoyed a wonderful meal of *arroz blanco, frijoles negroes,* and *lechon asado* (roast pork with rice and beans), until they became deathly ill and had to be transported back to the United States for immediate medical attention. It was discovered that they had been deliberately poisoned by pro-Castro agents, perhaps the first time there was an attempted assassination of a comic for doing an offensive impression. Only in the life of Lenny Bruce could a story like this ever be believed!

Whatever tension they had hoped to escape by running off to Cuba became far more pronounced when several U.S. critics initiated a campaign of moral outrage against a man whom they considered to be an agent of the devil. Columnists, pundits, radio personalities, politicians, all weighed in, condemning the filth that came out of Lenny Bruce's sick mind. It was while performing in New York that Lenny had been tipped off that the police were monitoring his appearances and tape-recording his every word.

Rather than feeling intimidated by the surveillance and attacks, Lenny delighted in the attention. For the next couple of shows, he avoided using a single obscenity, only coming close to the line just to tease the police and drive them crazy. It was just a game to him—and a fun one at that.

Reinventing Himself

During 1960, when Lenny was at the height of his fame, he worked even harder on his creative work. Not content with old material, or rehashing his best work that he had perfected after years of experience and hundreds of performances, he decided to reinvent himself from scratch—not unlike Judy Garland or Mark Rothko when they were forced to make adjustments during times of adversity. In Lenny's case, however, this was purely a matter of choice. He could easily have re-fined and developed his classic routines for the rest of his life but instead decided to start over again. One critic described this amazing transition as evidence of his remarkable creativity: "But the truth is that the creation of forty-five minutes of absolutely fresh material is the entertainment world's equivalent of writing a major novel. It is something that even a genius like Lenny Bruce could do only a few times in a lifetime."

Lenny's fire of rage burned with that much more intensity. He approached each show with the impossible goal of making sure the audience would never, ever forget him. This was a whole new genre of show business, something not quite pure entertainment, but something both hilarious and deeply disturbing.

The absolute pinnacle of his career occurred in the beginning of 1961, when Lenny was booked to appear in no less than Carnegie Hall, the most esteemed venue in America. Unfortunately, the night of the concert, there was a snowstorm that completely brought the city to a standstill. When Lenny trudged to the theater for the midnight show, expecting it to be canceled, he was absolutely shocked to see that the streets were packed with people making their way up Seventh Avenue. It looked to him like a death march in Siberia.

Lenny was so moved by the display of dedication on the part of fans that he gave what is regarded as the most brilliant performance of his career. By the time he whirled onto the stage in front of a packed house, he was a man truly possessed. He presented the best of his new material but mixed in improvisational riffs that were so inspired that they seemed both magical and seamless. More than anything he ever did, this single display of creativity generated a new movement in comedic performance, eventually spawning a new generation of social critics, like Hunter S. Thompson, George Carlin, Richard Pryor, and more recently Chris Rock.

Four-Letter Words and One Ten-Letter Word

The chronic drug use was taking a serious toll on Lenny's health. Soon after his appearance in Carnegie Hall, he developed weakness and a chronic fever, eventually collapsing. He had developed a staph infection in his blood from the meth injections, shooting his temperature up to a stunning 107. This gave new meaning to his being called hot-blooded. His body was iced down and flooded with antibiotics.

His mother, Sally, and his five-year-old daughter, Kitty, arrived to find Lenny in a coma, hovering near death. During the next month, they nursed him back to health, because Honey was far too drugged-out to be of use. When his ex-wife did come to visit him in the hospital and saw him hooked up to all the tubes and medical instruments, she imagined he was being poisoned and started ripping out all the intravenous connections. She had to be forcibly restrained and admitted into a psychiatric facility.

If there was a lesson to be learned from his close brush with death, it seemed to have escaped Lenny Bruce. In a weakened state, he resumed his performances—and his meth injections—resulting in several more collapses, hospitalizations, and narcotics arrests, the most serious of which occurred in Philadelphia in 1961. He was asked to pay a bribe of $10,000 by the authorities, which he negotiated down to $3,000, and then refused to pay altogether. Sealing his fate of persecution for the next years, he called a press conference and named the judge, detective, and others who had solicited the bribe. Some would say that this single act of recklessness is what encouraged police all over the country to mount a vendetta against him. But that is far too simple an explanation.

In reality, Lenny had made enemies from almost every constituency imaginable. He pissed off the liberals as much as the conservatives, ridiculing the democrats in power for their collusion with the establishment. He made jokes about John and Jackie Kennedy, attacked Marilyn Monroe, demeaned every other comedian in the business, broke every taboo he could think off. He commented that Eleanor Roosevelt had nice breasts. He talked about the Lone Ranger having a gay relationship with Tonto. He mentioned that St. Paul had given up fucking for lent. And in his worst transgression, which occurred a few years later, he observed that when John Kennedy was assassinated in a motorcade while riding through the streets of Dallas, Jackie was *not* leaning over to help her husband but rather to try and save her own ass and crawl on out of there.

It was four-letter words—and a certain ten-letter word—that would get him in trouble, but that was merely the excuse: it wasn't his language that was the problem as much as the content of what he was saying. All the focus on the language itself always puzzled and amused Lenny. Why were people getting so upset about just a four-letter word?

It wasn't like he was actually doing those things on stage (although he thought about it). He wondered why people were so offended and outraged, how it was possible that any sane, civilized person could become so upset over a word.

One week after his arrest in Philadelphia, Lenny was appearing in San Francisco at the Jazz Workshop, doing his most notorious routine, "To Is a Preposition, Come Is a Verb." Using the cymbals and drums for percussionist emphasis, he launched into a riff:

"To is a preposition,

Come is a verb.

I've heard these words my whole life, even when my parents thought I was sleeping.

"To come," Lenny hit the drum on the last syllable. "To come," he said again, this time louder.

"Did ya come?"

"Did ya come *good?*"

And so the monologue continued, playing with the words, singing their praises, highlighting their hypocrisy: words can be so ordinary in one context, but so dirty in another.

Lenny was arrested during the break, charged with obscenity. The officers took particular offense with his use of the word *cocksucker,* which they found particularly criminal.

"What?" Lenny challenged the sergeant as they hauled him away. "You've never had your cock sucked?"

This was just the beginning of his troubles. For the next few years, wherever he appeared, the police would monitor his activities with single-minded dedication. As mentioned at the beginning of this chapter, they even assigned Yiddish-speaking officers to surveillance, charged with the responsibility of writing down any Jewish words he might slip in that might be obscene, such as *putz* and *schlong* (both referring to penis). Lenny was hounded, dragged into court, and forced to defend himself, but he always managed to escape serving jail time, even when he was successfully convicted. After all, these were minor misdemeanors, and he attracted good legal representation, even though he kept firing his lawyers to defend himself. Things were getting so hot for Lenny that he decided to head for England in the spring of 1962 to broaden his international appeal and spend a month doing his act for the more staid British audience. If he ever expected that they would be far more polite, he couldn't have been more wrong.

Reminiscent of the audience's riots in Paris over Nijinsky's dancing, the London audiences were incensed by his provocative behavior.

At the Establishment Club, people not only screamed out their own obscenities to protest his act, but they also started throwing hard objects at the stage, crashing glasses against the walls. Fistfights broke out in the seats. Mass protests and walkouts ensued.

If Lenny was disturbed by the riots he was causing, he didn't show it. Instead he actually tape-recorded the insurrections and played them back for the audience the next night, ridiculing how rude and obscene that English people could be. This did not exactly endear him to the public, and he was mercilessly skewered in the papers by critics and politicians, eventually deported and not allowed back in the country again.

For the rest of his performing life, Lenny would be dogged by cops, both in uniform and undercover, who recorded everything he said and did, arresting him for the slightest transgression defined by the prosecutors as obscene, especially the four-letter words and the one ten-letter word. Comedian George Carlin would eventually immortalize these words in his ode to Lenny Bruce—the seven words you can't say in public: shit, piss, fuck, cunt, cocksucker, motherfucker, and tits.

Lenny was always amazed—and delighted—at all the attention he could stir up just by uttering a few words in public that everyone used in private. He was also incensed by all the time, manpower, and money that was wasted persecuting him instead of genuine criminals. So he was a crazy drug addict? But who was he hurting besides himself? So he said a few naughty words out loud? Why weren't they going after the real bad guys?

Another time when Lenny was in San Francisco, appearing at the Jazz Workshop, two teachers had been persecuted for homosexuality and were being demanded by some of the local media to surrender their jobs. Lenny wondered what all the fuss was about, as he'd never heard of a child complaining to his mother, "Today in school I learned five minutes of geography and ten minutes of cocksucking." What's the big deal with cocksucking, anyway? he wondered, saying he couldn't imagine a better way to spend a lazy afternoon. In truth, Bruce's own favorite pastime was to sit on the toilet and shoot some meth into his arm, while one of his lovely groupies gave him a blow job.

Trials and Tribulations

Lenny Bruce was arrested fifteen times between 1961 and 1962. It became even worse in the years that followed. For the last years of his life, he would spend more time on legal briefs than preparing comic material. Whereas early in his career he loved to carry around dictionaries, where he would make a point to extract interesting words to stick into his monologues, by the 1960s he was carrying suitcases of law books and state statutes. He had become so obsessed with his own defense and so determined to protect his right to freedom of speech that he virtually gave up his work in order to prepare his cases. Every penny of the thousands of dollars he had earned would go to pay his legal fees. Eventually, he would declare bankruptcy and become a pauper.

There have been whole books written about the legal battles of Lenny Bruce and their significance within Constitutional Law and First Amendment rights of freedom of speech. Some of the most famous lawyers came to his defense—William Kunstler and Melvin Belli, to mention a couple.

The judges didn't know quite what do to with Lenny Bruce. He was just as wild and uncontrollable in their courtrooms as he was on stage, demanding that he be heard and insisting he be allowed to do his act in front of them. He believed that if only he could demonstrate the artistry of his performance, the judge would understand the political significance of what he was attempting to do.

The judges couldn't just lock him up and throw away the key, because Lenny had so much support among a good portion of the intellectual and media elite. Beat poet Allen Ginsberg organized a petition on behalf of Lenny, protesting his treatment and declaring:

We the undersigned are agreed that the recent arrests of nightclub enter-tainer Lenny Bruce by the New York police department on charges of in-decent performance constitute a violation of civil liberties as guaranteed by the first and fourteenth amendments to the United States Constitution.

The petition went on to compare Lenny to other satirists, like Mark Twain and Jonathan Swift, and to object most strenuously to his persecution. "Whether we regard Bruce as a moral spokesman or simply as an entertainer," the petition ended, "we believe he should be allowed to perform free from censorship and harassment." The document was signed by no less than comedian Woody Allen; writers James Baldwin, Joseph Heller, Norman Mailer, James Jones, William Styron, John Updike, Gore Vidal, Susan Sontag, Henry Miller, and Lillian Hellman; singer Bob Dylan; actor Paul Newman; psychoanalyst Theodore Reik; cartoonist Jules Feiffer; Robert Gottlieb, Managing Editor of Simon & Schuster; and dozens of others.

In spite of the protests, Lenny Bruce was convicted of obscenity in New York. The prosecutor, Richard Kuh, pleaded to the judge that Bruce receive the maximum sentence allowable, declaring that he had shown absolutely no remorse.

When given an opportunity by the judge to respond to that accusation, Bruce replied, "I'm not here for remorse, but for justice. The issue is not obscenity, but that I spit in the face of authority."

The judge sentenced Lenny Bruce to four months in prison, a verdict that was eventually reversed on appeal. In fact, when all was said and done, Lenny was eventually exonerated from all of his many arrests, never serving prolonged prison time after his initial arrests. He was, however, sentenced to drug rehabilitation by one court in California, a fate that Lenny considered worse than death, because he hated shrinks and all that they stood for.

Dr. Keith Ditman, the psychiatrist at UCLA who was assigned to his case, found Lenny to be both charming and essentially a kind and misunderstood man. He also diagnosed him with acute paranoia and deep depression, and he believed Lenny to be deeply disturbed and borderline psychotic, beyond anything to do with his drug addiction. Dr. Ditman recommended hospitalization for treatment, but Lenny managed to find his way out of the doctor's clutches, preferring his own version of therapy—hundreds of milligrams of methedrine, followed by barbiturates and hallucinogens, as needed

The Long, Hard Fall

Paranoia refers to irrational fears and delusions that people are out to get you. In Lenny's case, he had reason to fear that he was being persecuted—because he was. But that's not to say that his own madness was not playing a significant role in behavior that was becoming increasingly irrational and self-destructive. He required reporters, friends, even members of his audiences, to take lie detector tests before he would speak to them.

When he had been rolling in dough earlier in his career, he had built his dream house in Los Angeles, equipped with every possible convenience for a drug-addicted, paranoid maniac who was becoming out of control and really was being followed by the police. Every room in the house was wired with surveillance and recording equipment that served two purposes: to keep a complete record of his own ramblings and thoughts as they came to mind and to record conversations with anyone who visited him, in case they might testify against him at a later time. He spent the most effort of all designing the master bathroom, with a special toilet located adjacent to a hypodermic syringe dispenser and a hidden disposal slot where he could hide the used needles.

During the last two years of his life, from 1965 to 1966, Lenny had stopped performing almost completely to devote himself to his legal defense. When he wasn't reading law books, he was using whatever money he could find, mooch, or steal to feed his drug habit and support his harem of young groupies, who hung out at his house all day and competed for the honor of spending the night in his bed.

Lenny had, by this time in 1966, virtually withdrawn from the world. His weight ballooned to over two hundred pounds, fed by unrelenting indulgences in pastries and drugs. Kitty was now nine years old and he would continue to see her when Sally brought her to visit. When he wasn't too depressed or too drugged out, he could still be a doting father, and Kitty positively adored him. Honey, as well, would sometimes come to visit, and they would even occasionally resume their sexual relationship for brief intervals. Actually, by this time, it took considerable work to help Lenny complete his favorite verb: to come. Girls would take turns, spending twenty-minute shifts, taking care of his sexual needs; more often than not, the acts would remain uncompleted.

After all those years acting like Lenny's sister, or best friend, Sally now played the part of the Jewish mother. She nagged him to see a doctor, to eat better, to take care of himself, to be a better father, but he was by this point too far gone. Even if he wanted to seek help, he had no money left to pay anyone; he could barely scrape together enough funds to keep his drug habit going.

On August 3, 1966, Lenny Bruce ate what was, for him, an unusual meal—a full breakfast of eggs, sausage, potatoes, and toast, instead of the usual diet of candy bars and cokes that he had been living on for months. He then went into his office, the floors littered with pornography depicting explicit scenes of sadism and masochism, as well as stacks of legal briefs. He sat down at his manual typewriter and continued working on a monograph about freedom of speech that he hoped to someday publish. He fancied himself now (delusionally) a legal scholar. He had written a sentence that began, "It appears that the conspiracy to interfere with the Fourth Amendment const . . . ," but then abruptly ended.

We'll never know what was going on in his deranged mind when he took his accustomed place on the throne of his toilet. He tied the sash from his bathrobe around his arm and injected himself with morphine, a lethal dose that was most likely accidental. He was never very good with a needle.

Lenny was discovered keeled over on the floor by the toilet. His final indignity is that when the police came, they posed his body in an unnatural angle, turned over to face the cameras, conveniently situated next to his drug stash. They then allowed as many photographers as possible to take his picture.

Lenny Bruce was pretty much persecuted to death. He was arrested over and over again for the most petty misdemeanors. His enemies spent millions of dollars in taxpayers' money—and years tying up the courts—for the kind of legal cases that usually take less than an hour to settle. He was frequently barred from practicing his profession and earning a living, because club owners were threatened as codefendants by prosecutors. He was left a pauper, trying to defend himself. Finally, authorities knew he was emotionally fragile, strung out on drugs, teetering on the edge of madness, and then they pushed him over the cliff. Even the prosecutors who convicted Lenny in his New York trial admitted that he was innocent, but they had proceeded anyway under political pressure. He was martyred in the cause for creative expression.

Rehabilitation

In what can only be regarded as a miracle, Lenny Bruce was recently forgiven for his transgressions, long after his death, by the State of New York. In the first such pardon in the state's history, Governor George Pataki declared in December 2003 that he was taking this action to celebrate his commitment to upholding the rights of the First Amendment of the U.S. Constitution.

Because he'd died thirty-seven years ago, Lenny did not comment publicly on the latest development in his case (nor is he expected to in the near future). One of his lawyers, Martin Garbus, spoke on his client's behalf when he said that this action represented just the kind of "appalling hypocrisy" that Lenny would have satirized in his next performance: "I think Bruce would be laughing and furious at the same time."

CHAPTER ELEVEN

Brian Wilson
Afraid of the Water

T he waves were rolling in with relentless regularity, building, folding in on themselves, before crashing on the shore. The swell seemed sinister and alive, like a giant, undulating monster of the sea. This was Malibu on a hot summer day in 1976, just the sort of scene that had been immortalized in the Beach Boys' hit "Surfin' USA."

There was a lineup of a few dozen surfers out past the break, jockeying for position. Some of them were sitting idly on their boards, talking, watching a pod of dolphins swim by, but most were staring out toward the horizon, waiting for the telltale bulge that signaled an incoming set. All of a sudden, one guy broke loose from the pack, paddling hard, before being crunched by a wave and pulled under. His board popped up like a cork, but it seemed like forever before the guy's head emerged, his mouth sputtering water.

A man in his late thirties, slightly pudgy, with a beard and long, brown, straight hair to his shoulders, was pacing back and forth on the sand, wondering if the wiped-out surfer was OK. He was standing awkwardly, shifting from one foot to the other, while his green terry cloth robe blew open from the wind, revealing a blinding white belly hanging out over his shorts. He could feel the cold water try to swallow his feet, and he took a few steps out of range, looking over his shoulder at the people watching him with uneasy scrutiny.

He thought seriously about backing out of this stupid stunt, but with a film crew from *Saturday Night Live* standing by to record every moment of this attempt to overcome his fear of water, this was not an option. To make matters worse, the exuberant and persuasive efforts of John Belushi and Dan Aykroyd, first pushing, and then forcibly pulling him into the water, made it impossible for him to resist.

Brian Wilson staggered into the ocean, holding a longboard, trying to balance it under his arm as he started to wade into the water. Before he got three steps, he lost his balance, starting to fall, before he was righted by his companions, who were having their own troubles. The two comics were dressed in police uniforms that they had donned in order to issue Brian a citation for "failure to surf." Then they dragged him to the beach to prove himself.

The man most responsible for launching the surfing craze in America, who sold twenty million records just about this sport alone, had never been on a surfboard in his life. In fact, he was afraid of the water. He was afraid of a lot of other things as well, like losing his mind. But on this particular day, on his thirty-fourth birthday, it was time to set things right.

When Brian hesitated his forward progress, after being thrashed by a wave breaking on shore, Belushi and Aykroyd continued to shove him forward, yelling encouragement. They didn't seem to notice that the man was frozen with terror.

His wife, Marilyn, standing by on shore, thought about calling the whole thing off at this point. It was a stupid idea anyway; everyone knew that her husband was panic-stricken about the water. It was one thing for him to pose for publicity photos, ankle deep in the surf, holding a board in his hands, and another for him to actually enter the ocean.

Brian stood for one agonizing moment after another, feeling the waves break just in front of him, almost knocking him on his butt. He thought about turning around. He wanted so badly to just get the hell out of the danger zone, to get back on solid, dry ground, but he had already been through so much in the last few years. He had mostly silenced the voices inside his head. He had gotten himself out of bed after years of confinement. He was out in the world again, almost enjoying himself. He was like a kid who finally discovered the childhood he was never allowed to have.

Taking a deep breath to calm himself, Brian Wilson launched himself forward, face down on the board (facing the wrong way), his large belly preventing him from digging very deep with a few feeble paddles. He was still wearing the terry cloth bathrobe, which was now drenched and clinging like a deflated sail. He propelled himself a few yards toward the onrushing wave only to meet the incoming swell. The water rushed up to smash his board head-on, blinding him, flipping him up and head over heels, driving him down into the gritty sand not far below, pounding him on the ocean floor. Now he was flailing about, trying to regain his feet, and only wanted to find his way back to the safety of the beach. But when he looked back over his shoulder toward shore and saw the crowd gathered there hooting and hollering, he knew he couldn't give up. It was just like he'd been practicing over and over the last few years in other areas of his life: when a wave knocks you on your ass, you pick yourself up and push forward again. Whatever it takes.

Brian remounted the board and tried again, only to meet the same fate. He hated to lose, hated to give up, but he realized that this little adventure wasn't really about surfing; it was about trying to overcome his fear of the water. This was enough for one day. It had to be. Feeling defeated, he stumbled, then crawled onto the shore.

Down but Not Out

From his first hit at the age of nineteen with the song "Surfin'" to the dozens of early surfing tunes that would come after—"Surfin' USA," "Surfin' Safari," "Surfer Girl," "Surf City"—Brian Wilson would emerge as one of the greatest songwriters and composers of the twentieth century, widely acclaimed for the originality of his music. He would go on to become America's most popular and creative musician, producing songs that literally defined a generation. He wrote about surfing, then he wrote about many other aspects of the sixties, about the powerful youth culture of his generation, including songs about exuberant spirit ("I Get Around," "Fun, Fun, Fun," "Do You Wanna Dance?"), cars ("409," "Little Deuce Coupe"), and the California lifestyle ("California Girls"), and also writing what is considered by many (including Paul McCartney!) as the greatest single popular-music recording ("Good Vibrations") and album (*Pet Sounds*) of all time.

Brian Wilson is one of the most accomplished songwriters of popular music, as well as the most prolific during his active years. In a two-year span, 1964 and 1965, the Beach Boys released eight different albums, six of which were produced and arranged by Brian, including his having written sixty-three songs. After this initial surge of hits, celebrating fun in the sun, he turned to the deeper subjects of his own lifelong insecurity, with "In My Room" and "Wouldn't It Be Nice?" before being fired from the band for his increasingly bizarre and unmanageable behavior.

Next came a solo career that surged and sputtered until Brian finally stopped touring altogether, then stopped writing, and finally succumbed completely to mental illness. Brian may have been counted down, but he was not out: in the last few years, he has initiated one of the all-time greatest comebacks. In 2004, after a gestation period spanning almost four decades, Brian Wilson finally completed and released perhaps his greatest masterpiece, *Smile,* the work that has truly made his legacy secure.

A Story of Hope

Brian Wilson's story, the last one in this book, was chosen specifically because it is a tale of resilience and triumph against all odds. Brian was written off a dozen times, a hundred times, as a certified card-carrying psychotic kook. He was paralyzed with insanity, suicidally depressed, confined to his bed for over three years, morbidly obese, drug addicted, unable to form a coherent thought. He has been called "rock's most famous nutcase."

Then, to make things still worse, after making progress, with a rather unconventional therapist, to address his emotional problems, the good doctor kept him under complete, hypnotic control, cutting off all Brian's other relationships, moving into his house (and sending *Brian* to the guest cottage!), claiming authorship for his music, and charging him millions of dollars for the privilege.

During these long years of bizarre behavior, almost everyone gave up on Brian Wilson. His brothers considered him a lost cause, as did the rest of his band. When he wasn't in the throes of madness, he was utterly under the control of the Svengali doctor who plied him with drugs, made all his decisions, and kept him passive and compliant but inaccessible to anyone else.

All of the other lives reviewed in this book ended badly—in suicide, drug overdoses, hospitalization, or death by overindulgence. But Brian Wilson managed to beat back the mental illness, if not keep it at a safe distance. He lost weight and started exercising. Even more amazingly, be began creating music again, returning to a project he had begun three decades earlier and had appeared irretrievably beyond reach. His therapist actually helped with a lot of this progress, even with the collateral damage, and then—with the help of his family—Brian managed to extricate himself from the relationship with that therapist, which had become pathologically dependent.

So this, our final tale, is a story of hope. Regardless of the inevitable setbacks that Brian Wilson may experience in the years ahead, he has proven that it is possible to overcome the most debilitating symptoms of madness—hallucinations, compulsions, addictions, paralyzing fears, depression, panic, agoraphobia, dependencies, and a host of other problems—and still reclaim his rightful place as one of the most innovative composers of our time.

The Sensitive and Nervous One

Brian Wilson's father, Murry, may have owned a machine shop, but in his heart he was a songwriter, waiting for his big break. He was a big guy, gregarious and commanding, always needing to be the center of attention—and not one to put up with any lip from anyone. His wife, Audree, was his opposite in many ways—quiet, compliant, and accessible. Together they formed what was considered a traditional relationship in the 1930s, with Murry firmly in charge.

Murry had devoted his working life to trying to make a go of his business, even sacrificing an eye in an industrial accident. The Wilsons settled in a mostly working-class neighborhood in Hawthorne, California, not far from LAX Airport. It wasn't a bad place to raise a family.

The Wilsons gave birth to three boys, Brian, Dennis, and Carl, each born two years apart, beginning in 1942, and each displaying the classic signs of birth order. Brian, the eldest, seemed the most poised. Dennis, in the middle, was the problem child, nicknamed "Dennis the Menace." And Carl was the baby.

If Murry had hoped that his musical interest had been passed on to his sons, he must have felt considerable relief (and jealousy) to discover that his firstborn had perfect pitch. By eleven months, before he could even talk, Brian could hum the melodies of songs in perfect imitation. Reminiscent of Mozart, by age three he could play chords on the piano and sing in perfect key.

Musical enrichment in the home environment not withstanding, the Wilson's house was a terrifying place. Murry was far more than a strict disciplinarian; he was sadistic in the beatings that he would inflict on the boys at the slightest show of defiance. He dished out punishment with a belt, his fists, or any object nearby, with ruthless disregard for the damage inflicted on the children. Murry's own explanation for the beatings was simple—he was only doing to his kids what his father had done to him.

It was during one of Murry's rages that he allegedly hit Brian on the side of the head with a bat, permanently destroying Brian's hearing in one ear. From the time he was six years old, Brian could be observed listening to music with his head turned to one side so that he could hear out of his good ear. He would never be able to listen to music in stereo.

Although Dennis was the rebellious kid in the family, and the one who got the brunt of Murry's most violent outbursts, Brian was the sensitive one. From the time he was in elementary school, he wet his bed most nights. Once he reached adolescence, he excelled in sports, playing quarterback for his high school football team and center field for the baseball team. Yet in spite of his natural athletic gifts, he would fold under pressure. Whenever he was inserted in a game, with something critical on the line, he would fall apart. He just wasn't built to withstand much tension. Or more likely, he had been subjected to so much chronic stress throughout his childhood, living under the constant threat of abuse, that he developed extreme anxiety that would remain with him throughout his life.

Three-Part Harmony

Brian loved all the things an adolescent is supposed to love: cars, girls, sports, and especially music. Ever since he was old enough to walk, he had sung in a church choir. He seemed to spend almost every waking moment that was not otherwise scheduled playing the piano, sometimes for hours at a time. There were also whole days that went by when he would do nothing else but lie on the floor with his good ear directed toward the hi-fi and listen to records and then compose his own variations of what he heard. He loved George Gershwin, classical composers, the Four Freshmen, and anything else with complex harmonies. He would spend hours locked in his room listening to the same records over and over again, duplicating, then embellishing the sounds on the piano and Hammond organ. He taught himself to play bass as well, his performance instrument in years to come. But most distinctive of all was his pure falsetto voice, which sounded as if it had been issued forth from an angel.

It was Brian's youngest brother, Carl, who introduced Brian to rock and roll (especially Chuck Berry), after Carl had taken up the guitar. Dennis, always the rebel, was the last to pick up an instrument, in his case the drums, because they helped him to act out some of his frustration and anger. Between the three of them, they had a band.

Whenever the kids found themselves on long car rides, they would immediately launch into sing-alongs, fifteen-year-old Brian directing the harmonies. Even grumpy Murry would tolerate the noise in the backseat, soothed by the angelic voices of his boys. And whenever Dennis or Carl would refuse to cooperate with Brian's singing direction, Murry would threaten them with dire consequences. Compliance, therefore, was not a problem.

By 1959, surfing was the "in" thing in Southern California. The movie *Gidget,* with Sandra Dee and Bobby Darin, was a big hit. Dennis was the only one of the brothers to join the new popular sport, hitting the beaches with the nine-foot board purchased by their father, one of the few loving acts that Dennis could ever remember. Whether one surfed or not, there was a whole new language that was developing, as well as a culture to be celebrated.

Brian had been fooling around writing songs ever since he was a kid, but it was a collaboration with his older cousin, Mike Love, that led to the creation of his first marketable song: "Surfin'." It was during this time that Murry and Audree had gone to Mexico for a vacation, leaving the boys with $250 in grocery money to feed themselves. The boys used most of the money, plus a contribution from Love, to purchase a set of drums and rent guitars and amplifiers to record Brian's first song.

When Murry walked in the door and saw all the equipment in the living room, he launched into one of his terrifying rages. Before he could start throwing things, all four boys quickly went to their instruments and started playing the tune. It was like music soothing the beast: Murry's anger dissipated as he heard the boys play.

If he liked the song, he refused to give the slightest indication. Instead he told the boys that it was amateurish and poorly arranged. This only made Brian, and especially Dennis, more determined that they were going to get it professionally recorded.

It was when a fifth member, Al Jardine, joined their group in 1961 that opportunities started to open up. Al was a nineteen-year-old folk singer with contacts in the music industry and a flamboyant singing style that added some life to their performances. Al managed to convince some friends who owned a small recording company, Guild Music, that surfing songs were going to be the next craze. The owners, Hite and Dorinda Morgan, agreed and the first song was recorded in less than hour.

"Surfin'" turned out to be a modest success, making its way up the charts from number 118 on *Billboard* all the way to number 75 a few weeks later. It sold over fifty thousand copies, not at all bad for a first recording, and enough to persuade the Morgans to sign up the Beach Boys to record more surfing songs, including "Surfin' Safari" and "Surfer Girl"—both big hits. Brian Wilson was now the reigning king of surfing music in the world.

Disharmony

Murry was now convinced that his boys had a future and therefore converted the garage into a rehearsal stage where the boys could practice. This was as much his dream as theirs, as it had been his grandest ambition to make it in the music industry. He would manage the band, negotiate their recording contracts, and write their music, or so he believed. It was the latter demand that Brian rejected unequivocally. He was still afraid of his father but not so much that he would back down from the only thing in life that was important to him: writing music.

It was while they were practicing that a neighbor, Gary Usher, five years older than Brian, stopped by the garage to see what the music was all about. He was not only a musician himself but also a lover of hot rods. When he and Brian immediately hit it off, they decided to collaborate together on some songs, beginning with "The Lonely Sea" and continuing over the next few years with some of the Beach Boys' classic hits, including "409" and "In My Room," which contained Brian's most revealing and personal lyrics, about his own loneliness and personal troubles. By this time, Brian was sleeping in the music room with his piano, the only place he felt safe.

In Gary, Brian found not only someone he could trust but also someone who spoke his language. Brian didn't have the words to describe how he felt inside—he would always feel self-conscious as a lyricist—but Gary could seem to read his mind and write the words that Brian could not express himself. Yet Gary recognized the core of vulnerability in his friend, even at such an early age, commenting, "He was sensitive to the point of being unbalanced. He was esoteric and very eccentric."

Usher was among the first to observe not only the extent of Brian Wilson's emotional vulnerability but also his remarkable talent. "True genius is spontaneous," he noted about Brian's style of music composition. "Rarely does a real genius sit down and plot what he is going to do. It doesn't work that way! . . . Brian made records because it was all he could do; all he ever wanted to do. It was straight from the heart and he loved doing it."

During the summer of 1962, Murry negotiated a contract for the boys with Capitol Records, cutting himself in for a hefty management fee. Brian was spending more and more time alone in his room composing music. It was during one of those times that his father burst into the sanctuary after he heard something on the piano that he didn't like and started screaming at Brian over some mismatched chord. Rather than taking the verbal beating, this time Brian lashed back, telling his father to go fuck himself. At the age of twenty, Brian finally exerted his independence to get away from his father's stifling influence. He moved out of the house, earning his own money by playing fraternity parties at USC and UCLA.

Brian hooked up with a roommate and new friend, Bob Norberg, an electronics whiz who collaborated with Brian to set up recording equipment in their apartment. This allowed Brian, for the very first time, to invent his trademark *overdub* method of recording several tracks laid over one another. In the future, this would allow him a level of creative innovation in making music in which he could layer dozens of different sounds, harmonies, and rhythms (immortalized in "Good Vibrations" and "Heroes and Villains").

Love and Success

In October 1962, when Lenny Bruce was being arrested for obscenity at the Troubadour Club in Los Angeles, just down the street at the Pandora Club, the Beach Boys were playing the sweet, innocent melody of "Surfin' Safari," which had reached number one in the city and number ten nationwide. While the Beach Boys were performing, wearing their cute matching outfits and singing perfect harmonies, girls in the audience were swooning in ecstasy at the handsome musicians. Among them were the three Rovell sisters: Diane, Marilyn, and Barbara, sixteen, fourteen, and thirteen, respectively.

During the following years, these girls, and their family, would play a crucial role in Brian's life, beginning the second week of their meeting when they invited the Beach Boys to their conservative Jewish home. Marilyn, the middle daughter, was totally infatuated with both Carl and Dennis, and Brian had taken up with Diane, the eldest. These were innocent crushes for girls this young, and the boys seemed to be more amused by the attention than anything else. But far more than the flirtations, Brian became immediately attached to the Rovells' household, which was so unlike his own.

Irv and Mae Rovell could sense in Brian a vulnerable, needy, and sensitive young man who was floundering, and they decided to do whatever they could to make him feel welcome. During the ensuing months, although Dennis and Carl would visit on occasion, Brian was practically living there. Mae would cook meals for all the members of the band, plus any of their friends who happened to be around. They made their home into Beach Boys Central, the headquarters for all their social and business enterprises. It was a strange mix of cultures, between the observant, Jewish, middle-class family in Fairfax and the prototypical icon of gentile fun-loving superficiality.

Brian began spending the night at the Rovells, where they had arranged a bed for him in the living room. Mae and Irv seemed to enjoy his company just as much as the girls did, and they engaged him in a wide range of conversations into the late hours of the night. It wasn't clear anymore which daughter in the house Brian was actually attracted to, because he flirted with all of them, as they did with him. But it was ultimately Marilyn with whom he fell in love, even though she was just fifteen and he was twenty-two. Once the secret got out, Diane, the eldest, said to him a line that would soon become the title of another hit record: "Don't Hurt My Little Sister."

Capitol Records wanted to take advantage of the success of the first surfing song and so released in 1963 a whole album of surfing songs, *Surfer Girl*, which also contained several of their car songs—"409" and "Little Deuce Coupe." It stayed on the *Billboard* chart for almost a year, going as high as number four. Ironically, at this same time, Brian enjoyed his first number-one hit by writing "Surf City" for two friends in the group, Jan and Dean. Brian Wilson had finally arrived, at least within their limited genre.

Fun, Fun, Fun

If the Beach Boys' success was cause for celebration at the Rovells, all was by no means well in the Wilson household. Murry was like Judy Garland's stage mother, multiplied by a factor of ten. He was not only controlling, manipulative, and living vicariously through his children's success, but he was often violent and abusive. During recording sessions, Murry would become so irate that he would scream and slap the boys, humiliating them in front of their friends. Brian, as the eldest and leader of the group, would bear the worst of his tirades. If only Capitol had taken a lesson from Louis B. Mayer at MGM, they would have banned Murry from the studio altogether.

As the Beach Boys were gaining recognition toward the end of 1963, they were booked in front of larger concert audiences, now numbering in the thousands. Brian, unfortunately, suffered from a crippling case of stage fright, not unlike the pressure he felt on the football fields in high school. He would fortify himself with a bottle of wine before he could go on stage, and even then he'd be shaky. He complained that with only one good ear, he couldn't hear properly. Even worse, as long as he was performing, he didn't have enough time to write more music. Besides his new love for Marilyn, it was all he lived for.

Brian began skipping out on many of their bookings, complaining of fatigue. What was unknown to others at the time was that he had begun to experience disturbing hallucinations. "At night I started to hear voices in my sleep," he confessed. "They weren't anything I could make out, but they sounded to me like screams. Loud, terrifying screams that darted past me like goblins in a haunted house. I used to lie in bed, waiting to return to the studio. The only way I kept the screams at bay and kept myself together was to work."

Whether Murry and the boys noticed something was wrong with Brian or not, they realized they had to honor his request to hire a replacement for him to fill in when they were on tour. Al Jardine would soon become a permanent member of the band, allowing Brian more freedom to stay home by the piano. They did persuade Brian to join the concert circuit on a few more occasions, most notably during "comeback" tours in 1976, and again the last time the original Beach Boys ever played together, on the fourth of July, 1983, in front of an audience of a half million people in Atlantic City. But each time Brian would join the group for performances, he would eventually succumb to crippling anxiety that would force a return to seclusion.

Not unlike the writing of Sylvia Plath, Virginia Woolf, or Ernest Hemingway, Brian Wilson's songs almost always came from his personal experience. He would write about his pain and loneliness and disorientation later, but at this point he was merely describing what he lived every day, events with which every teenager or young adult could relate. While he and Mike Love were cruising around in the car one day, they were laughing at Dennis's various exploits with groupies, who followed him everywhere. There was one young girl who had been especially persistent—she stole her father's Thunderbird, telling him she was going to the library but then went to visit Dennis for a rendezvous.

Brian and Mike found this so hilarious that they wrote a song about it, "Fun, Fun, Fun," which contains the line embedded in so many memories from this time. Almost everyone from this generation who is now reading this cannot help but sing along: "She'll have fun, fun, fun till her daddy takes the T-Bird away."

The Shadow of the Beatles

The song "Fun, Fun, Fun," released in 1964, would reach as high as number five on the charts, but it was their next single, "I Get Around," that would earn them their first number-one hit as a group. (Brian had written "Surf City" for Jan and Dean.) It was while they were working on this record that there would be an event that would finally lead to Brian's psychological emancipation from his father, a battle that Dennis had been waging single-handedly for years.

Murry had showed up to the studio, even against express orders by Brian to stay away. It was bad enough that his glaring presence would make everyone nervous, but he would constantly interrupt the flow, announcing with complete disdain that what they were doing was garbage.

"I disagree," Brian said as calmly as he could, hoping that would end it. It never did.

Murry persisted in attacking the arrangement, the instrumentals, the harmonies, everything he could think of, everything they had done. The guitars weren't loud enough. The drums were too loud.

Finally, Brian had taken enough, not just from this barrage but from all of his life. He told Murry that he was the producer now, that his father was nothing but a washed-up old man who was jealous of their success.

Murry started laughing at this point, calling Brian a loser, and that was when everything changed for Brian—in that moment. "Something in me snapped," Brian recalled. "I couldn't take any more of his abuse. I wouldn't."

With the rest of the boys watching in astonishment, Brian jumped out of his chair, lifted his father up and threw him across the room.

"Time seemed to freeze. Then, righting himself, my dad shot me the same kind of dark, hateful look he wore when I was a child and he had beaten me with a two-by-four."

The difference this time, however, is that Brian was bigger and stronger than his father. And for the first time in his life, Murry could see that his son had inherited his rage even if he so rarely allowed himself to express it.

The elation that Brian would feel at standing up to his father, not to mention enjoying a number-one hit, would not last long.

A new group coming out of England, the Beatles, knocked the Beach Boys off the top of the charts. When this new sensation arrived in America at the end of 1964, they took the country by storm, virtually controlling the first five positions in the rankings.

The Beatles represented the single greatest threat to Brian, besides his father, but also the greatest stimulation. The Beatles fired Brian's sense of competition and artistic ambition. He adored their music, admired their creativity and innovation, and this, more than anything else, would push him to reach new levels of his own inventiveness, even if it literally drove him crazy. If the Beatles conquered the United States, then the Beach Boys returned the favor by becoming the number-one group in England.

"Then I just have to create a new song to bring me up on top," Brian vowed, once he was knocked off the top of the charts. "That's probably my most compelling motive for writing new songs—the urge to overcome an inferiority feeling." Brian admitted that he was never motivated by money with his writing, but to prove something to himself, to the world, and mostly to his father: that he really was the best songwriter in the country.

Besides writing music, the one grounding element in his life was the total infatuation he felt for Marilyn, about which he was still trying to keep a secret from his family because she was still only fifteen. He also knew that of even greater concern to his anti-Semitic parents would be that she was Jewish. He believed that Irv and Mae Rovell would support their relationship; after all, they now treated him like a son. But he knew that once word got out about his relationship with Marilyn to his own parents, there would be hell to pay. His prediction was correct: once Murry learned of their engagement, he commented what a scandal it would be for his son to have little, Jewish children.

Brian was reluctant to join the group on their next scheduled tour of Australia, but against his better judgment, he agreed to go. It didn't take more than five minutes after he boarded the plane to realize that he had made a huge mistake, that he should never have left Marilyn alone (convinced she would forget him), and so he demanded that the pilot send a telegram right away, instructing Marilyn to expect his call. During the weeks he was away, he called her at all hours of the day and night, even with the time change, pleading with her to marry him.

As expected, once he returned and announced his engagement (the Novells did agree to the union once Marilyn turned sixteen), Brian's family was livid. Murry couldn't believe this cherished firstborn was going to marry a Jew, and perhaps that was part of the attraction for Brian: he had chosen a mate who would put more distance between him and his father. Murry seemed to have drawn Dennis and Carl into a conspiracy to sabotage the relationship, because they hid Brian's birth certificate so he was unable to obtain a marriage license. Nevertheless Brian and Marilyn persevered, and they were married in a civil ceremony in December 1964.

A Fractured Mind

Within weeks of the marriage, Brian developed a friendship with another in a series of dependent relationships with older guys who would influence and control him. Loren Schwartz was a musician and an early proponent of the power of drugs to set one's creative energy free. He introduced Brian to the pleasures of marijuana, and in no time, the two buddies were hanging out and getting high with other like-minded folks—David Crosby (from Crosby, Stills, and Nash), Roger McGuinn (from the Byrds), Tony Asher and Van Dyke Parks (both of whom would someday become Brian's writing partners).

Marilyn was immediately concerned that her new husband, not the most stable of guys in the first place, was choosing to spend his discretionary time smoking pot. To add to the tension in their new marriage, Brian was expected to join the group on a new concert tour. They were all waiting at LAX airport to board the plane for Houston when Brian imagined that Marilyn, who was there with others to say farewell, was giving Mike Love an amorous look. Marilyn found this amusing, but also disturbing, because she couldn't even recall looking his way and felt no attraction whatsoever to Mike Love. Still, Brian was insistent that this was not something that he had hallucinated. So Brian and Marilyn started to argue just as the boys boarded the plane.

As soon as he was seated, Brian began to lose complete control of himself. He started crying and sobbing at a pitch that alerted everyone around that there was something terribly wrong. The flight attendants tried to calm him down, but Brian started to become more and more agitated. He put a pillow up against his face to muffle the sounds of his screams, which he could not seem to restrain. All he could wail, over and over again, was, "She doesn't love me. She doesn't love me."

Once the plane landed in Houston, Brian refused to get off the plane until it returned him to Los Angeles immediately. His brothers were eventually able to pry him loose from his seat and had no choice but to send him home the next day.

Reflecting on what he was thinking at the time, Brian said, "I was driven by obsessions, extreme behavior, demons, and fears; I was an oddball with a deadpan delivery, so out of it I was hip. Everything I did or thought was aimed at creating music that would make people happy and also keep them away from me, and because I was successful, my weirdness was accepted."

One positive outcome from this crisis was that Brian was finally able to convince his brothers to release him from the demands of touring. He had earned the freedom to stay home from then on and devote himself to creating new music. He was desperately trying to save himself before he went completely mad.

As if he didn't already have enough problems to deal with, Brian was feeling incredible pressure to stoke his creativity, regardless of the risks, so he could keep pace with John Lennon and Paul McCartney. In 1965, when he was offered the opportunity to try LSD for the first time with Loren Schwartz, Brian jumped at the chance. During the next year, he would try it dozens of times, against the intense pleadings of his wife, Marilyn, who could already see widening fractures in her husband's fragile mind. She tried everything to break up the destructive relationship between Brian and Loren, including moving out for a period of time. But throughout his life, Brian would almost always have some dominant male in his life, a likely replacement for his father.

On and off the Road

Without the stresses of touring, Brian could devote himself full time to creating new music. He wrote and produced his second number-one hit for the group, "Help Me, Rhonda," about a depressed guy who was begging his lover to help him recover. And then, several months later, in the summer of 1965, he wrote one of his most enduring tunes, which still evokes memories in anyone over the age of fifty: "California Girls."

As successful as his compositions were becoming, Brian could still not escape the shadow of the Beatles (as well as other competing groups, like the Rolling Stones). He longed to escape from the genre of feel-good car and surfing tunes and do something deeper and more meaningful. For this, in December 1965, he turned to Tony Asher, one of the friends he'd met through Loren, to create what would become his most ambitious and enduring musical legacy. He'd even announced to Marilyn ahead of time, without the least bravado, that he intended to create the greatest rock-and-roll album ever made. There are many, forty years later, who would agree that he managed to accomplish this goal.

While the Beach Boys were away touring, Brian and Tony collaborated on *Pet Sounds,* a concept album of individual songs that would be the first one to hang together thematically and hold its own with anything ever written in the pop music scene. It would contain some of the best material, and most memorable lyrics, of any popular music ever written: "Sloop John B," "Wouldn't It Be Nice," and the autobiographical "I Just Wasn't Made for These Times."

Tony Asher had quit his job in advertising to come to the aid of Brian during his time of need, but it was by no means an easy arrangement. Brian's work habits were as erratic as his social behavior. He would sleep at weird times, stare at the television for hours, and only really get revved up to work by midafternoon. When he was disappointed with the way a track was turning out, he would break out in tears or do an imitation of Murry's rage. He even expressed regrets that maybe he had chosen the wrong Rovell sister, and he'd be better off with Diane or Barbara. Asher hung on only because he could see the outcome was worth it.

If Brian's emotional stability was suspect, his professional judgment was spot on. He controlled every facet of the production: writing the music, collaborating on the lyrics, laying down most of the voice tracks himself. He hired the best studio musicians he could find to play the instrumentals and only used his brothers for the harmonies and backup vocals. By the time he was done, it was the most expensive musical production ever. And he delivered exactly what he said he would: a deep, melancholic collection of songs about the pain of growing up. According to music critic Terrance Terich, it "absolutely drips with depression, loneliness, and alienation. The despair of Brian Wilson is palpable and real, yet set to such exquisite music and words that we have no choice but to go along for the ride and empathize."

The album may have been ultimately recognized as an artistic masterpiece, but the other members of the band were resistant, finally going along because they felt they had little choice. They found the lyrics too complex and abstract and the music too inaccessible. The executives at Capitol Records also had their doubts about its commercial success. Where were the cars, the surfing, the California girls in the songs?

When the album was released in the fall of 1966, it was initially not as successful as the previous records they had released. It broke briefly into the top ten but was the first studio album from the Beach Boys in three years that never achieved certification as a Gold Record. Singles released of individual tracks only did reasonably well. "Sloop John B" reached number three on the U.S. charts and number two in England; "Wouldn't It Be Nice" reached number eight in the United States; and "God Only Knows" (the first rock song with "God" in it) charted at number two in England, where Paul McCartney said that the album absolutely blew him out of the water: "I love the album so much, I've just bought my kids each a copy of it for their education in life. I figure no one is educated musically 'til they've heard that album." McCartney was especially intrigued with the way his fellow bass player wrote bass lines that redefined the way the instrument could be used (not unlike the experimental work of jazz artist Charles Mingus in a different genre).

Pet Sounds was a resounding critical success, and Brian Wilson was lauded as a genius, *the* genius of the American music scene in the 1960s. He was rushing against time—against the madness that was relentlessly closing in on him—to create as much as he could before he fell completely apart. His next work, and perhaps his greatest, was to be a mini-symphony, a single song that would take over six months to record and cost more money than any other single record in history.

Good Vibrations

More and more often, Brian would speak in the language of "vibrations." He would feel "good vibes" or "bad vibes," depending on who was around, or what kind of energy was flowing in the environment. This would become so important to him that he began to rearrange his house in order to maximize the vibrations in the air. He actually built a huge sandbox in the middle of his living room and had truckloads of sand, by the ton, brought in and distributed in the box, where he then placed his grand piano. He claimed that the vibes were better for creating music when he could feel sand between his toes. (Unfortunately, the sand also got into the keys and gummed up the works.) Then he moved out all the furniture on the ground floor and erected a tent—costing (in today's money) hundreds of thousands of dollars—in fabric and velvet, with cushions for smoking hashish. This was all about creating the right vibrations in his life.

The song "Good Vibrations" would become Brian Wilson's greatest single work. He was so demanding about its production that it was recorded in four different studios, over the course of twenty different sessions. Brian employed both classical and rock musicians to play a variety of unusual instruments on the piece, including a Theremin, an eerie-sounding electronic instrument that was used in horror movies to signal danger or impending doom.

Singer Linda Ronstadt recalls watching Brian Wilson compose music in a studio during this time. She was just mesmerized by his creative process. One time, he was stumped by the challenges of putting together a complex harmony in multiple keys, juggling the parts of a half dozen different voice lines, plus the symphonic instrumentation. He was talking to himself, muttering over and over again, "You can't get it right. You've got to get it right. You can't figure it out, can you? You just have to go to the piano."

Ronstadt watched in awe as Brian would then sprint over to the piano and start playing a boogie-woogie tune, in a different key, and with different chords, than anything he had been composing at the time. "He'd just rage on the piano for about two or three minutes," she said, shaking her head. "Then he'd stop playing and he'd walk back to the mike and he'd just throw the part down that fast."

Linda Ronstadt, among the most experienced and well-trained musicians on the scene, had never seen anything like it in her life. "Clearly, while he was playing this boogie-woogie song on the piano, he was figuring out these very complex harmony clusters in some other part of his brain—in another key, in a completely different genre. And I was just staggered."

Ronstadt was not the only one who couldn't figure out how Brian Wilson managed to do what he did, to break so much new ground, and to do so with such an unusual method and eccentric behavior. He had never had a single music lesson in his life, yet he understood, intuitively, just how to blend together instruments, harmonies, melodies, and chords that had never been combined in that way before.

Unlike *Pet Sounds,* "Good Vibrations" was not only regarded as one of the most original pieces of popular music ever written but was also a huge commercial sensation, soaring to number one and selling close to a million records the first week. This would be Brian's last hurrah, at least in terms of any significant completed work for the next thirty-five years.

Unfinished Symphony

As deeply as Brian had gone in his latest works, he wanted to still carve out new ground. He wanted to create music that was more than entertaining, that was also mystical. For this new project, he needed a different sort of lyricist altogether, someone who could write words to music that would be so different that there was no existing point of reference. For this, he turned to another of the fellows he had met through Loren: Van Dyke Parks, an intellectual folk singer who spoke in the complex streams of consciousness of a Virginia Woolf novel. Brian wasn't sure he understood the guy completely, but he admired his way with words.

Van Dyke was as much a poet as a lyricist, and when he teamed with Brian to write the music for what would someday become *Smile,* they had truly formed a partnership that was intended to rival Lennon and McCartney and Rodgers and Hammerstein. Unfortunately, Brian's unstable mental state, coupled with his increasing use of drugs to manage his anxiety, made the collaboration doomed from the start.

Capitol Records had already printed a half million album covers, waiting for Wilson and Parks to complete the compositions, but progress had stalled. Up until this point, the executives, engineers, and musicians put up with Brian's weirdness, because he was deemed a genius and his behavior the product of creative eccentricity. But this was obviously no longer the case. Brian was now in the throes of a full-blown psychotic breakdown. He had become paranoid, believing that there were listening devices all around him. He would agree to hold conversations only in the swimming pool, where he believed his enemies (especially his father) could not listen in. He became delusional, thinking that the movies he was watching had special messages embedded in them just for him.

In the spring of 1967, *Smile* was abandoned by the studio as an unfinished symphony, brilliant perhaps, but unlikely to ever be completed. The Beach Boys, too, were considered washed up and obsolete, replaced by Jefferson Airplane, the Grateful Dead, Rolling Stones, Jimi Hendrix, Janis Joplin, Fleetwood Mac, the Who, the Doors, and Led Zeppelin. For the next twenty years, while Brian was virtually housebound, the Beach Boys would become relegated to a bunch of hasbeens on radio stations that played "oldies but goodies."

Descent into Madness

Brian and Marilyn had their first child, Carnie, in April 1968, although by that time Brian was retreating further into his own world. The other brothers, as well, were struggling with their own problems. Dennis, in particular, had become mixed up with a group of fanatics devoted to sex orgies. The leader of the group and his harem actually moved into Dennis's home, where they practiced a dedicated schedule of having sex with the girls a half dozen times per day. It was an exhausting life, to be sure, but Dennis enjoyed the company of the charismatic fellow: by the name of Charles Manson.

Dennis actually supported Manson and his "family" of girls for many months during 1968 and 1969, sharing the spoils of the sex slaves and even helping Manson to record his song, "Cease to Exist," which they also included on their next Beach Boys album, *20/20*. Dennis brought Manson to Brian's home on occasion, but Manson's crazy eyes gave Marilyn the creeps. Knowing that Dennis had already gotten gonorrhea from one of the Manson girls, Marilyn disinfected the toilets every time they left. Even in his own demented state, Brian could feel Manson's bad vibrations and became convinced that something awful would happen around this man that everyone was calling a wizard.

Dennis eventually kicked Manson out of his house, after Manson threatened to slit Dennis's throat with a hunting knife, but they still remained in contact. Dennis had contributed over $100,000 to support the group, including giving Manson a new Mercedes-Benz. It was several months later, in August 1969, that Charles Manson and members of his so-called family committed the Sharon Tate massacre, earning a place in history as one of the craziest mass murders ever.

When Brian and Marilyn found out about what Dennis had brought into their home, they realized how lucky they had been. Brian had been rude to Manson whenever he showed up, refusing to speak with him and yelling at Dennis to get him out of there. Manson would just glare at Brian with those scary eyes, then turn his attention back to the naked women squirming on the floor, waiting for his direction.

The decade of the 1970s was one of turmoil and lawsuits for the Beach Boys. By the end of 1969, they were on the verge of bankruptcy. Their bookings dried up. They sued Capitol Records for unpaid royalties and severed their relationship. (Soon they would begin suing one another.) And the final straw was, without consulting Brian, his father sold the rights to all of Brian's early songs, which were owned by Murry's management company. Then he took the money and ran. Without creative leadership, the next years would be bumpy for all the members of the band, surviving on a few concerts playing their older hits, living on their royalties and savings.

Brian had become so depressed that he would rarely leave his room. He threatened at times that he would kill himself, even going to the trouble to dig his own grave, but he couldn't sustain interest in any one thought for very long. Marilyn and his brothers could see what was happening to him, but they felt powerless to do anything: Brian simply refused help from anyone. The only thing that gave him any relief was getting high.

Marilyn and Brian's second daughter, Wendy, was born in October 1969. Brian would be a rather withdrawn father to the girls. After Wendy was born, Brian stopped functioning any longer as a husband to his wife and became instead an invalid and third child.

Recovery, of a Sort

When Murry died of a heat attack in 1973, both Brian and Dennis refused to attend their father's funeral. Brian was moved to his own private quarters in the house, and although he was no longer sleeping with Marilyn, he was enjoying the company of her sister Diane, as well as another woman, Debbie Keil, who was completely devoted to him. None of the three women knew about the other until a blowup occurred when

Debbie sneaked into the house only to find Diane already there. The fight that ensued awakened Marilyn, who didn't know that either her sister or this groupie had been intimately involved with her husband.

During the next two years that Brian remained virtually house-bound, he ballooned up to 240 pounds, subsisting primarily on junk food and drugs. He had added cocaine to his "repertoire" of drugs, and when that was taken away, and his access to money was cut off, he smoked five packs of cigarettes a day and gulped overly sweetened coffee by the mug—anything to get a buzz.

Marilyn tried repeatedly to get her husband help, but Brian consistently refused, remaining holed up in his room, sneaking alternative ways to get drugs. She tried hiring guys to keep twenty-four-hour watch over Brian and monitor his activities, but Brian was sneaky and always found a way to outfox them. The big mystery was how a drug-addled, obese, unwashed, unkempt blimp managed to juggle relationships with three women at the same time. Obviously, there remained something besides his star power that others still found charming, attractive, and desirable.

Marilyn found a couple of conventional therapists, who tried to help Brian, before she discovered Eugene Landy in 1975. The psychologist fancied himself an expert in addictions and had already worked with actors Gig Young, Richard Harris, and Rod Steiger, as well as singer Alice Cooper. Landy was an aspiring songwriter himself, who had previously tried producing and collaborating with the jazz musician George Benson, who fired him for being too controlling.

"My people developed distrust," Benson explained later, "when he made them sign a power of attorney that they didn't understand, and he got all my mail and all my checks."

If Marilyn was looking for someone with a radical approach to getting through to her husband, she sure found it in Landy. He believed he would have to exert complete control over his patient's life, and with the assistance of several minions, he intended to provide twenty-four-hour around-the-clock supervision. Many of Landy's plans were well conceived and executed—cutting off Brian's access to drugs, improving his diet, getting him involved in an exercise program, helping him to lose weight, reteaching him the basic social skills that he had forgotten—like bathing, table manners, and making conversation.

"I had to be crazier than Brian," as Landy once described the essence of his method. "There is only room for one crazy person in Brian's head, and that's got to be me. I have to be the ultimate power in this situation. . . . How do you make a guy get out of bed after so long? Explain it to him first? No. You throw water on him first. That's just what I did. I warned him, and then threw water on him and he got up."

As strange as his method appeared to Marilyn and Brian's family, they couldn't argue with the results. Landy did manage to get Brian out of bed and back to rudimentary working order. He lost weight. He stopped drugging. He even started writing music again. The only side effect was that he became pathologically dependent on Landy to control every facet of his existence. Even Landy admitted this was by design.

Nobody was allowed access to Brian without Landy's approval. If the studio wanted to negotiate a deal, they had to go through Landy. If a friend wanted to visit, first he needed Landy's permission. When Lorne Michaels was negotiating to produce a special about the Beach Boys (including the scene in which Brian tried to surf), he showed up at the house with Dan Aykroyd and John Belushi in tow. Belushi had brought pizza and beer for the occasion—from one glutton to another—and Brian scarfed up the food and alcohol in record time, the first he'd had in a long time. Landy was livid at this breach of his control and made Belushi apologize.

When Brian hosted *Saturday Night Live* in July 1976, it was with Landy appearing within his constant view, holding up cue cards of encouragement. It was an awkward, exploitative, and painful performance on live television, in which Brian was forced to do a skit about a singer suffering from debilitating stage fright. It was immediately after this debacle that everyone else in Brian's life banded together to prevent further such humiliations.

Regardless of whether one agrees or not with Landy's unconventional methods, there could be little doubt that he crossed the ethical line by meeting his own needs in the relationship and taking advantage of his disoriented patient. He was charging the Wilsons over $1,000 per day for his services, 365 days per year, *plus* writing himself in for a percentage of royalties for any songs Brian wrote while under his care. Landy figured he was entitled. The Psychology Board of the State of California eventually disagreed, suspending his license when word got out about exactly what he had done.

Marilyn and Brian's brothers were trying to extricate him from Landy's control but found it difficult to be alone with him long enough to do so. Eventually, they had to mount a "coup," in which Marilyn informed Brian about how much money had been paid—hundreds of thousands of dollars—during a time when their financial situation was precarious. Brian become furious at what he finally understood was overt manipulation. During a confrontation with Landy, Brian went after him physically, which the doctor claimed was good therapy.

In 1977, Landy was replaced by a bodyguard, Rocky Pamplin, an ex-professional football player with the New Orleans Saints, and then a model who had appeared as a centerfold in *Playgirl*. He was gorgeous, and before weeks had gone by, he had seduced Marilyn, in what would become a long, messy affair right under the nose of unsuspecting Brian (who was having his own affairs).

Say what you will about Landy, but once his treatments stopped, Brian regressed with respect to his physical and mental health. Marilyn added other "watchers" to the payroll, but none of them—nor Landy before them—had really addressed the real core of his issues: his terrible lack of self-esteem, his insecurities, his unresolved issues related to his abuse and relationship with his father, and his likely biologically based mental illness, which required careful medical supervision, not illicit or hallucinogenic drugs.

One of the saddest incidents of all in Brian's crumbling life was a day in 1977 when Paul McCartney came by the house to visit. Paul and Brian had met on a few occasions and regarded each other with the respect that would be expected from two of the greatest living popular-music composers.

Paul had heard about Brian's troubles and had come by to visit and offer support. But when Brian heard that McCartney was there, he immediately ran to hide, locking himself in his room. He felt too insecure and fragile to meet with the one man he admired most.

Not knowing what else to do, and unwilling to give up after making the trip to Brian's house, Paul just stood there, staring at the locked door. He began knocking, first softly, then loudly, begging to be let in. All he heard in response was the sound of Brian sobbing.

Emancipation

Brian continued to slip out of touch once again, relying on old sources to obtain drugs any way he could. He would disappear for days, sometimes hitchhiking as far as San Diego, or even Mexico. He was recognized a few times by other musicians, who offered to pay him in drugs if he would help them produce their records.

Marilyn had decided that she had had enough and suggested a separation, to which, surprisingly, Brian readily agreed. He had found out about his wife's affair with Rocky and believed he would be better off now on his own. This was not, unfortunately, to be the case.

Brian was committed to a psychiatric hospital in 1979, where, for the first time, he received conventional, intensive care and was diagnosed with *schizoaffective disorder*, a psychotic condition that includes features of both schizophrenia and manic depression (similar to Nijinsky). Perhaps his friend Van Dyke Parks had him pegged in a far more compassionate way, by noting that Brian had suffered from "an absence of unconditional love—love that had no contingencies, no hooks, no fine print, no exploitation in the subclauses." Regardless of whether he was labeled (variously) paranoid schizophrenic, manic-depressive, or a victim of drug-induced psychosis, he was certainly in trouble and desperately needing to be stabilized. He occupied himself on the ward playing the piano in the dayroom and even tried writing some music when he could concentrate. A few months later, he was released, having made significant progress.

Meanwhile Dennis was doing his own out-of-control fatal spin, secretly supplying Brian with drugs on the side, as well as engaging in an assortment of crazy behavior that would have given his brother a run for his money. Eventually, he became involved with the fifteen-year-old friend of his daughter, Shawn, who just happened to be the illegitimate daughter of Mike Love (at that time, Dennis's bitter enemy). Dennis would impregnate the girl, marry her, and then in December 1983 die in an accidental drowning; he was so high on drugs and alcohol that he could have been pickled.

When Brian heard the news of his brother's death, he was devastated. More than anything, he couldn't understand how Dennis, so much stronger than him, could be dead while he was still alive. "Despite the way drugs and alcohol had ravaged him, I still thought of Dennis as all muscle, good looks, and charm. He was one of my best friends."

Brian would be returned to Landy's care once again, this time at the instigation of the remaining Beach Boys, who desperately needed their leader for creative inspiration and could think of no other alternative. They hated the psychologist and distrusted him, but he was the only one who could put a dent in Brian's madness and get him in good enough shape to work. Perhaps it was worth any price for his help.

The association between Brian Wilson and Landy would continue for the next several years, during which time the psychologist would so embed himself in his patient's life that he installed himself as producer. In the beginning of 1988, at the instigation of Brian's family, ethics complaints were lodged against the doctor. After reviewing the case, the Board of Medical Quality Assurance suspended the psychologist's license, but that was still not enough to extricate Brian from Landy's undue influence.

It wasn't until 1990 that Brian once again earned his independence from Eugene Landy, after having sued him to end their relationship. Even after the California Superior Court intervened to protect Brian Wilson against further manipulations from his therapist, Brian remained grateful to Landy. "I don't regret it," Brian said about their years together. "I loved the guy—he saved me. Exercise saved me. There is no drug in the world like it. He pushed me beyond my limits and stopped me being fearful of the world."

Struggling Back

With the freedom from the dependent relationship came renewed energy in Brian's fifties and sixties to begin writing music again, first releasing a solo album, *Imagination,* dedicated to his brother Carl, who was then battling cancer. Brian then resumed work on his magnum opus, *Smile,* which had lain dormant for over thirty-five years.

Brian remarried in 1995 to Melinda Ledbetter, and they adopted three children. After years of estrangement, he has reconnected with his daughters, Wendy and Carnie, who formed their own musical group, Wilson Phillips, along with Chynna Phillips, the daughter of John and Michelle Phillips, from the Mamas and Papas. Brian even helped produce their first recording, which sold over four million copies.

Brian's mother, Audree, died in 1997, and his last remaining brother, Carl, died of cancer in 1998. Brian was the last Wilson of the Beach Boys—and the least likely one to have survived.

Smile

The album *Smile,* first begun in 1967 with Van Dyke Parks, was finally completed, thirty-eight years later, and released in 2004. "I wanted to get it out before I died," Brian said in an interview, admitting that it grated on him all these years to have this unfinished business weighing on his mind. This ranks as the longest case of overcoming writer's block in history.

Going back to his unfinished masterpiece has not occurred without risks for Brian. In the beginning of 2004, just before he was about to embark on the concert premiere of *Smile* in London, he was so flooded with memories about the past that he took himself to the emergency room of a hospital. "I had to have a lot of strength to recall the bad memories, to put that behind me and to go on with it and learn."

Although Brian is now well enough to be performing, he confesses that he still has auditory hallucinations in spite of the medications he takes to control them. Interestingly, it is the same phenomenon that produces disturbing voices in the form of auditory stimuli that permits Brian to hear all the unusual melodies and complex harmonies that have been the signature of his compositions. Who else could have ever had the ability to hold onto so many layers of discordant sounds?

In an interview following his *Smile* concert tour of 2004, Brian talked about the dialogue that took place inside his head. To paraphrase, the voice says this to him:

"You're OK. You're OK. You're going to be OK," but he doesn't feel reassured. Standing backstage, he can hear the impatient rustling of the audience.

Another voice, also inside his head, chants, "You're gonna get it. Yes, you're gonna get it. You'll get it for sure." He covers his ears with his hands and shakes his head, *hard,* hoping to dislodge the annoying voices. Sometimes this works, but this time it doesn't.

"You're OK. . . . You're gonna get it . . ." The voices keep alternating, getting louder, sometimes just whispering.

"You OK?" one of the stage assistants asks him, knowing that something is terribly wrong.

Brian nods his head, not at all convincing. "I'm afraid," he thinks to himself, momentarily drowning out the voices. "I'm so afraid."

"What are you so afraid of?" he hears another voice ask, but this one he is pretty sure is not a hallucination. It's the voice of his therapist, who's been helping him deal with the stage fright and the voices that have plagued him most of his adult life. This voice inside his head calms him for a moment. He takes deep breaths the way he has been taught. Then he bends over and pukes his guts out into the bucket that is kept nearby for exactly this contingency.

As shaky as he feels, this is the best it's been for years. He's been through so much—the depressions, the drugs, being kept a prisoner by his former therapist, the lawsuits with his brothers, but now he's on the mend, relatively speaking.

"You're gonna get it. Yes you are," the voice repeats over and over. He is just about to scream when he hears the announcer's disembodied voice: "Ladies and Gentlemen, Brian Wilson."

Brian Wilson's *Smile* tour began shakily enough, just as one would expect after so many years out of circulation. But the critical acclaim, the thunderous and prolonged standing ovations, and the personal satisfaction of having conquered his greatest fears have given him a new lease on life. "I love to make people happy," Brian confessed. "I'm happier now than I've ever been. I got standing ovations wherever I went in Europe. I feel young. I feel happy. Isn't that something?"

In spite of the hugely popular reception he is receiving, it is hardly all roses for Brian, who still struggles at times. He still finds it difficult to have meaningful conversations and sometimes appears shaky at best.

Although he is forcing himself to talk to the media, one interviewer described him as so brittle that she thought about ending the conversation for fear that she might wound him in some way. "I've never met anyone so bewildered, so fragile, so clearly close to the edge. Even the simplest things seem to elude him. Over the course of an hour, he asks me my name four times."

Obviously, Brian has his good days and his bad days. He still struggles with depression and will always have to fight with all his heart to keep himself on a reasonable, stable footing. At sixty-three, he finally appears to have found some sense of peace with himself, even as he continues to battle lingering personal difficulties. With the help of his wife, Melinda, his children, and a herd of faithful supporters watching his back, he appears to have boosted himself to the point where he can express his creative genius once again.

Brian Wilson is still afraid of the water. But that terror will not stop him from riding the waves of his own creativity, even if it means occasionally wiping out. Whether out of courage, or desperation, he is driven to seek the best in his own divine madness.

CHAPTER TWELVE

Interpretations of Meaning in the Lives of Creative Geniuses

M y first reaction, upon completing the final story, was to feel depressed. The individuals profiled in this book have been populating my world—and invading my dreams—for the last months. I hope they've touched you as well.

I would be less than honest if I didn't admit that one of the reasons I haven't been able to sleep much lately is that I so closely identified with many of the people profiled in the book. I hold no delusions of grandeur (well, maybe a few) that I can ever be compared to a creative genius, but like most people, I like to think that at times, I can be rather imaginative. Maybe that is one reason why, during unguarded moments, I found it difficult to separate myself from the subjects. There were times when I found myself thinking like Plath, or feeling the despair of Woolf, or experiencing the anger of Bruce. And I can tell you this: it was a terrifying experience.

Were They Really "Mad" After All?

One reason I selected each of these folks, beside the fact that they fulfill the basic qualifications of being both extraordinarily creative and mad, was that I wanted to learn more about them. I wanted to find out what drove them to create, and—more important—what drove them crazy. Were they born that way and subject to fate beyond their control? Or did they *become* mad because of the choices they made?

These are questions that are not only critical for a psychologist who helps people deal with their demons, as well as trains other therapists to do the same, but for *anyone* who wishes to make sense of his or her own internal struggles to remain reasonably sane in a world that has become increasingly stressful. So what have we learned from our study of these ten lives?

There is a counterpoint to the whole premise of this book: that few of these creative geniuses were either mad or mentally ill. Such labels are bestowed on individuals who deviate from the norm, and by all accounts, each of the individuals profiled here certainly qualified. Our whole system of psychiatric nomenclature is built on the premise that deviations from consensual "reality," in the form of imagery, mood fluctuations, and especially conventional behavior, signify psychopathology. See the following list, which compares the parallel symptoms of creativity and madness, each with different names for similar behavior.

Parallel Symptoms of Creativity and Madness

CREATIVITY	MADNESS
High energy	Mania, insomnia
Heightened senses	Mood disorder
Eccentricity	Erratic behavior
Emotional expressiveness	Emotional volatility
Spontaneity	Impulsiveness
Risk taking	Recklessness
Single-mindedness	Obsessiveness
Unusual perceptions	Distortions of reality
Visions	Hallucinations
Big ideas	Grandiosity
Fluency of ideas	Flight of ideas
High standards	Perfectionism
Feelings of giftedness	Narcissism

There is little doubt that each of the artists in this book were highly unusual people. They all suffered mightily for their art. Most of them relied on alcohol or drugs to self-medicate the disturbing symptoms. Some even ended their own lives to stop the pain.

But to call any of them truly mad is to disparage and disrespect their creative identity. After all, how could you be expected to function so far outside the norm in one area (art, writing, dance, performance) and not exhibit such behavior in other domains?

"Men have called me mad," admitted Edgar Allan Poe, "but the question is not yet settled whether madness is, or is not, the loftiest intelligence—whether much that is glorious—whether all that is profound—does not spring from disease of thought, from moods of mind exalted at the expense of general intellect."

I still wonder whether someone like Lenny Bruce was really all that crazy, as opposed to being a visionary who was so misunderstood. OK, he was depressed and paranoid. And he sought to dull his pain with drugs. But he was as much driven mad by a system that found him threatening, an assault that few of us could have withstood with our sanity intact.

And what about Marilyn Monroe, Judy Garland, and Brian Wilson, also victims of such manipulation and abuse? Their behavior certainly demonstrated a high degree of disturbed and destructive conduct, but again, how many people could survive the kinds of experiences that they suffered?

The answer is surprising: *lots* of people—even *most* people. Human beings are amazingly resilient. Many children who are exposed to drugs or who are subjected to abuse or violence are messed up for a while, but most of them turn out just fine. However, there is indeed a relatively high incidence of mental illness among close relatives of those who also suffered these problems (such as Hemingway and Woolf for sure, as well as Nijinsky, Plath, and Monroe). Yet even with this greater risk, most of the relatives of mentally ill people lead normal lives, apparently unaffected by the supposedly tainted genes.

Even among extraordinarily creative people, we could easily focus not on those who were mad but on the vast majority of them who were quite high functioning in their personal lives. For every van Gogh or Rothko, there are two, three, or ten Pissarros or Braques; for every Beethoven or Schumann, there are so many more Brahmses or Bartóks; for every Woolf, Plath, and Hemingway, there are a legion of Melvilles;

for every Brando or Monroe, there are far so many more Paul Newmans and Tom Hankses. So the first idea to keep in context is that madness is in the eye of the beholder.

Are Madness and Creativity Really Connected?

There is an ongoing dispute about whether madness and creativity are indeed correlated. Some psychiatric critics have objected in the strongest possible terms to portraying madness as a muse, as the source of pain and suffering that drives creative output. Certainly Plath, Woolf, and van Gogh believed it even though there is not much empirical research to support the connection that creative productivity is enhanced by the presence of mental illness and especially debilitating depression.

Some mental health experts insist depression is a *disease,* not a condition or a state of mind. As such, rather being glorified as some sort of heroic inspiration it should be consistently classified as an affliction like cancer or diabetes.

Most likely, insanity is not an all-or-nothing phenomenon but rather a matter of degree. Regardless of notable exceptions, like scientist John Nash, composer Robert Schumann, or dancer Vaslav Nijinsky, who were schizophrenic and severely disturbed, a moderate amount of madness can lead to creative innovations.

Extraordinary creativity is about thinking outside the box. It is quite literally about seeing things invisible to "normal" people, in the same way that Mingus could hallucinate melodies; Nijinsky, dance movements; Woolf, stream of consciousness prose; Bruce, mad routines; and Wilson, inspired harmonies, in times of madness. Under such conditions, there are periods of heightened consciousness, the sort that fueled creative frenzies by Sylvia Plath during one of her writing binges or Mark Rothko during one of his painting marathons.

One conception of insanity is that it involves a state of irrational, illogical thinking that is not based in so-called collective reality. Yet it is precisely this rather unusual cognitive activity that leads to novel problem solving. It is also the heightened emotional sensitivity and awareness often associated with psychic pain and suffering that helped Marilyn Monroe, Judy Garland, and Sylvia Plath to deepen their artistic expression. In that sense, symptoms of anxiety and agitated (rather than vegetative) depression can actually become adaptive and functional for the creative genius. They produce states of hyperawareness—

of self and the environment—that contribute to new discoveries and methods of exploration. One need only think of artists like van Gogh or Pollock or Rothko, composers like Beethoven and Schumann, or musicians like Judy Garland, Brian Wilson, Charlie Parker, and Charles Mingus to appreciate the ways their inner pain led to achievements that would not have been otherwise possible.

Mania and hyperactivity, such as that seen in the cases of Hemingway, Plath, Mingus, Woolf, and Bruce, also helped to fuel their creative binges. Also the lack of inhibition evident in the behavior of Nijinsky, Garland, Monroe, Bruce, and Mingus allowed them to experiment with alternative ways of thinking, creating, and being. One definition of creativity is—in fact—the ability to make unusual associations between apparently unrelated elements. One example of that is the way that Mingus combined features of the classical composers with evolving jazz scores and doing so with an instrument (the string bass) that had never before been used in a lead role.

Of course, there are corrosive side effects to madness that also sabotage productivity. *Chronic stress syndrome* refers to the ongoing effects of anxiety that over time take a toll on the neurological, endocrine, and cardiovascular systems in the body. That is one reason why so many of the subjects in this book relied on drugs and alcohol to help soothe the more annoying symptoms. It also lends support to the idea that too much madness sabotages any possible opportunity to communicate novel ideas or products. That is what Sylvia Plath meant when she said, "When you are insane you are busy being insane—all the time. . . . When I was crazy, that's *all* I was." Yet there was a gestation period for her, and for Woolf, such that when they recovered, they were practically vibrating with creative energy to set their ideas to paper.

—⁓—

The following lessons can be derived from the lives of the creative geniuses profiled in this book and from how they struggled to reconcile their emotional instability with productivity in their art.

The Price of Creativity

The first conclusion that we may draw is that extraordinary creativity comes with a price. It is a given that any extreme deviation from the norm is going to be met with a certain degree of resistance at the very least, and usually a certain amount of envy and jealousy. Surely, you have experienced this in your own life when you have come up with your own bright ideas. Much to your surprise, people may not have been as grateful as you had thought and hoped. This does not apply so much to those circumstances where you have invented a novel solution to a problem that is bugging others, and for which they are thankful for your creative intervention, but rather in those circumstances when you have devised a whole new domain that others don't even understand. Throughout history, folks get poisoned (think Socrates), imprisoned (think Copernicus), burned at the stake (think Joan of Arc), or driven mad (think Lenny Bruce) when they deviate too far from expected norms.

In the case of our subjects, most of them were marked by trauma in early childhood and that followed them throughout their lifetimes. Judy Garland, Virginia Woolf, and Marilyn Monroe were sexually abused. Charles Mingus and Brian Wilson were physically abused. Lenny Bruce and Vaslav Nijinsky were neglected. Mark Rothko and Ernest Hemingway suffered emotional abuse of different sorts. Lord Byron, the English writer, was seduced at the age of nine by a nanny and thereafter found it difficult to sustain any permanent relationship except an incestuous one with his sister. I could go on, but the point is clear: most of these people felt damaged early in life and so sought healing, if not redemption, through their creativity.

Another factor to consider is that there are different kinds of creativity, which rely on different thought processes and talents, thereby producing different effects. It would appear from one study of writers who have won the Pulitzer or Nobel Prize that the more innovative and "far out" the creative product, the more likely that mental illness is present. According to the author of the study, "The ability to see the world in a completely novel way may come with a unique price tag. The mental processes that underlie this type of creative thought may be more tied to unhealthy processes than is creative thought that is more founded in a traditional style."

In the *Kabbalah,* the seminal book of Jewish mysticism, there is reference to the balance contained within all of life, the belief that—not unlike the *Tao* of *yin* and *yang*—the higher that one goes in any aspect of material or spiritual life, the lower that one also plummets. Therefore for any great burst of creative energy, it is impossible to sustain the momentum indefinitely, before a crash of some sort is inevitable. We all, it is said, must pay the piper.

Intensity and Sensitivity

One definition of madness is an extreme hypersensitivity to the world, as well as one's reactions to it. Crazy people are often viewed as over-reacting to things that happen in the world. Brian Wilson freaked out on an airplane because he missed his wife. Sylvia Plath went into a deep sense of mourning over the dissolution of her marriage. Mark Rothko and Virginia Woolf became unusually sensitive to criticism of their work. Marilyn Monroe, Charles Mingus, and Judy Garland threw (what were called at the time) "fits" when things didn't go their way.

Rather than lapse into psychological jargon and label this behavior as narcissistic or evidence of an underlying mood disorder, keep in mind that it was this same exquisite sensitivity to their environments, as well as their own strong emotional states, that permitted them to create such memorable works. Without their intense feelings and passions, Plath's poetry, Bruce's monologues, Mingus's music, Nijinsky's dances, Garland's performances, and Wilson's greatest songs would have been empty by comparison. Perhaps they never would have been written at all.

In a sense, such intense awareness of self—and the world—is an essential feature of greatness in creative pursuits, whether in art, music, literature, or theater. So-called mood disorders really mean the ability to experience deep emotions beyond the range of most people.

Even though depression is known to slow down both thought processes and the energy that supplies constructive action, it also promotes a degree of contemplation that would not otherwise be possible. In a study of creativity among so-called relatively normal-functioning geniuses, including Sigmund Freud, T. S. Eliot, Pablo Picasso, Albert Einstein, Igor Stravinsky, and others, it was noted that during the time of their breakthroughs in artistic or scientific achievement, they felt incredible pressure and despondency. All of them experienced depression and anxiety of one sort or another.

There is some merit to the idea that what does not kill you makes you stronger. Even among people who are not involved in creative pursuits as a profession, resilience is often developed as a result of surviving some type of adversity. This could take place while on a trip in which you become lost or in any other situation in which you are required to rely on resources that you didn't know you had or invent a new way of solving problems, but in most cases, the growth takes place when you are required to reach beyond your known limits.

Binges of Creativity

Let's look at a list of traits that are associated with innovation and extraordinary productivity, regardless of whether the field is in the sciences, arts, music, drama, commerce, or literature:

- High energy level
- Willingness to take risks, regardless of consequences
- Impulsivity and sometimes poor judgment based on snap decisions
- Ability to function at a high level with little sleep
- Feeling of being special and gifted, if not chosen for greatness
- Flood of ideas
- Strong drive and grand ambitions, regardless of the costs
- Feelings of euphoria associated with creative pursuits, as well as life in general
- Emotional volatility and sensitivity
- Unrealistic expectations for self and others that lead to higher performance
- Overconfidence in one's abilities
- Charisma and sense of personal power that is persuasive and influential
- Gregarious, engaging, and highly talkative

Although not an exact duplication, the same characteristics that are common to sustained creative innovation are also common to *hypomania* (a milder version of the mania associated with bipolar disorder)—with a few exceptions that have been noted in the stories in this book—paranoia, sexual acting out, and drug use to control or augment the symptoms.

In one study of the founding of America, the author believes that it is primarily mania that fueled the birth of this country. Many of the founding fathers, from Christopher Columbus to William Penn, Alexander Hamilton, and Andrew Carnegie, displayed messianic zeal for their ideas. Throughout history, it is not enough to *have* new ideas unless you are able to *sell* them—with unrestrained passion. In order to do so, it helps if you can function on little sleep and work in sustained binges of productivity in which new breakthroughs become possible (as with Plath and Woolf).

Seeing and Hearing Things That Don't Exist

One person's hallucinations are another person's "visions." Of course, whether these voices or images are labeled as crazy or not depends on how useful they are. A voice telling you to kill all the firstborn sons in your neighborhood is significantly different than one that tells you how to construct a new mathematical formula or lyrics to a song.

One contemporary poet, Thomas Disch, described creativity as "the ability to see relationships where none exist"; that is, to envision a reality that is invisible to so-called normal people. The "inspiration" that makes those who can do that great is also the "plague" that drives them mad. It was because Brian Wilson could hear voices that he learned how to become attuned (with only one functioning ear) to sounds that escaped others' attention.

Each of us hallucinates every night of our lives in the form of dreams. The lucky or misfortunate few who hear voices during the day may in fact have the wires crossed in their brains. What they label *voices* or *hallucinations* may merely be the residual dream images from REM sleep that have crossed over from one hemisphere to the other. According to this model, schizophrenia may actually be a kind of waking reality that is processed by the dreaming brain.

There are many cultures in which being insane is a sign of greatness. It is a required qualification to be a healer, a sign of holiness. Such people are believed to be touched by God. They are given a gift that allows them to see beyond the mortal world. In these cultures, shamans are specifically approached by those in pain because of the shaman's ability to access hallucinations. Rather than being interpreted as signs of madness, these visions are viewed as gifts from the gods that are to be honored. If any self-respecting Indian medicine man, Zulu *sangoma,* or Amazonian *brujo* were to admit that he does not actively hallucinate, he would lose all credibility within his community.

I am not urging that you necessarily start talking to others about your own auditory and visual hallucinations, but I am suggesting that these experiences occur on a continuum of intensity and frequency rather than an all (crazy) or nothing (sane) phenomenon. Most of us could profit from paying more attention to our inner experiences, especially if we can manage to harness these voices in constructive ways to guide our decisions and give more life to our original ideas. One difference between creative geniuses and the rest of us is that they are more willing to trust their inner voices even when others might caution otherwise. Of course, this same stubbornness could also get one in a lot of trouble!

Solitude, If Not Isolation

Creative efforts almost always involve a stage of incubation in which free-flowing thoughts and ideas are left to roam where they will, without the person's feeling the need to make sense of what is going on, much less to explain it. Mark Rothko, in fact, regretted one thing most of all in his life—that he had ever talked about or explained his art. For a painter, like Rothko, Gauguin, van Gogh, or Pollock, complete isolation was critical in order to get the work done, even if they went stir-crazy in the process. For writers, like Hemingway, Woolf, Dostoyevsky, Faulkner, or Plath, they too had to tolerate long periods of time in their own insufferable company in order to complete their masterworks.

Isolation may be good for creative thought, but it doesn't make for the best social skills. In spite of how much you might admire the people in this book and the brilliant work that they did, you would not want one of them in your home for any length of time, or even at a dinner party with others you liked. Imagine how amusing—and obnoxious—it would be to spend time with Lenny Bruce or Vaslav Nijinsky or Ernest Hemingway. We are talking about a group of people who were so self-centered, so used to being on center stage, that they found it difficult to communicate in any sort of meaningful way when they were not the focus of attention.

Emotionally challenged people seek out as much solitude as they can, feeling secure and safe only when they are sure that nobody around can hurt them. That is one reason why Brian Wilson was content to spend so many years in bed. It is also what makes such wounded people so ripe for creative innovation. When the composer Pyotr Tchaikovsky became so agitated at the prospect of his impending marriage, he fled to a life of isolation in the countryside, where he could devote himself entirely to composing music and could avoid any further emotional entanglements that might threaten him.

The more isolated you are, the more insulated you become from the usual influences of conventional media, and potentially the more original your products will be. This may not be true in science as much as in the arts, and certainly not to extreme degrees. (Even Rothko and Pollock benefited tremendously from their ongoing dialogues with the other abstract expressionists.) But a certain amount of time alone is necessary for any substantial creative output.

If the benefit of isolation is that the work gets done, the downside is that there is a significant lack of support and nurturance around most of the time. When you consider those who are already acutely vulnerable and overly sensitive, sometimes the worst thing they can do is isolate themselves from loved ones. This is another price paid for choosing a life of creativity.

Yet seeking a balance in life between time alone and time with others is not only the key to life satisfaction but also to enduring stamina. One of the major lessons of these stories is how important it is to ask for help when it is most needed. That, unfortunately, is part of the sickness of insanity: these people are unable to see clearly just how disordered they have become. Without such awareness, there is little motivation to seek help, in spite of what others might plead.

Could They Have Been Helped?

So many of the individuals who have been profiled in this book sought the help of professionals with less than satisfactory results. In the case of Judy Garland, Marilyn Monroe, Mark Rothko, and Brian Wilson, their therapists were incompetent, unethical, or both. In the case of others, such as Vaslav Nijinsky, Ernest Hemingway, and Virginia Woolf, psychiatry, psychopharmacology, and psychotherapy were not advanced enough to provide the type of care that is currently available. Drugs like lithium (for bipolar disorder) and Prozac (for depression) could have made a huge difference. Instead of Nijinsky being administered insulin shock, Sylvia Plath and Ernest Hemingway given electroshock, or Virginia Woolf given jugs of milk, current knowledge in psychopharmacology could have at the very least reduced their symptoms. There is also considerable scientific evidence that demonstrates conclusively that debilitating depression is best treated by a combination of antidepressant medication and psychotherapy.

Those with serious drug and alcohol addictions (Monroe, Bruce, Garland, Rothko, Wilson, Hemingway, Mingus) could have benefited from inpatient treatment centers that are available today. Such programs would have helped them not only to detoxify but also to get them away from their unhealthy environments, which were contributing to their abuse, so that they could develop new habits that could have kept them off their past addictions.

As most of the individuals (except Bruce, Wilson, and perhaps Mingus) lived during a time when psychotherapy was synonymous with insight-oriented, orthodox psychoanalysis, they were not offered the kind of structured, action-oriented treatments that are currently available. So many of these individuals did indeed suffer from unresolved issues of the past that would have lent themselves to analytic work, but they needed much more than that. As victims of trauma and abuse, they needed opportunities for more expressive therapy to work through the kind of depression that represented extreme helplessness and anger.

Throughout the writing of this book, I fantasized frequently about what I would have done if each of these people showed up as my patient for help. Certainly, a few of them, like Nijinsky, I would have immediately referred for medication consultation to manage his most distressing symptoms. And others, like Garland, Bruce, Hemingway, Mingus, and Monroe, would have needed immediate drug intervention and participation in support groups (like Alcoholics or Narcotics Anonymous) to maintain their sobriety. It's really unfortunate that these people did not receive the kind of constructive interventions that are now readily available.

Because so many of their problems took place within a context of their relationships, it would now be standard operating procedure to initiate couples therapy for Ted Hughes and Sylvia Plath, Marilyn and Brian Wilson, Mary and Ernest Hemingway, Vincente Minnelli (or Sid Luft) and Judy Garland, Arthur Miller and Marilyn Monroe, Honey and Lenny Bruce, Romola and Vaslav Nijinsky, Susan (or Judy) and Charles Mingus, Mel and Mark Rothko. In every case, miscommunications and misunderstandings sabotaged the potential support that could have been possible. In several cases, extremely dysfunctional (Garland), dependent (Monroe), and abusive (Hemingway) relationships could have been addressed. And though they may not have been remedied, they could at least have been improved. Such support would have helped these couples to stop repeating the same destructive patterns over and over again.

All of the women—Marilyn, Sylvia, Judy, and Virginia—would have profited from feminist approaches to therapy, which focus on issues of empowerment. Each of these women had appeared (and acted) crazy because it was adaptive behavior for them in situations where they had no voice of their own. Women during those times, in particular, were objectified and given no direct access to the market for their art without the access and control of men like Ted Hughes, Louis B. Mayer, and Lee Strasberg. A feminist therapist would have helped them to develop greater resourcefulness and independence so that they would not have needed to remain so dependent and helpless. It is more than a little ironic that Plath and Woolf, in particular, were inspiration for the very development of the feminist approach to therapy.

I don't mean to imply that if one of these people sought the care of a professional today that there would be 100 percent agreement on the best course of therapeutic treatment. Quite the contrary, actually, because there is more debate than ever about which one, among dozens of alternatives, would provide the best results. Nevertheless I think that today any reasonably competent and ethical therapist would provide far different care than what was provided to Marilyn Monroe and Brian Wilson, in particular. It would be critical to enforce clear boundaries in the therapy and most of all not to get sucked into the patient's celebrity. Many of the therapists allowed themselves to become seduced by the fame and notoriety of their patients, and in so doing, they ended up exploiting their patients in ways that paralleled what they had experienced earlier in life with authority figures.

What all of these individuals needed the most was understanding of their divine madness and its consequences. I am not saying that psychotherapy, or present-day psychopharmacology, would have cured them. But it surely could have reduced their suffering and could even have saved some of their lives. I also don't believe that this reduction of pain and self-destructive behavior would have significantly reduced their creative productivity, and from all available evidence on the subject, it would most likely have improved the quality and quantity of their work. When you consider the number of lost days that these folks spent in drugged, psychotic, or depressed stupors, it is mind-boggling to consider what else they could have accomplished.

Is Madness Divine?

We are now back to the question that began our inquiry, except a more useful way of framing it is not *whether* there is a connection, but rather *what form* it takes to provide guidance in the ways we conduct our lives. "Beauty is inspired by madness," said the French writer André Gide, but it is also "written by reason."

We could all do with a little madness in our lives if that means greater spontaneity, playfulness, constructive risk taking, and experimentation in the ways we do things. So often, people become locked into stifling routines, drive the same route to work every day, engage in the same conversations, with the same people, in the same ways. As such, daily life can feel stale and boring, just as you might feel stuck in relationships, in a dead-end job, or in repetitive patterns that seem circular.

It isn't necessary to be certifiably insane in order to enjoy greater creativity and impulsiveness in the ways we relate to others, nor does choosing a creative path necessarily lead to increased madness. For the subjects in this book, who died tragically and before their times, they lacked one crucial characteristic that you most likely possess, as a function of choosing to read a book such as this: a desire to know yourself better through the lives of others who traveled before you. Sure, Marilyn Monroe, Sylvia Plath, and Virginia Woolf read Freud. Brian Wilson read self-help books prescribed by his doctor. Others, like Rothko, Bruce, Mingus, and Hemingway, also read widely, but in many cases they were afraid to confront their insecurities. Even when they entered therapy, it was with a determination to hide themselves as much as possible.

We are all a little crazy, some more than others. And we all have the capacity to be far more creative in the ways we work, and play, and live our lives. "There must be provision for the adjustment of tensions between pleasure and pain for the experience of beauty," said Mark Rothko. He seemed to understand, at least intellectually, that there are always risks associated with looking into the void.

—∿— Notes

Chapter One—The Nature of Madness and Creativity: Myths and Realities

1–2   See the book by psychiatrist Kay Jamison (1993) for a catalogue of prominent artists and composers who suffered bipolar disorders. She suffered this illness herself. In addition, a study by Post (1994) of almost three hundred world-famous men also supported a close connection between creativity and psychopathology.

There are many sources that debunk what is called the myth of a relationship between madness and creativity. In a review of the complex connection, Lauronen, Veijola, Isohanni, Jones, Nieminen, & Ishohani (2004) found some links but not as clear a correlation as generally believed.

The data on incidence of bipolar disorder in the general population and in creative people is from Jamison, but some (see Schlesinger, 2002) would say these figures were inflated based on a biased and limited sample.

The study of one thousand creative individuals was done by Ludwig (1995).

3   The quote is from Victor Frankl (1962), p. 104.

An excellent survey of the theories related to creativity and madness can be found in Barrantes-Vidal (2004).

3–4   Studies on the similarities between psychotic thought processes and creativity were conducted by Rothenberg (1990).

4   The interviews with prominent artists and writers were conducted by Jamison.

The question about resilience was investigated by Poole (2003).

5   The quote is from Styron (1990), p. 62.

7   The quote is from Poe (1848/1948), p. 356.

7 One conclusion to this debate, presented by Barrantes-Vidal, is that moderate amounts of some forms of madness might facilitate creative enterprises, whereas more severe forms (especially chronic vegetative depression) would diminish creativity because of the sheer lack of energy and will.

Chapter Two—Sylvia Plath: Perfected in Death

9 Nobody knows, of course, what really happened during that fateful early morning of February 11, 1963. This re-creation is based on several accounts described in the important biographies of her life, including Alexander (1999), Butscher (2003), and Hayman (2003). Most of what is known about what actually occurred is based on testimony by her physician, Dr. Horder, her neighbor and friend, Jillian Becker (2002), her nurse Myra Norris, and police investigations that ruled the death a suicide. Much of the material used throughout this chapter is based on these three biographies, plus Plath's own journals and letters, as well as her published writing.

11 The poem "Edge" was published along with three others to accompany her epitaph in *The Observer* (1963) of London. It is included in her collection *Ariel,* which was first published two years after her death.

The lines from "Edge" that seem to signal her intention of taking the children with her are these:

> *Each dead child coiled, a white serpent,*
> *One at each little*
> *Pitcher of milk, now empty*
> *She has folded*
> *Them back into her body as petals*
> *Of a rose close when the garden*
> *Stiffens and odors bleed*
> *From the sweet, deep throats of the night flower.*

12 See *The unabridged journals of Sylvia Plath* (2000) and *Letters home* (1975), the collection of letters written to her mother throughout her years at Smith and in England.

Ted Hughes insisted that he destroyed one volume of her journal to protect their children, and another volume was lost.

12   Plath's first poem was published at age eight in the *Boston Herald*:

> *Hear the crickets chirping*
> *In the dewy grass.*
> *Bright little fireflies*
> *Twinkle as they pass.*

15   This is a journal entry, November 3, 1952, from *Unabridged journals*, p. 149.

16   This is from *The bell jar* (1963/1971), p. 121.

17   This account of Plath's loss of speech was reported by Alexander (1999) in his interview with her friend Wilbury Crockett, who visited her in the hospital and worked to train her to relearn language by playing a word game of "Anagram."

       This excerpt from Plath's journal is dated June 20, 1958, *Journals*, p. 395.

18   This is from an article by Beam (2001) entitled "The mad poet's society," which appeared in *The Atlantic Monthly*.

       Her doubts about her failures are reported in Alexander (1999), as well as to a boyfriend, Peter Davison (1986).

19   This is from a journal entry about her first meeting with Hughes and the violence of his poetry, *Journals*, p. 212.

20   Ted Hughes's personal papers, letters, and correspondence were only released after his death in 1998. Because he remained silent about his wife for thirty years after her suicide, it was only learned relatively recently about his version of what took place during their passionate relationship. From reading both their papers, it is clear that there was indeed a period in their marriage when they were monogamous, devoted, and supportive of each other.

22   The friendship between Anne Sexton and Sylvia Plath is memorialized in "The Barfly Ought to Sing" by Sexton, which is in Alexander (1984).

23–24   This is an excerpt from *Journals*, November 7, 1959, p. 524.

24   See Silverman & Will (1986).

       The account of the last days of Sylvia Plath are described in the books by Ronald Hayman and Jillian Becker.

25   See Becker.

26   Ted Hughes's letter to Sylvia is from the poem "The Blackbird," in Hughes (1998), p. 162.

26   A number of psychoanalysts and psychologists have studied the case of Sylvia Plath for purposes of diagnosing her mental illness and exploring her core issues. Some of these sources include Claridge, Pryor, & Watkins (1990), Robertson (1995), and Silverman & Will.

27   Runco (1998) proposed the theory on how creativity affects depression.

Kaufman (2001b) dubbed "The Sylvia Plath Effect."

Ludwig (1995) conducted the study of a thousand distinguished creators.

Kaufman (2001a) cites external locus of control as a factor.

28   This is an excerpt from *Journals,* July 19, 1958, pp. 408–409.

The epitaph is in Alvarez (1963), p. 23.

28–29   See Alvarez (2000).

29   The connections between Plath and Sexton are discussed in Beam (2001).

30   See Butscher, p. 365.

Chapter Three—Judy Garland: Under the Rainbow

33   The description of this scene between Judy Garland and her daughter Liza Minnelli is intended as a generic one, based on several similar incidents that occurred during Liza's adolescence. It is based primarily on Shipman (1992) and Clarke (2000).

34–35   The list of her achievements and ranking as the greatest enter-tainer of all time comes from the PBS Web site and database, found at www.pbs.org.

38   Descriptions of Judy Garland's relationship with her mother come from interviews conducted by Clarke and Finch (1975).

The quote on the "Wicked Witch" is from Finch.

41   The interview about feeling ugly appeared in the *National Enquirer,* October 23, 1960.

42   The interpretation of *Oz* as a spiritual journey is from Clarke.

47   The account of her suicidal "gesture" was reported in all the local newspapers on June 21, 1950, earning headlines in the *Los Angeles Times.*

49 Garland's relationship with John Kennedy was reported in several newspapers during 1960 and also described in Clarke.

51 The interview about her ex-husbands was reported by John Gruen in the *World-Journal-Tribune* and also was described in Finch.

Chapter Four—Mark Rothko: Painted in Blood

56 This quote is from Breslin (1993), p. 17. This is the best biography about Rothko and a major source for this chapter.

57 The description by Moise of his brother is from Ashton (1983).

  The quote on Rothko's forced migration is in Fischer (1970).

58 The quote about Kate Rothkowitz is from Breslin, p. 29.

59 This quote is from his school publication, *The Cardinal,* published in October 1920 and cited in Breslin.

  Reports of discrimination against Jews at Yale is based on Oren (1986).

60 The quote on wandering into the art class is from Fischer.

62 The quote on teaching art to children is from Rothko's essay "New training for future artists and art lovers," cited in Breslin.

64 This quote is from Morris Calden, based on an interview by Bonnie Clearwater from the Archives of the National Gallery of Art, and is cited in Breslin.

  The manifesto is described in Clearwater (1984). The original letter is found in the *Archives of American Art.*

65 This is from the Letter to Clay Spohn, May 11, 1948, Clearwater.

65–66 Rothko was always secretive about his technique, not even allowing his daughter to watch him in later life without a certain reluctance. Based on reports from a number of his assistants over the years, this description is described in Breslin.

67 See Breslin.

68 This quote by Al Jensen is from a conversation with Rothko that he later transcribed and provided to Breslin from a third party.

  See Hess (1955).

69 This Rothko quote on the Four Seasons is from *Mark Rothko, 1903–1970.* London: Tate Gallery, 1987.

72   Bruce Ruddick was interviewed by the Mark Rothko Archive
           and cited in Breslin.

72–73   The story of the medical mistakes and mismanagement is re-
           viewed in a special section of the journal *Suicide and Life-
           Threatening Behavior*, *25*(3), Fall 1995, edited by J. T. Maltsberger.
           Articles about the way Rothko's case was handled were written
           by Lester, Klepser, & Weinberg. All agreed that Rothko was a
           very difficult patient, but that was no excuse for the lack of
           communication and cooperation among his physicians.

73   Albert Grokist's comments on his patient are found in Seldes
           (1978).

73–74   The account of Rothko's suicide is gleaned from several sources,
           including Breslin, Seldes, and an article by a journalist who was
           allegedly at the scene, Wilkes (1970).

Chapter Five—Ernest Hemingway: Living Up to His Legend

78   The Hotchner (1966) quote is on the shock doctors, pp. 279–280.

           The Hemingway quote on not being able to write is from
           Hotchner, p. 297.

78–79   The description of the suicide is based on Meyers (1999),
           Hotchner, and a memoir by M. Hemingway (1976).

79   The quote about playing Papa Hemingway is from Yalom &
           Yalom (1971), p. 487.

80   See G. Hemingway (1976).

81   Cases of the family legacy of mental illness are reported in Jami-
           son (1993).

83   The quote from "Nick Adams" stories on the conversation with
           his father is cited in Donaldson (1998).

84   The quote on having to be hurt like hell is described in Meyers,
           p. 36.

           The quote about lying is in Reynolds (1981), p. 4.

85   The quote from "The Big Two-Hearted River" is from the book
           In our time, cited and described in Donaldson.

86   The quote about his sexual abstinence in a letter to Katy Smith is
           described in Meyers.

88   The quote on shit-detector is from Hemingway (1958), p. 88.

          The quote on the principle of iceberg is from Hemingway, p. 84.

89   See Stewart (1974), p. 85.

91   The book about Hemingway's fetishes is by Eby (1999).

92   A review of scholarly articles analyzing Hemingway and his neu-
          roses is in Craig (1995).

97   The quote from David Bruce is based on a letter sent to a war
          correspondent, cited in Meyers, p. 407.

98   The quote on his fiftieth birthday to Scribner's is cited in Meyers.

101   The description of the aftermath of the suicide is described in
          M. Hemingway.

Chapter Six—Virginia Woolf: A Great Lake of Melancholy

104   The letter to Ethel Smyth is in Woolf's six-volume *Letters of
          Virginia Woolf* (1980).

          The quotation about "curious visions" is from Woolf's five-
          volume *The diary of Virginia Woolf* (1978), vol. 2, p. 283.

          The quotation about "sinking down, down" is from *The diary*.

105   The various theories about the causes of Woolf's mental illness
          are attributed as follows: genetic inheritance: Jamison (1993),
          neurobiology: Caramagno (1992), trauma of childhood sexual
          abuse: De Salvo (1989), dissociation from childhood trauma:
          Terr (1998), defective personality: Love (1977), separation-
          individuation issues with mother: Bond (1995, 2000), abandon-
          ment by depressed husband: Dally (1999), reading Freud:
          De Salvo and Bond (1995).

          The debate about whether Woolf's reading of Freud was danger-
          ous to her mental health is discussed in Dervin (1992).

106   The quote about growing up among the books is from a letter to
          her friend Vita Sackville-West in *Letters*.

107   Descriptions of all the mental illness in the Stephens family is
          based largely on Dally.

          Laura's actual condition and diagnosis have been debated almost
          as often as that of her stepsister Virginia. She has been described
          as schizophrenic, retarded, autistic, and antisocial, to mention
          a few.

108   The genogram was created by Mary Halunka.

109   The theory that Stephen was Jack the Ripper is discussed at length in De Salvo and in Harrison (1972).

The source of Stephen's abduction and assault of Woolf is described in De Salvo.

109–110   Much of the material on the childhood sexual abuse is based on De Salvo.

112   The quotation "I know the feeling now, when I can't spin a sentence . . ." is from her *Diary*, vol. 3, p. 174.

113   The quotation about the sound of waves is from *Diary*.

114   Woolf's description of her sexual abuse was reported in many different reports—in letters, conversations, and public lectures.

The quotation about "private nucleus" is in *Diary*.

116   Leonard Woolf's description of Virginia's manic episode is from Leonard Woolf (1964), pp. 172–173.

117   The quotation "Curious how all one's fibres seem to expand & fill . . ." is from her *Diary*, vol. 4, p. 176.

120   The quote is from *The waves* by Virginia Woolf (1931/1959), p. 7.

The quote on "intensity and intoxication" is from *Diary*.

A discussion of the unconscious processes involved in the creation of *The waves* is found in Charles (2004).

The quote on "what interested me" is from *Diary*.

120–121   The quote on how Woolf challenges us is from Charles.

122   The material describing Woolf's last two weeks is based on Marder (2000) and Woolf's *Letters*, vol. 6, 1936–1941, pp. 481–486.

123   The letter to sister Vanessa Bell is from *Letters*.

124–125   The description of what happened on March 28, 1929, with the "fertile illness" is based on Marder.

Chapter Seven—Charles Mingus: Musical Hallucinations

130   The quote on no joy and no love in the room is from Russell (1996).

Parker's quote is from Russell, pp. 345–346.

132   This quote from Mingus on being three people is from Mingus (1971), p. 3.

132–133   Life histories of jazz musicians are collected by Willis (2003).

134   This quote is from Mingus on his father's beatings, Mingus, p. 14.

134–135   The story of Mingus learning to fight from his father, and other material for this chapter, is based in large part on the biography by Santoro (2000).

136   The quotes from Britt Woodman are based on interviews by Santoro, p. 32.

137   The quote from Red Callender is from Gioia (1992), p. 334.

139   The quote from Mingus on his learning is from Hentoff (1979b).

140   The quote describing the music is from Santoro, p. 69.

   This Mingus quote to the reporter on the bass becoming an extension of himself is from Hentoff (1978).

141   Mingus's quote on Bird Parker is excerpted from the "liner notes" of his album *Mingus Dynasty.*

144   The scene talking to his therapist, Dr. Pollock, is from Mingus, p. 6.

145   The note at Bellevue is from Mingus, p. 338.

   The rant from Mingus is from Cerulli, Korall, & Nasatir (1987), pp. 16–17.

148–149   Quotes from Mingus about living in the neighborhood are from Hentoff (1972), p. 17.

149   The quote about the extended chemistry mix is from Santoro, p. 338.

151   The quote from Mingus about self-slavery is from Hentoff (1981), pp. 52–53.

Chapter Eight—Vaslav Nijinsky: A Method to His Madness

153   Much of this chapter is based on the psychiatric study of Nijinsky by Ostwald (1991) and the biography by Buckle (1971).

153–154   The story of his rage during rehearsals is from his sister's *Early memoirs,* Nijinska (1981).

156   An analysis of Nijinsky's diary can be found in Abenheimer (1946).

157   Nijinsky's handicap in so many other areas, while excelling in the dimension of dance, is consistent with much of Gardner's (1993) research on creative genius.

158 Nijinsky's confession about death to his sister is from *The diary of Vaslav Nijinsky* (2000), p. 162.

160 Nijinsky's writing about his masturbation fantasies is from *Diary*, p. 205.

162 The quote from Bronislava is from Nijinska, p. 316.

166 This quote is from Jones (1946), p. 46.

167 See Chaplin (1964), p. 192.

172 The quote from Nijinsky on his suffering is from his *Notebook on death,* quoted in Ostwald (1991), pp. 191–192.

173 Case note from Fritz Wieland, one of the staff at Bellevue, is from Ostwald (1991), p. 246.

175 Details of Alfred Adler's treatment of Nijinsky are from Ansbacher (1981, 1993).

For a discussion of Nijinsky's psychiatric diagnosis, see Stephens and Ostwald (1991).

177 Romola Nijinsky (1934, 1952) wrote her own books about her relationship with Nijinsky, as well as edited (and censored) his diaries in their first publication. (They have since been reedited by more objective scholars.) In these books, she told her version of his story, conveniently leaving out any details that didn't suit her or show her in the best possible light. A much more critical look at her motives and behavior can be found in Ostwald (1991, 1994).

The quote from Nijinsky from his *Diary* is included in the film *The diaries of Vaslav Nijinsky,* produced and directed by Paul Cox.

Chapter Nine—Marilyn Monroe: Killed by Kindness

180 The critical biography of other biographies about Marilyn Monroe is Churchwell (2004), and the encyclopedia about Marilyn Monroe is Riese & Hitchens (1987).

181 See Steinem (1987).

Material about Monroe's early childhood is based on Spoto (1993), Leaming (1998), and Summers (1986). It should be acknowledged that there are so many controversies and conflicting information reported in various sources about many aspects of her life (her death, for instance, which was said to be a mob hit, an accidental overdose, suicide, or FBI assassination) that whenever possible, I relied on several different sources.

182   Descriptions of Marilyn's physical abuse are described in Moes (1990) and Guiles (1984).

182–183   The incident of her sexual abuse, although questioned as to its accuracy by some sources (see Spoto), was reported by her in great detail during an interview in 1954 with Lloyd Shearer, a journalist. The story is repeated in Summers and mentioned many times in her life to other friends she trusted, although there is still no sure way to tell how much of the story actually happened as reported. This, of course, is often the case with regard to reports of sexual abuse in children. Churchwell covers the various versions of the reported abuse and rapes, noting that it was mostly male biographers, like Norman Mailer, who minimized or questioned whether these incidents ever occurred. Even if some of the reports were not as described, it is highly probable that Marilyn was assaulted sexually (as so many foster children are) more than once and that these experiences had a huge effect on her later development.

184   The quote from Marilyn on her naked fantasy is from an interview that appeared in *Time*, "To Aristophanes and back," 67(20), May 14, 1956, p. 74.

186   The quote on having the body of a woman is from Barris (1995), pp. 35–36.

189   The ideas about multiple intelligences and creativities come from Gardner (1983, 1993). Gardner describes one of the seven types of creativity as largely "interpersonal," meaning that certain extraordinary people are particularly influential in the domain of their personality and charisma.

The quote from Natasha Lytess is cited in Spoto, p. 138.

191   Accounts of Marilyn's suicide attempts are based on reports from Jim Dougherty, a reliable witness, considering his later job as a SWAT police officer. The incidents are described in Summers.

195   The quote from Strasberg is in Riese & Hitchens, p. 501.

196   The quotes from Marilyn on becoming an artist and notes on her problems from multiple sources are cited in Spoto.

196–197   Material on the Miller and Monroe early meeting and relationship is from Riese & Hitchens.

198   Margaret Hohenberg's professional lapses and conflicts of inter-
        est are documented in Spoto.

199–200 Marianne Kris's treatment of Marilyn, including overmedication
        and inappropriate pushing, are detailed in both Spoto and
        Leaming.

201   The quote from Billy Wilder is based on an interview by Sum-
        mers, p. 203.

202   The quote from Marilyn on Miller is from Kobal (1974), p. 613.

203   The note from Marilyn was published in *American Weekly,*
        May 1, 1960.

        The quote from Greenson in his letter to Kris was dated August
        20, 1962, and is cited in Spoto.

204   There are sources (Summers) that claim that Kennedy and
        Monroe had a love affair lasting several years, but the best docu-
        mented and most objective accounting of the evidence is pre-
        sented in Spoto, who details three to four probable meetings
        between them. Marilyn talked a lot about her relationship with
        Kennedy, but she was not considered a reliable witness consider-
        ing her tendency to exaggerate.

205   It is clear that Marilyn Monroe had absolutely no privacy in her
        life. Her desperate note to the Strasbergs to help her escape
        appeared in *The Daily Mirror* of London, August 5, 1981.

207   The biographies on Marilyn are split on the subject of her sup-
        posed affair with Robert Kennedy, just as they are on the presi-
        dent. Even Norman Mailer, who wrote one of the first
        biographies on Marilyn alleging an affair with Bobby Kennedy,
        eventually retracted the claim. From reviewing all evidence now
        available, there is nothing definitive that points to anything
        more than a brief sexual encounter with John and nothing other
        than a friendship with Bobby.

208–209 Greenson's explanation of his treatment plan was discovered in
        his professional papers after his death. His report is presented in
        Spoto. Although Spoto and Brown & Barham (1992) are the
        most critical of all the biographers about Greenson's conduct,
        others, such as Leaming and Summers, judged him to be gener-
        ally compassionate and well meaning in his actions. Given that
        Greenson's own diagnosis of his patient was that she had a bor-
        derline personality disorder, in addition to depression, paranoia,

and possibly schizophrenic features, one would think the last thing he would have wanted to do was expose his family to the dangers of manipulation, hysteria, narcissism, and other characteristics of such a destructive personality.

210   The quote from Natasha Lytess is from Guiles (1969), p. 97.

The quote from Marilyn on searching for her identity is from Steinem (1972).

212   One of Greenson's colleagues, Robert Litman, an expert on preventing suicide, was given the job of doing a psychological autopsy on Monroe's death, just as he had been asked by the coroner to do for other celebrities who died under suspicious circumstances (John Belushi, Natalie Wood, William Holden, Freddie Prinz, Janis Joplin). Reluctant to place blame on any of his fellow doctors, he nevertheless concluded that a lack of communication between the attending physicians had led to needless overmedication. From reviewing the evidence available, he also surmised that Marilyn had been reaching out for help and actually wanted to be saved at the last minute. His report can be found in Litman (1996).

Speculation regarding Eunice Murray's role in Marilyn Monroe's death is described in detail in Spoto and Churchwell.

Lee Strasberg's eulogy to Marilyn can be found in its entirety at: http://marilynmonroepages.com/memorial_2002_3.html.

213   For further discussion of Marilyn Monroe's significance as a cultural icon, see Churchwell.

Chapter Ten—Lenny Bruce: Sick and Dirty Comic

215–217   The dialogue for the stand-up routine is adapted from Bruce (1984), pp. 28–29.

218–219   The description of Bruce's drug activity is based on reports by Goldman & Schiller (1971).

220   The quote from Kenneth Tyson of the *London Observer* is from the documentary by Baker (1972).

The quote from Lenny on his humor's being based on destruction and despair is from Cohen (1971).

221   The quote from Lenny on divorce is from Weaver (1968), p. 74.

221–222   Material on Lenny's childhood comes from Milstein (1959) and Deikel (1974).

224   The quote from Lenny on appearing in contests is from the best biography on him, Goldman & Schiller.

234   The quote on his creative innovation is from Goldman & Schiller, p. 340.

235–236   The description of Lenny's wondering about why people got so upset from four-letter words is based on a recollection by Kenneth Tyson from the documentary by Baker. The excerpted dialogue from "To is a preposition, come is a verb" is from the same film.

239   Information about Lenny Bruce's trial is from Krassner (1996) and Collins & Skover (2003).

241   The admission by his prosecutors of Lenny's innocence is described in Kofsky's book (1974) on the social significance of Lenny Bruce and also in the film by Baker.

The quote by Bruce's lawyer on his pardon is from Kifner, Collins, & O'Donnell (2003).

Chapter Eleven—Brian Wilson: Afraid of the Water

243–245   The description of Brian Wilson's first surfing experience is from Gaines (1986) and from the film *Brian Wilson: I just wasn't made for these times,* directed by Don Was and produced by Larry Shapiro.

246   Quote on "rock's most famous nutcase" is from an article by Bill Holdship that appeared in the *Bay Area Music* magazine, December 12, 1991.

251   The quote from Gary Usher about Brian's eccentricity is in Gaines, p. 73.

The quote from Gary Usher about Brian's creative genius is from 1987 and is included in Abbott (2003), p. 287.

253   The quote from Brian about hearing voices is from his autobiography, *Wouldn't it be nice,* Wilson (1991).

255   The quotes from Brian describing the fight with Murry are from Wilson, p. 92.

The quote from Brian about his motive is from Wilson.

256	Brian Wilson's relationship with Loren Schwartz and his introduction to drugs is described in Gaines and in Granata (2003) as well as from Wilson's autobiography.
257	The quote from Brian about being driven by obsessions is from Wilson.
259	The quote from music critic Terrance Terich about *Pet Sounds* is from www.Treblezine.com.

259 The quote from Paul McCartney is from Abbott, p. 288.

For a complete track-by-track-analysis of *Pet Sounds,* including its significance in the history of popular music, see Granata.

260–261 The quote from Linda Ronstadt is in the film *Brian Wilson: I just wasn't made for these times.*

264 The quote from George Benson is from White (1994), p. 310.

The quote from Landy on his method is from Gaines, p. 285.

267 Brian Wilson's diagnosis of schizoaffective disorder is from the disclosure by his wife, Melinda, on the *Larry King Show,* August 20, 2004.

Van Dyke Parks's "diagnosis" of Brian is quoted in White, p. 333.

The quote from Brian on Dennis's death is in Wilson, p. 313.

268 The report on Landy's suspension of his license appeared in "Brian Wilson's Svengali has his wings clipped as he gives up his license to shrink," *People Weekly, 31*(15), 1989, p. 97. The description of his therapy practices was based on interviews that appeared in Gaines.

The quote from Brian Wilson about Landy's help is based on an interview with Sean O'Hagen in 2002 and is cited in Granata.

268–269 The discussion by Brian Wilson of his writer's block is from an interview with Cathy Maestri in *The Press-Enterprise* (Riverside, CA), October 20, 1999.

269 The quote from Brian Wilson about going to the emergency room because of bad memories associated with *Smile* is from an interview that appeared in the *Toronto Star* based on a report by the Associated Press, October 1, 2004.

The discussions about Wilson's continuing hallucinations is from an interview with Deborah Solomon that appeared in the *New York Times,* July 4, 2004, and from an interview on *Larry King Live* on August 20, 2004.

269–270   The description of the voices before performing on stage for *Smile* is based on an interview with Wilson by Fiona Sturges that appeared in *The Independent* on June 21, 2004.

270   The quote from Brian Wilson on being happy is from an interview with Bernard Weintraub that appeared in the *New York Times* on September 12, 2004, after the release of *Smile*.

The interviewer quote about Wilson's current instability is from Sturges.

Chapter Twelve—Interpretations of Meaning in the Lives of Creative Geniuses

274   For a discussion of the ongoing debate on whether madness is correlated with creativity, see Barrantes-Vidal (2004).

275   For a discussion of chronic stress and its effects on mental and physical health, see Sapolsky (1998) and Restak (2004).

275–276   A discussion on the price of creativity can be found in Ludwig (1995).

276   The quote on Pulitzer and Nobel Prize–winning authors is from Kaufman (2001a), p. 312.

277   One of the strongest critics of depression having been overromanticized is Peter Kramer (1993, 2005), author of several books (including *Listening to Prozac*) about the benefits of antidepressant medication. He builds a case that depression, in particular, is hardly "divine" or "sacred" or "inspirational" but rather is a medical disease that requires chemical intervention. Of course Kramer is also responsible, more than anyone, for the popularity of Prozac and other "cosmetic" drugs that are designed to balance moods.

The study of creative genius was undertaken by Gardner (1993)

For a study of those who have changed their lives as a result of some adversity that they faced while traveling, see Kottler (1997).

278   The study of hypomania among America's founders, as well as the list of features associated with creativity and manic episodes, is from Gartner (2005).

279   The ideas about waking reality and dreaming are from Griffin & Tyrrell (2004).

See Kottler, Carlson, & Keeney (2004) for a discussion of the ways that indigenous healing practices make use of altered states to promote healing.

For a wonderful story about a medicine man who was unable to have a vision and about how he sought help for his problem, see the story by Brad Keeney in Kottler & Carlson (2003).

281   For a review of research on the benefits of antidepressant medication, see Kramer (2005).

284   The quote is from Rothko (2005).

—⁓— References and Further Reading

Abbott, K. (2003). *Back to the beach: A Brian Wilson and the Beach Boys reader.* London: Helter Skelter.

Abenheimer, K. M. (1946). The diary of Vaslav Nijinsky: A pathological study of a case of schizophrenia. *Psychoanalytic Review, 33*(3), 257–280.

Alexander, P. (Ed.). (1984). *Ariel ascending: Writings about Sylvia Plath.* New York: HarperCollins.

Alexander, P. (1999). *Rough magic: A biography of Sylvia Plath.* Cambridge, MA: Da Capo Press.

Alvarez, A. (1963, February 17). A poet's epitaph. *The Observer.*

Alvarez, A. (1999, September 15). How black magic killed Sylvia Plath. *Guardian.*

Alvarez, A. (2000). *Where did it all go right? A memoir.* New York: Morrow.

Anderson, W. T. (1992). *Reality isn't what it used to be.* New York: Harper-Collins.

Ansbacher, H. L. (1981). Discussion of Alfred Adler's preface to *The diary of Vaslav Nijinsky. Journal of Individual Psychology, 37,* 131–152.

Ansbacher, H. L. (1993). Alfred Adler's description of the case of Vaslav Nijinsky in light of current diagnostic standards. *Archives of General Psychiatry, 50,* 669.

Arnold, E. (1987). *Marilyn Monroe: An appreciation.* London: Hamish Hamilton.

Ashton, D. (1983). *About Rothko.* New York: Oxford University Press.

Baker, F. (1972). (producer and director). *Lenny Bruce without tears: A documentary.* Fred Baker Films.

Barrantes-Vidal, N. (2004). Creativity and madness revisited from current psychological perspectives. *Journal of Consciousness Studies, 11*(3–4), 58–78.

Barris, G. (1995). *Marilyn: Her life in her own words* (pp. 35–36). New York: Citadel Press.

Beam, A. (2001, July/August). The mad poet's society. *The Atlantic Monthly.*

Becker, J. (2002). *Giving up: The last days of Sylvia Plath.* New York: St. Martin's Press.

Bell, Q. (1972). *Virginia Woolf: A biography.* Orlando: Harcourt Brace.

Bond, A. H. (1985). Virginia Woolf: Manic depressive psychosis and genius. *Journal of the American Academy of Psychoanalysis, 13*(2), 191–210.

Bond, A. H. (1995). Virginia Woolf: Manic depressive psychosis and genius. In B. Panter, M. L. Panter, E. Virshup, & B. Virshup (Eds.), *Creativity and madness.* Burbank, CA: Aimed Press.

Bond, A. H. (2000). *Who killed Virginia Woolf?* Lincoln, NE: Human Sciences Press.

Breslin, J. (1993). *Mark Rothko: A biography.* Chicago: University of Chicago Press.

Brown, P., & Barham, P. B. (1992). *Marilyn: The last take.* New York: NAL/Dutton.

Bruce, L. (1984). The money I'm stealing. In K. Bruce (Ed.), *The almost unpublished Lenny Bruce.* Philadelphia: Running Press.

Buckle, R. (1971). *Nijinsky.* New York: Simon & Schuster.

Butscher, E. (2003). *Sylvia Plath: Method and madness.* Tucson, AZ: Schaffner Press.

Caramagno, T. C. (1992). *The flight of mind: Virginia Woolf's art and manic depressive illness.* Berkeley: University of California Press.

Caws, M. A. (2001). *Virginia Woolf.* New York: Woodstock.

Cerulli, D., Korall, B., & Nasatir, M. (Eds.). (1987). *The jazz word.* New York: Da Capo Press.

Chaplin, C. (1964). *My autobiography.* New York: Simon & Schuster.

Charles, M. (2004). The waves: Tensions between creativity and containment in the life and writings of Virginia Woolf. *Psychoanalytic Review, 91*(1), 71–97.

Churchwell, S. (2004). *The many lives of Marilyn Monroe.* New York: Metropolitan Books.

Claridge, G., Pryor, R., & Watkins, G. (1990). *Sounds from the bell jar: Ten psychotic authors.* New York: St. Martin's Press.

Clarke, G. (2000). *Get happy: The life of Judy Garland.* New York: Random House.

Clearwater, B. (1984). Shared myths: Reconsideration of Rothko's and Gottlieb's letter to the *New York Times. Archives of American Art Journal, 24*(1), 23–25.

Cohen, J. (1971). *The essential Lenny Bruce.* New York: Ballantine.

Collins, K. L., & Skover, D. (2003). *The trials of Lenny Bruce: The fall and rise of an American icon.* Naperville, IL: Sourcebooks Mediafusion.

Craig, R. J. (1995). Contributions to psychohistory: Hemingway "analyzed." *Psychological Reports, 76,* 1059–1079.

Dally, P. (1999). *The marriage of heaven and hell: Manic depression and the life of Virginia Woolf.* New York: St. Martin's Press.

Davison, P. (1986). *Contemporary authors' autobiographies.* Detroit: Gale Research.

Deikel, S. M. (1974). The life and death of Lenny Bruce: A psychological autopsy. *Life-Threatening Behavior, 4*(3), 176–192.

Denzin, N. K. (1989). *Interpretive biography.* Thousand Oaks, CA: Sage Publications.

Dervin, D. (1992, spring). Who's afraid of who killed Virginia Woolf? *The Journal of Psychohistory, 19*(4), 463–471.

De Salvo, L. (1989). *Virginia Woolf: The impact of childhood sexual abuse on her life and work.* New York: Ballantine.

Donaldson, S. (1998). *Ernest Hemingway, American writers retrospective supplement.* New York: Scribner.

Eby, C. (1999). *Hemingway's fetishism: Psychoanalysis and the mirror of manhood.* Albany: State University of New York Press.

Finch, C. (1975). *Rainbow: The stormy life of Judy Garland.* New York: Ballantine.

Fischer, J (1970, July). Mark Rothko: Portrait of an artist as an angry man. *Harper's Magazine, 241,* 16–23.

Frank, G. (1975). *Judy.* New York: HarperCollins.

Frankl, V. (1962). *Man's search for meaning.* New York: Washington Square.

Gaines, S. (1986). *Heroes and villains: The true story of the Beach Boys.* New York: Da Capo Press.

Gardner, H. (1983). *Frames of mind.* New York: Basic Books.

Gardner, H. (1993). *Creating minds.* New York: Basic Books.

Gartner, J. D. (2005). *The hypomanic edge: The link between (a little) craziness and (a lot) of success in America.* New York: Simon & Schuster.

Gergen, K. (2001). *Social construction in context.* Thousand Oaks, CA: Sage Publications.

Gioia, T. (1992). *West coast jazz.* New York: Oxford University Press.

Goldman, A., & Schiller, L. (1971). *Ladies and gentlemen: Lenny Bruce.* New York: Random House.

Granata, C. L. (2003). *Wouldn't it be nice: Brian Wilson and the making of the Beach Boys.* Chicago: A Cappella Books.

Griffin, J., & Tyrrell, I. (2004). *Dreaming reality.* Great Britain: Human Givens Institute.

Guiles, F. L. (1969). *Norma Jean: The life of Marilyn Monroe.* New York: McGraw-Hill.

Guiles, F. L. (1984). *Legend: The life and death of Marilyn Monroe.* New York: Stein and Day.

Harrison, M. (1972). *The life of H.R.H. the Duke of Clarence and Avondale.* London: W. H. Allen.

Hayman, R. (2003). *The death and life of Sylvia Plath.* New York: Sutton.

Hemingway, E. (1958). The art of fiction (interviewed by George Plimpton). *The Paris Review, 18.*

Hemingway, G. (1976). *Papa.* Boston: Houghton Mifflin

Hemingway, M. (1976). *How it was.* New York: Ballantine.

Hentoff, N. (1972, January 30). Mingus: I thought I was finished. *New York Times,* p. 17.

Hentoff, N. (1978). *The jazz life.* New York: Da Capo Press.

Hentoff, N. (1979a, March 5). Mingus ah um. *Village Voice.*

Hentoff, N. (1979b, March 12). Mingus dynasties. *Village Voice,* pp. 34–35.

Hentoff, N. (1981, August). Mingus: You'd be playing, and he'd yell, "get into yourself." *The Progressive,* pp. 52–53.

Hershman, D. J., & Leib, J. (1998). *Manic depression and creativity.* Amherst, NY: Prometheus.

Hess, T. (1955, summer). Reviews and previews. *Art News, 54*(4).

Honos-Webb, L. (2005). *The gift of ADHD.* Oakland, CA: New Harbinger.

Horsley, C. B. (1999, November 19). Mark Rothko: Silence is so accurate. *The City Review.*

Hotchner, A. E. (1966). *Papa Hemingway.* New York: Random House.

Hughes, T. (1998). *Birthday letters.* New York: Farrar, Straus & Giroux.

Jamison, K. R. (1989). Mood disorders and patterns of creativity in British writers and artists. *Psychiatry, 52,* 125–134.

Jamison, K. R. (1993). *Touched with fire: Manic depressive illness and the artistic temperament.* New York: Free Press.

Jones, R. E. (1946). Nijinsky and Til Eulenspiegel. In P. Magriel (Ed.), *Nijinsky: An illustrated monograph.* New York: Henry Holt.

Kamiya, M. (1965). Virginia Woolf: An outline of a study on her personality, illness, and work. *Confinia Psychiatrica, 8*(3–4), 189–205.

Kaufman, J. C. (2001a). Genius, lunatics, and poets: Mental illness in prize-winning authors. *Imagination, Cognition, and Personality, 20*(4), 305–314.

Kaufman, J. C. (2001b). The Sylvia Plath effect: Mental illness in eminent creative writers. *Journal of Creative Behavior, 35*(1), 37–50.

Kifner, J., Collins, G., & O'Donnell, M. (2003, December 24). No joke! 37 years after death Lenny Bruce receives a pardon. *New York Times*, p. A1.

Kobal, J. (1974). *Marilyn Monroe: A life on film.* London: Hamlyn.

Kofsky, F. (1974). *Lenny Bruce: The comedian as social critic and secular moralist.* New York: Pathfinder Press.

Kottler, J. A. (1997). *Travel that can change your life.* San Francisco: Jossey-Bass.

Kottler, J. A. (2003). *On being a therapist* (3rd ed.). San Francisco: Jossey-Bass.

Kottler, J. A., & Carlson, J. (2003). *The mummy at the dining room table: Eminent therapists reveal their most unusual cases.* San Francisco: Jossey-Bass.

Kottler, J. A., & Carlson, J. (2005a). *How clients transform their therapists: Stories of therapist personal transformation.* New York: Routledge.

Kottler, J. A., & Carlson, J. (2005b). *Their finest hour: Master therapists share their greatest success stories.* Boston: Allyn & Bacon.

Kottler, J. A., Carlson, J., & Keeney, B. (2004). *American shaman: An odyssey of global healing traditions.* New York: Routledge.

Kramer, P. D. (1993). *Listening to Prozac.* New York: Viking.

Kramer, P. D. (2005). *Against depression.* New York: Viking.

Krassner, P. (1996, August 1). Lenny Bruce: The man who said too much. *Los Angeles Times.*

Lauronen, E., Veijola, J., Isohanni, I., Jones, P., Nieminen, P., & Isohanni, M. (2004). Links between creativity and mental disorder. *Psychiatry, 67*(1), 81–98.

Leaming, B. (1998). *Marilyn Monroe.* New York: Crown.

Litman, R. E. (1996). Suicidology: A look backward and ahead. *Suicide and Life-Threatening Behavior, 26*(1), 1–12.

Love, J. (1977). *Virginia Woolf: Sources of madness and art.* Berkeley: University of California Press.

Ludwig, A. M. (1995). *The price of greatness: Resolving the creativity and madness controversy.* New York: Guilford Press.

Marder, H. (2000). *The measure of life: Virginia Woolf's last years.* Ithaca, NY: Cornell University Press.

Maltsberger, J. T. (1995, Fall). *Suicide and life-threatening behavior, 25*(3).

McLean, A. L. (2002). Feeling and the filmed body: Judy Garland and the kinesics of suffering. *Film Quarterly, 55*(3), 2–15.

Meyers, J. (1999). *Hemingway: A biography.* New York: Da Capo Press.

Milstein, G. (1959, May 3). Man it's like satire. *New York Times Magazine*, p. 28.

Mingus, C. (1971). *Beneath the underdog.* New York: Vintage Books.

Moes, E. C. (1990). Validation in the eyes of men: A psychoanalytic interpretation of paternal deprivation and the daughter's desire. *Melanie Klein and Object Relations, 8*(1), 43–65.

National Alliance for the Mentally Ill, "Lithium and creative work." [http://www.nami-nyc-org/diagnosi/mrbipol.html].

Neihart, M. (1998). Creativity, the arts, and madness. *Roeper Review, 21*(1), 47–50.

Nettle, D. (2001). *Strong imagination: Madness, creativity, and human nature.* Oxford: Oxford University Press.

Nijinska, B. (1981). *Early memoirs.* Austin, TX: Holt, Rinehart and Winston.

Nijinsky, R. (1934). *Nijinsky.* New York: Simon & Schuster.

Nijinsky, R. (1952). *The last years of Vaslav Nijinsky.* New York: Simon & Schuster.

Nijinsky, V. (1934/1971). *The diary of Vaslav Nijinsky.* New York: Simon & Schuster.

Nijinsky, V. (2000). *The diary of Vaslav Nijinsky: The unexpurgated edition* (edited by J. Acolcella). New York: Farrar, Straus & Giroux.

Oren, D. A. (1986). *Joining the club: A history of Jews and Yale.* New Haven: Yale University Press.

Ostwald, P. (1991). *Vaslav Nijinsky: A leap into madness.* New York: Lyle Stuart.

Ostwald, P. (1993). Genius, madness, and health: Examples from psychobiography. In P. Ostwald & L. Zegans (Eds.), *The pleasures and perils of genius: Mostly Mozart* (pp. 167–190). Madison, CT: International Universities Press.

Ostwald, P. (1994). The god of the dance: Treating Nijinsky's manic excitement and catatonia. *Hospital and Community Psychiatry, 45*(10), 981–985.

Plath, S. (1963/1971). *The bell jar.* New York: HarperCollins. (Originally published in 1963 under the name Victoria Lucas)

Plath, S. (1975). *Letters home: Correspondence 1950–1963* (edited by A. Plath). New York: Perennial.

Plath, S. (1962/1998). *The colossus and other poems.* New York: Vintage Books.

Plath, S. (1965/1999). *Ariel.* New York: Perennial.

Plath, S. (2000). *The unabridged journals of Sylvia Plath* (edited by K. Kukil). New York: Anchor Books.

Poe, E. A. (1848/1948). In J. W. Ostrom (Ed.), *The letters of Edgar A. Poe* (Vol. 2). Cambridge, MA: Harvard University Press.

Poole, R. (2003). Kind of blue: Creativity, mental disorder, and jazz. *British Journal of Psychiatry, 183,* 193–194.

Post, F. (1994). Creativity and psychopathology: A study of 291 world-famous men. *British Journal of Psychiatry, 165,* 22–34.

Restak, R. (2004). *Poe's heart and the mountain climber: Exploring the effect of anxiety on our brains and our culture.* New York: Harmony Books.

Reynolds, M. (1981). *Hemingway's reading: 1910–1940.* Princeton, NJ: Princeton University Press.

Riese, R., & Hitchens, N. (1987). *The unabridged Marilyn Monroe: Her life from a to z.* New York: Congdon & Weed.

Robertson, M. (1995). Sylvia Plath: A blind girl playing with a slide rule of values. In B. Panter, M. L. Panter, E. Virshup, & B. Virshup (Eds.), *Creativity and madness.* Burbank, CA: Aimed Press.

Rothenberg, A. (1990). *Creativity and madness: New findings and old stereotypes.* Baltimore: Johns Hopkins University Press.

Rothko, M. (1987). *Mark Rothko, 1903–1970.* London: Tate Gallery.

Rothko, M. (2005). *The artist's reality: Philosophies of art.* New Haven, CT: Yale University Press.

Runco, M. (1998). Suicide and creativity: The case of Sylvia Plath. *Death Studies, 22,* 637–654.

Russell, R. (1996). *Bird lives!* New York: Da Capo Press.

Santoro, G. (2000). *Myself when I am real: The life and music of Charles Mingus.* New York: Oxford University Press.

Sapolsky, R. M. (1998). *Why zebras don't get ulcers* (2nd ed.). New York: Henry Holt.

Schlesinger, J. (2002). Issues in creativity and madness part one: Ancient questions, modern answers. *Ethical Human Sciences and Services, 4*(1), 73–76.

Seldes, L. (1978). *The legacy of Mark Rothko.* Austin, TX: Holt, Rinehart and Winston.

Shipman, D. (1992). *Judy Garland: The secret life of an American legend.* New York: Hyperion.

Silverman, M. A., & Will, N. P. (1986). Sylvia Plath and the failure of emotional self-repair through poetry. *Psychoanalytic Quarterly, 55*(1), 99–129.

Spoto, D. (1993). *Marilyn Monroe: The biography.* New York: Cooper Square Press.

Steinem, G. (1972, March). The woman who died too soon. *Ms.*, p. 42.

Steinem, G. (1987). *Marilyn.* New York: New American Library.

Stephens, J. H., & Ostwald, P. (1991). A formal diagnosis of Nijinsky's psychosis. In P. Ostwald (Ed.), *Vaslav Nijinsky: A leap into madness.* New York: Lyle Stuart.

Stewart, D. O. (1974). An interview. *Fitzgerald-Hemingway Annual.*

Sturges, F. (1994, June 21). Brian Wilson: Just wasn't made for these times. *The Independent* (online edition). [http://enjoyment.independent.co.uk/music/interviews/story.jsp?story=533414]

Styron, W. (1990). *Darkness visible: A memoir of madness.* New York: Random House.

Summers, A. (1986). *Goddess: The secret lives of Marilyn Monroe.* New York: Onyx.

Terr, L. C. (1998). Who's afraid of Virginia Woolf? Clues to early sexual abuse in literature. In A. Solnit, P. Neubauer, S. Abrams, & A. Dowling (Eds.), *The psychoanalytic study of the child.* New Haven, CT: Yale University Press.

Underwood, A. (2005, March 14). The gift of ADHD? *Newsweek*, p. 48.

Weaver, J. (1968). The fault, dear Bruce, is not in our stars but in ourselves. *Holiday, 44*(5).

White, T. (1994). *The nearest faraway place: Brian Wilson, the Beach Boys, and the southern California experience.* New York: Henry Holt.

Wilkes, P. (1970, April 19). *New York Times Magazine*, pp. 32–84.

Willis, G. I. (2003). Forty lives in the bebop business: Mental health in a group of eminent jazz musicians. *British Journal of Psychiatry, 183,* 255–259.

Wilson, B. (1991). *Wouldn't it be nice: My own story.* New York: Henry Holt.

Woolf, L. (1964). *Beginning again.* Orlando: Harcourt Brace.

Woolf, V. (1931/1959). *The waves.* Orlando: Harcourt Brace

Woolf, V. (1978). In A. Bell (Ed.), *The diary of Virginia Woolf* (Vols. 1–5). Orlando: Harcourt Brace.

Woolf, V. (1980). *The letters of Virginia Woolf* (Vols. 1–6). London: Hogarth Press.

Yalom, I., & Yalom, M. (1971). Ernest Hemingway: A psychiatric view. *Archives of General Psychiatry, 24,* 487.

About the Author

Jeffrey A. Kottler is one of the most prolific authors in the fields of psychology and education, having written sixty-five books about a wide range of subjects. He has authored a dozen texts for counselors and therapists that are used in universities around the world and a dozen books each for practicing therapists and educators. Some of his most highly regarded works include *On Being a Therapist, The Imperfect Therapist, Compassionate Therapy, Making Changes Last,* and *The Mummy at the Dining Room Table.*

He has also authored several highly successful books for the public that describe complex phenomena in highly accessible language: *Beyond Blame; Travel That Can Change Your Life; Private Moments, Secret Selves; The Language of Tears;* and *The Last Victim: A True-Life Journey into the Mind of the Serial Killer.*

Kottler has been an educator for thirty years. He has worked as a teacher, counselor, and therapist in a variety of settings: preschool, middle school, mental health center, crisis center, university, community college, and private practice. He has served as a Fulbright scholar and senior lecturer in Peru (1980) and Iceland (2000), and has worked as a visiting professor in New Zealand, Australia, Hong Kong, Singapore, and Nepal. He is currently professor and chair of the counseling department at California State University, Fullerton.

Poetry

Photographs